THIRD MAN TO
FATTY'S LEG

AN AUTOBIOGRAPHY

Steve James

First published in 2004 by
First Stone Publishing
A Division of Corpus Publishing Limited
PO Box 8, Lydney,
Gloucestershire GL15 6YD

This edition published in 2005 by First Stone Publishing.

© 2004 Corpus Publishing & Steve James

Cover design: Sarah Williams

ALL RIGHTS RESERVED

No part of this book may be reproduced or transmitted in any
form or by any means, electronic or mechanical, including
photocopying, recording, or by any information storage and
retrieval system, without permission in writing from the
Publisher.

ISBN 1 904439 41 1

MORAY COUNCIL LIBRARIES & INFO.SERVICES	
20 36 14 35	
Askews & Holts	
B.JAM	

CONTENTS

To Jane, Bethan, Mum, Dad and 'Budgie'.

WHAT THE PAPERS SAID

'No ghost-writer haunts this particular story. The title of the book is obscure, but the contents are not. The writing is sharp, often funny and the account of his 19 years at Glamorgan, and two Tests with England, is told in wonderful detail and with refreshing honesty. What shines from the pages is that rarest of things, self-knowledge. Steve James has written a perceptive and enjoyable book.'

MIKE ATHERTON, *SUNDAY TELEGRAPH*

'Compellingly honest…his account of his two Test caps in 1998 is a classic of self-deprecation.
James paints a vivid portrait of the professional cricketer's life and has a good eye for the characters he mixed with.'

SIMON WILDE, *SUNDAY TIMES*

'Nasser Hussain's glum, charmless and angry ghosted bestseller might have been a fair portrait of its pouting subject, but as a worthwhile read it was not a patch on the illuminatingly fresh, witty and wholly diverting life of a fellow county cricket captain (and two-cap wonder) which the cultivated Steve James wrote himself.'

FRANK KEATING, *THE SPECTATOR.*

'An extraordinarily honest and absorbing autobiography… James is brave in his discussion of opponents, team-mates and dressing room politics. A fascinating record of interesting times.'

ED SMITH, *SUNDAY TELEGRAPH*

'[Steve James] has a good, analytical brain which he uses to dissect his batting technique and he has two "hums", humour and humility, which add up to a third – humanity. He laughs at himself frequently, accords credit where it is due for certain of his successes, and displays a sensitivity towards team-mates and opponents which is rare in this hard-nosed age. He is refreshingly honest about his shortcomings, not only as a batsman, but also as a captain and occasionally as a human being.'

DAVID LLEWELLYN, *THE INDEPENDENT*

'Why does anyone read cricket autobiographies? I only ask because, like lots of cricket fans, I seem to have read many and enjoyed very few. The lifeless prose. The old matches reheated. The skimpy childhoods. The nicknames. The endless bloody nicknames. The genre has become soiled and debased, to the point that often the only issue of interest is whether they call it "An Autobiography" or "The Autobiography". But every year or two, one book rises from the mire. Recent examples include PCR Tufnell's louche memoirs and the elegantly straight bat of MA Atherton. Such books do the almost impossible: they tell you things you want to know and things you didn't know already. And what we really don't know, and really want to know, is essentially: what is it like? The uncountable millions of us who will never play professional, let alone international, cricket, other than in hallucinatory bursts at four o'clock in the morning. What is it like? Steve James's book is one of the few that tells us.
Fascinating insights...withering self analysis...the pleasure is in the detail.'

MARCUS BERKMANN, *WISDEN CRICKETER*.

ACKNOWLEDGEMENTS

I would like to thank John Sellers for his bravery in agreeing to publish this book, and for his unstinting guidance and advice. Thanks also for the carefully-placed advice from all those who have painstakingly read all, or some, of the manuscript; to my mum and dad, to my wife, Jane, and to Ian Williams. Thanks to all who have helped with the collection of photographs; the professionals – Huw Evans, Huw John, Chris Tinsley at the South Wales Argus, Russell Cheyne, various at Allsport; and the amateurs – Mike Powell and David Shufflebotham. Thanks also to Dr. Andrew Hignell for the statistics.

My father always told me that I should be nice to the people on the way up because I would almost certainly meet them on the way down. So I would like to think that I have been most grateful to all those who have helped me throughout my sporting career. To Monmouth School (especially Graham 'Budgie' Burgess, to whom I am indescribably indebted), Lydney CC, Lydney RFC and the universities of Swansea and Cambridge for their varying types of education.

Special thanks to Glamorgan CCC for providing me with 19 marvellous years; to its players, staff and coaches, for their fun and companionship, and for providing most of the material for this book.

Also thanks to those who have helped and encouraged so much with my early attempts at journalism – Paul Tully, Neil

Manthorp, Mark Tattersall, Edward Bevan, Scyld Berry, Peter Mitchell and Jon Ryan.

But, most of all, thank you to all my family, including my sister Karen. Thank you for putting up with my moods. And, to my late Grandma 'Tish', thank you for setting me on the road to professional cricket from an early age by offering me £10 for every hundred!

PREFACE

I could have asked someone much more famous than me to write a foreword to this book. Maybe my old university chum, Mike Atherton (he gets enough mentions in this book anyway), or the current England coach, Duncan Fletcher, or a mate from the world of rugby, such as Mike Hall or Gwyn Jones.

I know how good I was, how good I could have been and what I did to get that far. And it will not add any weight if someone famous says it. Not in my opinion anyway. They are hardly going to be derogatory, are they? I had a decent county career and I might have played more for England. There again, I might not have played at all. I was fortunate enough to have represented Glamorgan during arguably the most successful period in their history. And I reckon I played some part in that. Not bad for a Gloucestershire boy.

I've enjoyed some wonderful times, meeting some wonderful people and visiting some wonderful places. So I make no apologies for telling my story. I hope I don't upset too many people, but, if I do, it is because I have tried to be candidly honest and balanced about myself, so I think I should apply the same criteria to those I have met, whether friend or foe. I love writing – and no, this is not ghosted; I have written every single word – and hope I can enlighten you as to what it is like to be a professional cricketer... what it is *really* like, especially the mental turmoil, for an introverted worrier like myself. And I want to tell you about the characters, the anecdotes, the humour, the banter, the graft, the thrills, the disappointments, the cynicism, and the disagreements that have coloured my life in sport.

I have always been more of an observer than an attention seeker, often in awe of those around me, sometimes too much so, but I have a good retentive memory so there is plenty to relate. From an early age, I knew that I wanted to be a sportsman. It was either going to be rugby or cricket. Those were the sports with which I was reared. I know it is a clichéd story, but when I went to have my little chat with the careers master at school, I told him I wanted to be a cricketer. Rugby hadn't turned professional then, so there was no choice. My only concession was that I would go to university first. Then cricket.

The Forest of Dean, where I grew up, is a no-nonsense area, where masculinity is often defined by one's performances on a rugby field, so there was no chance of football being the future. My father played cricket for Lydney in the summer and rugby for Lydney in the winter. That was his life. And so it became mine. And beyond.

But I might never have guessed that all this would lead me to Glamorgan and Wales. My family are English and I had an English upbringing, until I went to Monmouth School. If only I had discovered earlier that my maternal grandmother was from Kenfig Hill in south Wales, then things might have been so much easier. Then the subject of my history O-level project might have been Wilf Wooller rather than W. G. Grace. Then all this Welshness might have been easier to comprehend.

Before I knew it, I was captain of the Welsh Schools cricket team. There was no turning back. In 2002 I captained Wales to victory over England in the first one-day international (albeit unofficial) between the two sides. It was one of the proudest moments of my life. I bet my parents never expected to read that.

But as for rugby, which shirt do I still yearn to wear? The red rose or the three feathers? We shall come to that. The answer may have something to do with the fact that Foresters are often described as being neither English nor Welsh, but a breed of their own. Confused? So am I.

The title of this book? Well, anyone who saw me bat knows that I scored a ridiculous proportion of my runs down to third man, so the first part is self-explanatory. The second part is more obscure. Fatty's Leg is an indication that this book, amongst other things, reveals some of the ludicrously appealing jargon used inside a cricket dressing room. Have you seen the cult film *Twin Town*? It's a Welsh film, but you don't need to be Welsh to enjoy its humour. Its words often filled the Glamorgan dressing room. I didn't fall off a ladder like Fatty, but my knee is now like Fatty's Leg. You'd better read on...

Steve James
Cardiff
April 2004

CHAPTER ONE

RELUCTANT HERO

I may have achieved some things in cricket of which many only dream, but they have never come easily; rarely confidently. For this is one cricketer for whom the mental battle has raged long and hard.

The County Ground, Taunton, September 1997. Eleven runs to win, and the County Championship is Glamorgan's. I walked to the wicket with Hugh Morris while our team mates began their celebrations in the dressing room. Left-arm spinner Dean Cosker had just trapped Somerset's last man, Ben Trott, LBW to preface wild revelry amongst the thousands of Welshmen present, as well as the many others watching on a special TV broadcast from BBC Wales. I had already scored 1,766 first-class runs that season, more than anyone else in the country. Confidence should have been high...

As a boy, I had spent countless hours at my parents' home in Lydney day-dreaming of such a moment. I would walk down the steps to the wonderfully manicured lawn, listening to the cheers of the crowd. I was the hero, the one to win the match with breathtaking brilliance and bravery; a triumph crafted with decisive precision. Time and time again (I was still pursuing this sad, lone ritual well into my teens), I either scored the winning runs or grabbed the winning try. But that day at Taunton, at the most euphoric of moments (the one I always cite when asked of my cricketing highlight), the dream was replaced by a recurring nightmare. I did not want to bat.

All afternoon I had been hoping that we would bowl out Somerset before they scored the 277 required to make us bat again. I spent many hours of my professional career doing the same, mentally inventing ways of postponing the hour of truth, when I put myself on the line by walking out to bat.

It is not that I was scared to bat; just often scared of failing. This fear had its roots in the old three-day first-class cricket, a lot of which I played at Cambridge University. In those matches it was traditional for the side batting first (rarely Cambridge – we were too overawed and subservient to countenance such bravado) to declare just before the end of the first day's play, leaving the opposition openers a difficult 20 minutes to negotiate till the close. I used to hate those periods. Often, I would spend most of the day silently willing the opposing skipper to bat through.

And this insecurity explains why I was such an avid watcher of the evening weather forecast. Rain the next day meant no pressure. It was not that I didn't want to play cricket – I devoted my life to it, for God's sake – but it was a mind game, which eased the stress. Confidence can be an elusive commodity. But there must be something positive in my mental make-up. What I could do, in the vernacular of Mike Powell, my Glamorgan team mate, was 'get my head on' when the time to bat arrived. I was often described as possessing a sound temperament. Early in my career, John Steele, the second-team coach, asked the whole of the team to say which characteristic of the chap sitting to their left they would most like to possess. The one to my right said "his temperament".

Once I was 'in', I was able to focus and forget about what had happened previously, repeating the same simple and obvious mantra to myself, "watch the ball", time and time again. For some reason, large scores became my domain, my speciality even. Before I batted, I wrapped myself in a cocoon of concentration, which my colleagues knew not to interrupt unnecessarily, slavishly adhering to a series of superstitious preparations. Left pad on first, boot laces tied so tight that blood was barely able to reach my toes. Long-sleeve shirt, sleeveless sweater on, unless the temperature was above 90F (rare in Wales!), left glove with the Velcro done up. Then a series of stretching and fast feet exercises to sharpen me up while ensuring I stayed out of view of the opposition – don't ask me why. Then, if we were at home at Sophia Gardens, it was a thump of the board at the top of the stairs, which bears the names of the 16 Glamorgan players to have represented England:

M.J.L. Turnbull
J.C. Clay
A.D.G. Matthews
A.J. Watkins
W.G.A. Parkhouse
J.E. McConnon
P.M. Walker
I.J. Jones
A.R. Lewis
J.G. Thomas
M.P. Maynard
S.L. Watkin
H. Morris
R.D.B. Croft
S.P. James
S.P. Jones

And then out to the middle, pausing momentarily to practise a straight drive on the move. A quick exchange of good lucks with my partner and the right glove Velcro done up before facing my first ball. I was never one to set myself targets. I had many an argument about this with the various sports psychologists brought in to aid our mental preparation. For me, there are too many variables in the game of cricket to set goals. The next ball. That is as far ahead as I could think. It might have been my last. That might sound fatalistic but to me it was highly realistic. Funny how none of this had ever entered my head on the lawn of Foxhill in Lydney.

So now captain Matthew Maynard was changing near me that day in the dressing room at Taunton. "It's a day like this that I wish I was an opening batsman," he said. "You can open if you want," I replied, only half seriously. "Alright then," he retorted with a hint of anger and astonishment. "Nay, you're okay," I mumbled, as the magnitude of the situation hit home. Glamorgan were about to win the Championship for the first time since 1969 and there was a good chance that I was going to be out there when the winning runs were hit.

I remember thinking that Somerset might bowl part-timers to get it over with quickly, but, as we walked to the middle, I saw England seamer Andy Caddick marking out his run. It wasn't his short one. Whyte & Mackay, the whisky distillers, were sponsoring some individual awards that season, and Caddick was a frontrunner for top bowler. He wanted a couple more scalps to ensure that prize and, with good reason, he fancied his chances against me. There was always a bit of an added edge in the contests between us, and he was never short of a word or two of encouragement for me. This had begun when Caddick appeared for Clevedon against Lydney in the now defunct Three Counties League, through the occasional second-eleven encounters while the New Zealand-born Caddick was qualifying, then finally to the County Championship.

There was an occasion in 1999 when I became particularly incen-sed with him. On a bouncy Taunton wicket he had stood at the end of his run and announced in the most belittling manner to everyone in the ground: "Come on, Stevo [nobody else has ever called me that], get yourself out now before you make a complete arse of yourself." He then swaggered down to fine leg at the end of the over to continue the tirade, shouting, "Come on, lads, we've got him rattled; he doesn't like it up him."

In truth, he was making the ball talk that day – it was swinging round corners, and I was scarcely able to lay a bat on him. Generally, sledging did not bother me over much. But this was different – public and puerile. When I got down to the non-striker's end, John Hampshire, that most no-nonsense of Yorkshiremen cricketers and now an umpire, was there. He said: "If anyone 'ad said that to me, they'd 'ave 'ad me bat rownd their 'ead."

I did not last much longer; Graham Rose trapped me LBW at the other end. But when Caddick arrived to bat later in the game, I pleaded out loud with Darren Thomas to exact some sort of revenge. "Please, Teddy, hit him on the head for me." He did. First ball. I roared in from cover, laughing, which is not something of which I am proud now.

"You liked that, did you?" said Caddick. I had stooped to his level, and, as so often happens, he prevailed because he dismissed me first ball in the second innings. And two years later he broke my hand with a vicious lifter. I think I should have kept my mouth shut.

Caddick is a complex character. He is not universally liked in cricketing circles, but there is no doubting his pedigree as a bowler. On his day he can be world class, but – and this seems to madden people most – on his off days he can be ordinary and can exude an air that hints at a lack of effort and heart. I think he is a fundamentally decent bloke, who, if anything, tries a little too hard in befriending team mates. He did apologise to me when he broke my hand and was helpful in my desperate, albeit vain, efforts to conquer my phobia of going underwater when asked to scuba dive with the England squad in Lanzarote in 1997. But I always found it hard to divorce how players behave on the field from their characters off it. I always found it difficult to have a beer with someone who had been abusing me only a few hours beforehand.

Jacques Kallis spoke to me about this during his spell with Glamorgan in 1999. He said: "I can be a real cock on the field, but I reckon I'm okay afterwards." He most certainly is okay afterwards – generally reticent, but fun-loving and great company. When he first met up with me that season, he was most concerned. "Sorry, mate, did we give you a hard time at Lord's?" He was referring to my Test debut at Lord's in 1998. I did not know what he was talking about. I wasn't there long enough to be sledged.

All bowlers might have a word up close to you in their follow through, some more than others. It is designed to be a process of 'mental disintegration', as the Australians call it. But most of the comments, made in order to distract and disturb the batsman, are either rude or moronic. For instance, Steve Kirby, the Yorkshire quickie, currently regarded as county cricket's most garrulous exponent, is supposed to have said to Mike Atherton in his final season, "I've seen better batsmen than you in my fridge."

Generally, it pays for the batsman not to return the banter, as the bowler will almost always have the last word. But in my younger days, I could not resist a word back. Age mellowed me, and later I was more likely to turn away. My replies to bowlers were never the type to linger long in the memory, but others have been. At Trent Bridge in 2000, Glamorgan's young wicket-keeper/batsman, Mark Wallace, was attracting some pithy observations from Nottingham-shire's quick bowler, Paul Franks. So, having stolen a single, Wallace decided to follow Franks back towards his mark. "Look, Franksy, there are 10 blokes in our dressing room who think you are a twat. I'm not sure yet, so let's not make it 11."

And at Canterbury in 1992, Tony Cottey, our diminutive batsman, was being sledged non-stop by Kent's fast bowler, Martin McCague. Cottey resisted all that the 6ft 5in and 17st Australian had to throw at him, with a typically pugnacious century full of cuts and pulls. Near the end of the day, McCague limped off injured, and as he passed Cottey, there came from the little man: "What's the matter? Pulled a heart muscle?"

Back to Taunton, 1997. I had never been so nervous in my life, and a simple task suddenly became an almost impossible one. Caddick's first over was certainly eventful; he had me plumb LBW, but the cricketing gods were with me that day, and umpire George Sharp disagreed. I heaved a sigh of relief, then edged one straight to first slip. It was simple as far as slip catches go, but he grassed it. I could not believe it. Neither could Caddick. Then I added insult to injury by clattering a half-volley through the covers for four.

The rest is a blur. Morris got a single off the first ball of the second over bowled by Graham Rose. Caddick was at fine leg for the left hander and was supposed to move across to be there for me. But he neglected to do so. Not that I noticed. I did not even know how many we required to win. So when I tickled Rose's leg side ball down towards fine leg, I thought we might muster one, maybe two if we ran quickly. As usual, I ran the first quickly and turned ... to see Morris grabbing the stumps at the other end and thousands of Welshmen pouring on to the pitch.

Morris, arms aloft, was running in one direction while I went in the other, unsure of what was happening. "We haven't won, have we?" I said. But no one was listening. Even hours after the game I was worried that we had not scored enough runs to win. I kept conjuring up thoughts of the victory and the Championship that never was.

Adrian Dale, known affectionately to all as Arthur, had pleaded with me that if I happened to be out there when we won, to get a stump for him. I suddenly remembered. "Grab the stumps," I screamed to myself. I got two. Quickly, I became engulfed. Fans were banging my helmet, and a silly sort of claustrophobia set in. This was relieved when I was suddenly lifted above someone's shoulders. I was chaired towards the pavilion for a while. Moments later, I was on the floor and one stump and my bat were being wrestled from my grasp. I was helpless. I struggled but quickly gave up in order to escape. I had one stump. "But what about Arthur? He will be gutted," I thought.

I reached the pavilion to be met by Dale at the bottom of the steps. Lo and behold he had two stumps in his hand! Morris had given him one, and his brother, Gary, who is in the Metropolitan Police, had given him the other after using the long arm of the law to separate it from a cheeky souvenir hunter. All that worry for nothing. I was disappointed to have lost my bat though. I thought it might be valuable in years to come, maybe as an auction item in my benefit season, or, more likely, as a sentimental memento. More importantly, I wanted to keep it because I enjoyed using it so much. It was an easily distinguishable bat because it was obvious that some new stickers had been somewhat clumsily placed over those of the original maker.

I had been using Stuart Surridge bats for a second season after I had become sceptical of the quality of bats that Gunn & Moore were sending me. Professionals often talk of bat-makers having different shelves upon which they place their bats according to the quality of the player. At that stage, I felt that I was having enough problems with my batting without being consigned to one of the lower shelves. So my father, who ran a sports shop in Lydney for 26 years, arranged for a Surridge Enigma to be sent out to Zimbabwe where I was wintering. It had been intended for Paul Prichard, the Essex batsman, and was 2lb 8oz in weight with a thin, oval handle. Perfect. I noticed an E engraved on the shoulder of the bat. Only later did I discover that this meant that the bat was crafted by Eric Loxton, probably the most renowned bat-maker in the land. He worked for Slazenger, of which Stuart Surridge was a subsidiary. It felt magnificent in my hands – "Forget who makes it, it has to feel right in your hands," my father used to advise – and it played an enormous part in my rejuvenation as a cricketer from 1996 onwards. Late on in 1997, Stuart Surridge disbanded. A deal was struck with Slazenger, but I wanted to keep using that bat, so Slazenger stickers hastily had to replace the Stuart Surridge ones. So it was with much delight that I learnt some time later that this prized possession had been found by the *South Wales Echo* newspaper after they had launched an appeal.

At Taunton, the party began. Robert Croft, as he had done four years earlier when we won the Axa & Equity Law Sunday League Trophy at Canterbury, sang *Alouette* from the balcony, conducting his adoring crowd through his increasingly lewd verses. The singing continued in the bar downstairs, with Waqar Younis bizarrely entering the room wearing a Nelson Mandela mask. And another foreigner stood next to him, proudly wearing a Wales rugby shirt. Coach Duncan Fletcher had been presented with it by Matthew Maynard in an emotional presentation after the game, with the skipper adding: "Get as pissed as you want until November, and then begin the hard work again."

Tony Cottey scared the life out of all of us by wanting to throw himself off the bridge outside the ground into the river Tone. "I haven't done much for you boys this year, so I want to do this now," said the ever-so-inebriated little man from Swansea, who had endured a wretched season with the bat. He would have done it too – this is a man who has bungee jumped, parachuted and run countless marathons, as well as being a good enough footballer to have been on Swansea City's books when they were in the old First Division. He was released on the same day as Dean Saunders.

My excellent season prompted many commentators to say that it was fitting that I should have scored the winning runs. Really, it would have been more appropriate if Hugh Morris had hit them, because it turned out to be his last innings for Glamorgan. He was leaving to become Technical Director at the England and Wales Cricket Board (EWCB), but not before bowing out with a century in his final match. Our opening partnership had blossomed that season. He was a fine player, who, like me, had endured his fill of the vicissitudes of opening the batting. He had also experienced some torturous times as captain, accepting the job as a green 22-year-old before he was ready. This was in 1986 and Glamorgan were still the whipping boys of the County Championship. It was a difficult time for Morris and he eventually resigned in 1989, during a match against Gloucestershire at Bristol, with Alan Butcher taking over.

Morris and Butcher never really got on, mainly because, I think, Morris felt that the ex-Surrey man was after his job the moment he arrived in Wales (or maybe had even been promised it when signing). Whatever, they formed a formidable alliance at the top of the order. It was a standing joke that they seemed to spend so much time together out in the middle yet hardly said a word to each other. Apparently, Tim Robinson and Chris Broad operated in a similar *omerta* at Nottinghamshire. So much for batsmen communicating and building partnerships!

I wrote a piece for *The Cricketer* magazine in February 1998 in appreciation of Morris and, looking back on it, my most telling words were: "The biggest compliment I can pay him is to say that I was always surprised when he was out. To me, he rarely looked in trouble and I always yearned for his calmness and poise."

His career looked like ending early because of dodgy knees,

but as the emphasis on fitness increased, he took this on board and worked hard to strengthen his leg muscles in order to protect those knees. With this came bigger scores. I could not believe that he did not score a double hundred until 1996 (he first played in 1981) when he completed that milestone against Yorkshire, adding a further one in 1997 – 233 not out against Warwickshire, which was ended when he was felled by a wickedly-fast Allan Donald bouncer.

I remember a team meeting we had under Mike Atherton in my first year at Cambridge in 1989 prior to the first match of the season against Glamorgan, when the skipper naturally asked me for my thoughts on how to dismiss Morris. "Just bowl on a length outside off stump, he will nick it," I proudly announced, having witnessed that winter a torturous session Morris had had with then-coach Alan Jones. He seemed totally at sea with his batting; his feet and head were all over the place and he was edging the ball with alarming regularity. But he had obviously worked hard to rectify those problems because that first match of the season saw him score the first hundred of the season – much to the amusement of my new university colleagues!

I thought Morris was a decent captain of Glamorgan, despite some personal grievances over selection. That is not a view shared by my predecessor, Matthew Maynard, who questioned his tactical awareness in his recent book *On The Attack*. He was not instinctive like Maynard, but he was meticulous in his planning and keen for success. Indeed, he achieved that in 1993 when we won that Axa Equity & Law Sunday League title as well as finishing third in the Championship and reaching the semi-finals of the NatWest Trophy. He had retaken the reins that season after Maynard had deputised so ably during the 1992 campaign, when Butcher had been injured. Maynard had been a somewhat surprising choice as vice captain, given his colourful lifestyle, and Morris was miffed. But Maynard did reveal a clever cricketing brain as well as engendering a healthy respect from his players. The decision to make Morris captain was reached after the final game of that 1992 season against Derbyshire, when some typical Maynard bravado had tempted the Midlanders so close to our target that they were eventually bowled out. We all waited in the Beverley Hotel for the announcement – apart from Morris himself, who was on the way to London to see his girlfriend, Debbie.

Maynard was devastated, and he had some right to be. But it was not for me to become involved in such political manoeuvrings at that stage of my career. That had been my first full season in the first team and my relative success had been due in no small part to the confidence that Maynard had instilled in me. We travelled together that season and he was forever building me up. Once I was extolling the virtues of Middlesex's Mike Roseberry, who was having an extraordinary season, when Maynard shocked and motivated me in equal measure by stating that he thought that I was a better player. That got me thinking.

The committee took the safety-first option with Morris, and in a way I can understand their decision. Maynard is no shrinking violet when it comes to enjoying himself and I was worried about that side of things when he was eventually named as club captain in 1996. It is common knowledge that he likes a pint and a fag. And another. And another... His nickname is Ollie, after the infamous hell-raiser Oliver Reed and, until recently, Maynard celebrated this fact with a personalised number plate on his Jaguar sports car.

He does nothing by halves. When most people are tiring on a night out at, say, 1am, Maynard's night is only just beginning. The casino is an unavoidable diversion on the journey home. But, in fairness, his training sessions are equally lengthy. He has run marathons, too.

I thought that, as captain, he might struggle with the disciplinary side, but he changed his way of behaving in front of the team, especially during games. Instead of being seen at the bar late, he took himself off with other friends outside the squad if he felt that he needed to unwind. But I was surprised by the underlying theme in his book that he was content with what he had achieved in the game. He has a wonderful county record, with over 23,000 first-class and nearly 13,000 one-day runs. But for me his tally of four Tests and 14 One-Day Internationals does scant justice to one of the finest talents I saw in my time in the county game.

Whether his fast-living has contributed to this only he could truly say, but I do know that his behaviour on the 1994 England tour to the West Indies did not go down well with the management. He became known as the Shadow, such was his dependence on his friendship with Robin Smith, another well-known bon viveur, who likes to end every sentence with the word 'China'. Thus came Maynard's hysterical and self-contradictory advice to a team mate: "Be your own man, China." Maynard is amiable and generally good-natured, but he is easily led and influenced, as well as being determined to be the eternal youngster. A 38-year-old with dyed peroxide blonde hair is not one who is readily accepting the precepts of Father Time.

Maynard's admirable longevity in the professional game would suggest otherwise, but my suspicion is that his love of good-living has affected him. I think he is now a better player because the advancing years have taught him that he cannot continue burning the candle at both ends. He is much more selective in his revelry, and I think that his cricket has matured as a result. He has now become a big game performer for Glamorgan, rarely failing on the big occasion, as substantiated by his rousing century in the Benson & Hedges Cup Final of 2000.

The best innings I have seen from him, though, was in the Championship decider at Taunton when he plundered 142, reaching his century without a single. Most of those runs were made in near-Stygian gloom, with five lights glaring from the scoreboard light meter. What I remember most vividly about it was the manner of his on-driving – always considered as the most difficult of shots to play – against some excellent away-swing bowling from Caddick and Rose. To hit the exquisitely-timed on- drives as Maynard did that day was the work of a batsman on a different plane. Morris may have scored a nuggety, career-capping hundred, but it was not without its share of luck. Maynard required none of that fortune. Where Morris was the hard-working artisan that day, Maynard was a batting aristocrat.

In my formative years as a professional, I used to marvel at what I perceived as Maynard's extraordinary self-belief, exuding confidence and conviction at every sling and arrow thrown at him by the fickle master that is cricket. But I have come to learn that, beneath that self-assured exterior, there is a nervous side to his character. That surely must be the major reason why he has struggled so much when he has stepped up to the highest level.

There was a match in 2000 against Essex at Cardiff, which revealed a curious fallibility in Maynard's mental make-up. He scored 98 that day, but when on 97, he launched a fierce straight drive. It was a certain boundary and a certain century, but unfortunately non-striker Adrian Shaw was unable to move out of the way and the ball struck him. As a result, Maynard got only a single. He made a real fuss about this and was out in the next over, reaching the dressing room while cursing Shaw's folly.

It was ridiculous, but Maynard thought that it was fate that he was not to reach a hundred that day once Shaw had committed his 'sin'. I was genuinely surprised at Maynard's reaction. I thought he was stronger than that. After 1993 we endured two hapless seasons under Morris, and Maynard made it increasingly clear that he wanted the captaincy. Sometimes I felt that he went overboard in doing this, shaking his head at slip when he felt Morris had made a poor decision in the field. There was another surprising character in all this – wicketkeeper Colin Metson. He also made it obvious that he wanted a change of leader. I was stunned during the pre-season of 1995, while we were doing weight training in the National Sports Centre next to Sophia Gardens, to be confronted by him asking whom I thought should be captain. He went round all the other players asking the same. I cannot even recall my response, but I felt that it was not the appropriate thing to be doing. Morris was captain for that season, and that was that. Metson was a self-appointed shop steward and, in this role, he did do some sterling work concerning the standardisation and improvement of players' wages. He helped me when I was outraged to discover that I was earning less than workaday left-arm spinner Neil Kendrick. But it was ironic that when Maynard did eventually become captain, one of his first acts was to drop Metson and include Adrian Shaw. Shaw was by far the better batsman and most definitely a more popular team man, but nowhere near as proficient behind the stumps. Morris often used to walk around gravely proclaiming: "It will all come out in my book" – as much a reference to committee room shenanigans as Metson's meddling. But there was a curious entry in a question-and-answer piece he did for Metson's benefit brochure. Under the requested motto for life he entered: "Watch your back."

So why was the 1997 season so special? It was a settled team for a start. James, Morris, Dale, Maynard, Cottey, Croft, Shaw, Thomas, Waqar, Watkin, Cosker was the familiar cast, with Powell, Butcher, and Evans fulfilling bit-part roles. For just 14 players to be used in a season is remarkable, and 12 of those were reared in the Welsh youth system (Welsh Schools and Glamorgan Colts). Waqar and Gary Butcher, son of Alan and brother of Mark, were the exceptions.

Little heralded the success that was to come. The previous season had been moderate – tenth place in the Championship being tempered only with the promise of four batsmen (myself, Morris, Maynard and Cottey) all exceeding 1,400 Championship runs and all making double centuries. But the pre-season build-up had been good, with some prolonged clement weather meaning plenty of outdoor nets. And there was a real buzz about the place because of the two new arrivals – Duncan Fletcher and Waqar Younis. Waqar's coming was timely; a massive boost for the club. This was the first time that we had had an overseas bowler of such esteem and potency.

I remember being in the Beverley (as you can gather, a favourite watering hole for the Glamorgan team around that time) the previous season, standing with Adrian Dale, when Maynard came in to announce that we had just signed Waqar. Our delight was unconfined because we both realised that this could be the missing link. The Barbadian Ottis Gibson had previously been signed by Morris to be the strike bowler we needed to complement the unerring accuracy and probing of Steve Watkin, and the youthful promise of Darren Thomas. But he was a massive disappointment. At times he should not even have been in the side, such was his impotency. He clearly struggled on the slow home pitches and let that affect his general game. He was certainly talented. He could bowl quickly at times and swing the ball away from the right hander, too. And he could hit the ball as far as anyone I have ever seen. But he was not mentally up to the task of being an overseas player, which was clearly illustrated by two games in the August of his final season.

On both occasions we were batting last in a four-day game. The first was against Leicestershire at Swansea, and Gibson was sent to the wicket with instructions to play for a draw. But the spinners were on and he could not help himself, aiming big shots at every opportunity. Some came off but eventually he was bowled, to some quizzical looks from the balcony. Two games later, Kent came to Cardiff. It was a rain-affected match, and this time Gibson was instructed to go for his shots and win us the game. But this time he could not get the ball off the square, as we failed in our contrived chase by some 61 runs.

Waqar balanced our attack, which, with the spin duo of Robert Croft and Dean Cosker, could now compete on any surface. There were some early fears over his fitness, and he actually arrived with his foot in plaster from a stress fracture, but once physiotherapist Dean Conway had given him the all-clear he was superb. The club was very clever in structuring his contract so that it was heavily weighted towards bonuses, especially if we won the Championship. He immediately fitted into the dressing room, quickly hooking up with the younger lads who enjoyed sampling the nightlife.

A quick bowler cannot bowl flat out for a whole Championship campaign. There are times when an out-and-out pace merchant like Waqar has to rein himself in. But there are also times when he has to seize the moment and go for the kill. Waqar was excellent at recognising these situations. One of these critical scenarios occurred in the penultimate match of the season against Essex at Cardiff. The wicket was flat after a spell of particularly dry weather, which had left the square resembling the Gobi desert. And we were toiling in our effort to bowl out the visitors for a second time. Ronnie Irani, that renowned Welsh antagonist, was well established, along with Paul Grayson. Then, for some reason, Irani lofted Waqar over long on – not a particularly sensible shot against one of the quicker bowlers in the world.

Adrian Dale said to me: "That was one hell of a shot."

"Yes, for us," I replied. Indeed it was. Waqar was incensed and steamed in to bowl quicker than he had all season. Irani's stumps were soon rearranged by one of those trademark yorkers, and Danny Law's followed a moment later. Both were accompanied by some gentle words of advice as to the whereabouts of the pavilion from our Pakistani, which attracted the intervention of the umpires. But the tempo and atmosphere had crucially altered. What looked like a meandering draw was suddenly transformed into a winning position and, although we had some tremors on the way, we chased to win.

Waqar's presence lent the whole side a new aggression. Even I, normally the most reticent of players on the field, became occasionally vocal, sledging an old adversary, Kent's Alan Wells, at Canterbury, and then becoming embroiled in an unseemly contretemps with John Stephenson at Southampton. Wells had always irked me as an individual when he was captain at Sussex. He was an excellent player but, to me, he was a classic example of someone trying to be more aggressive when he was captain. He had made a lot of enemies doing this, prompting something of an exodus from Hove – himself, eventually, included. Wells' brother Colin was also released and, apparently, the two did not speak for a long time afterwards. Power can do strange things to people.

So, in the third game of the season, while I was batting on a spicy wicket on the first day, Wells kept on urging Dean Headley: "Come on, Deano – this bloke doesn't fancy it." He said it again and again, until I snapped, "Sorry, but we can't all be as f**king good as you." And then later, as Waqar steamed in, I suggested to him several times from my position at short leg that maybe he should send 'Mr. Popular' from Hove quickly on his way. I know that it doesn't sound much, but I rarely said a word on the field.

In the second round of the NatWest Trophy, I said plenty. It was an incident that was very much out of character, but actually shaped the destiny of the match. Hampshire had scored 302 with Robin Smith getting a hundred. In reply, we were 241 for six in the 53rd over (the NatWest was a 60-over competition then) with myself and Adrian Shaw at the wicket.

A muddle over a run ensued, and Shaw should have been run out at the bowler's end. But Shaun Udal made a horlicks of the throw, and disturbed the stumps while the ball was at least three yards away. My relief turned to indignation when umpire Ray Julian, obviously unsighted, gave Shaw out. I immediately voiced my displeasure as the Hampshire players gathered around. I could sense they were thinking of calling Shaw back when skipper Stephenson stormed in with: "Tell him to f**k off."

This was red rag to a bull for me. I lost it completely. Stephenson had been attempting to be aggressive with me ever since I'd come to the wicket, and now, in front of a live BBC Wales audience, I proceeded to tell him what I thought of him. I was screaming and swearing and ended up putting my glove to his nose as I offered to see him after the game. I can't recall saying anything memorable, just volleys of unprintable invective.

What was interesting was that none of his team mates attempted to intervene or help their leader. That said a lot to me. There had been rumours of serious discontent in the Hampshire dressing room, and here they were being validated before my eyes. Smith and Matthew Hayden, two big guys who would have scared the life out of me if they had been minded to butt in, were no further than ten yards away, yet they showed no sign of wanting to get involved. What they did do was call Shaw back, just before he reached the boundary edge. Stephenson just skulked back to his fielding position. From there I knew that the game was won. Hampshire were a broken side. What's more, adjudicator Chris Broad gave me man of the match for my 69 rather than Smith, and as I walked back to the dressing rooms at the back of the Hampshire pavilion, I heard an irate spectator berating Broad for his choice. "What James did was a disgrace to the game," he shouted. Now calmed, I realised an apology was in order, so I made my way to the

Hampshire dressing room. I was warned away by batsman Jason Laney, who said that Stephenson was in no state to be spoken to. The next season, Stephenson did make a point of speaking to me and was most contrite. After that, he never uttered a single word of aggressive intent to me on the field. Mike Kasprowicz, who joined Glamorgan in 2002, knows him well from their Essex days together, and reckons that he is one of the nicest people he has ever met. It is just that he suffers from what Kasprowicz terms 'white line fever', whereby one's personality undergoes a dramatic change once the boundary is crossed.

Kasprowicz reckons I suffered from it too. I did not often 'lose it' like I did at Southampton, but, by coincidence, did so twice with a Glamorgan colleague, Owen Parkin, the mildly eccentric swing bowler with a mathematics degree. He is highly intelligent, with a quirky sense of humour, but also very intense, and although we spent much time doing *The Daily Telegraph* crossword together, we also had our share of touchy moments. Firstly, in an internal practice match (I hated them, because things like this often happened) on a pre-season tour to Jersey, he began chirping me, prompting a heated verbal exchange, and I waited for him as he left the field. "Show some respect," I rather haughtily fumed.

Later, in 1999, on a white-hot pre-season day in Cape Town, Parkin wound me up during a game of football by mockingly heading the ball into the goal along the floor, to emphasise his side's superiority. My reaction was to slide into him, kneeing him in the ribs. I immediately apologised, acutely aware of my idiocy, but it did not prevent my team mates from branding me a loose cannon. Adrian Dale declared that the fact that I had 'a bit of mongrel' in me set me apart. Waqar was evidently also in no state to be spoken to at Southampton. BBC Wales sports correspondent Bob Humphrys was waiting for him as he ran triumphantly from the field having hit the winning runs. "How do you feel, Waqar?" Humphrys asked. "F**king great," was the reply.

I was lucky not to be disciplined for my actions. Ironically, two rounds later, Robert Croft was fined £1,000 for his part in a pushing incident with Essex's Mark Illott, and I was asked to be the player's representative at the disciplinary meeting. Further irony arrived later in the season in the shape of an interview with *Cover Point* video magazine. The interviewer? Stephenson's wife, Fiona!

For most of that season I was on top of the national batting averages. Graeme Hick pipped me at the end when my form deserted me in the last four games. I did dislocate the little finger on my right hand while dropping a dolly of a catch off Graham Thorpe at the Oval, but I cannot use that as an excuse for my relatively poor form at that crucial time. That lean spell cost me a place among the five *Wisden* Cricketers of the Year, a prestigious award only ever given to a cricketer once, and one I never achieved. Instead, skipper Maynard was honoured, with editor Matthew Engel noting that he had come into a rich vein of form at the crucial time while I had faltered. Indeed, it is an oft overlooked fact that while I averaged 68.26 (only Javed Miandad has averaged higher for Glamorgan – 69.43 in 1981) in first-class cricket, Maynard was not far behind with 65.00. Maynard did remark to me once in a quiet moment that he thought that I should have won the award, but I did have the consolation of a host of others, most notably the Professional Cricketers' Association Player of the Season, voted for exclusively by one's fellow players. Receiving that from John Major was one of my prouder moments. It meant that I had finally been accepted by my peers. They rated me.

I also met Jeffrey Archer that evening at the Café Royal in London, with him commenting: "We must get you into this England team." He was clearly not a man to be trusted! Neither was team mate Parkin, who dropped the trophy as we stumbled outside later that night. Going back to the start of that 1997 season, I remember the night before the first match, against Warwickshire at Cardiff. I was incredibly nervous because I would be facing Allan Donald the next day. I thought it was unfair that we should have to confront the fastest bowler in the world in the first match of the season. We had played the Wales Minor Counties side a couple of times as a warm up, but with all due respect to the likes of their opening bowler, Andrew Rowlands, it was not quite the same.

I always found the first game of the season the most nerve-wracking. Questions like "Will I still be able to do it?" were never far from my mind. We fielded first, which pleased me (predictably), but Warwickshire folded quickly and, by tea, Hugh Morris and I faced the South African.

It went better than I could have imagined. He did splatter my stumps just before the close, but by then I had reached 83. Hugh Morris went on to make his remarkable 233 not out before being poleaxed ("I wanted 300," he muttered to Dean Conway as he was stretchered off) and Adrian Dale (who has a reputation for always starting the season well) made a hundred.

I was happy with my contribution but I missed the subsequent one-day match because of a hip injury sustained in a collision with the rather large figure of Ashley Giles, who later that year, during the England fitness week in Lanzarote, astounded me with his remarkable aerobic fitness; a complete contrast to his lumbering image – he has been likened to "a wheelie bin" by one harsh commentator.

My form and confidence then dipped so low during the round of Benson & Hedges matches that, in the final one against Ireland (who included Hansie Cronje in their side), I asked Matthew Maynard if I could drop down the order – hardly the steely edge of an England aspirant, which I palpably was not at that stage. Thankfully, a trip to Headingley restored my faith; a hundred against Darren Gough and Chris Silverwood being a refreshing antidote. "Your bat looks big," commented Robert Croft, in reference to his perception of my solidity at the crease. Second innings half centuries for me and Morris prompted Scyld Berry in *The Sunday Telegraph* to write that "The opening pairs of several Test countries could not have equalled the batting of Steve James and Hugh Morris. James, once angular to the point of Roebuckian, has become fluent and high class, on the slow pitches at any rate."

I presume that Peter Roebuck, the former Somerset opener and now respected writer, must have also scored a lot of runs down to third man, but we will get to that later. For now, my season was underway after that one-day blip. I continued to bat down the order in one-day games – at number 6 – with some success, and my Championship form soared, with only one glaring failure. It was against Middlesex, complete with England selector Mike Gatting in their ranks, when I contributed 3 and 2 as we rolled over for an ignominious 31 in the second innings.

I don't recall feeling under undue pressure to perform in front of Gatting. It was more difficult to be batting for the first time in front of my future father-in-law, who came to watch on the last day. I was always curiously bothered by family and close friends watching me play. I once told my parents that I did not want them to come and watch after they had made the long trip to Cambridge and I had failed. I may have been influenced by Mike Atherton there, who told me that he hated his mother, Wendy, watching him. A few familial disputes ensued before I realised my folly. My parents were avid watchers of my career, and after that silly outburst, I was proud for them to share my triumphs as well as my failures. Often, friends joked that "I'd better get there at 11o'clock in case I miss you bat" and often they were right. Maybe I sometimes tried too hard to impress, born of insecurity and an inferiority complex. Therefore I was most satisfied by my performance when a group of friends made the train journey down from Lydney to watch the final day of the tour match against the Australians.

I remember the date well. It was July 18, 1997. I had narrowly missed a century in the first innings against the second-string tourist attack (although it did include my future team mate Mike Kasprowicz – "That was a fluke," he growled, as I hit him through the covers). But more importantly, I had fallen 15 short of becoming the first batsman in the country to 1,000 runs that season.

So there was much expectation that day. We were fielding at the start of play, and every time the ball came near me, the boys from Lydney, already well-oiled, would cheer raucously. "Pressure on," I thought. So it was with much relief, as well as no little pride, that I passed the landmark later in the afternoon. July 18 was unusually late for it to be passed – remember those good old days when batsmen passed it before the end of May? – but the rain of that wet summer was a significant factor. And, of course, the advent of four-day cricket has dramatically reduced the number of innings available to a batsman.

The match against Lancashire at Liverpool that season will also linger long in my memory for a number of reasons. Bizarrely, I was stranded on 99 not out for three nights after rain had intervened in the middle of the first afternoon. "Either someone is gobbing at me or it's starting to rain," said Lancashire captain Neil Fairbrother, with his typically northern humour, which manifested itself in my direction with him and Mike Watkinson singing *Lady in Red* as I walked to the wicket. They reckoned I looked like Chris de Burgh.

He was in a chipper mood anyway, having earlier talked his old mate Hugh Morris out. Fairbrother continually used to bawl "Don't forget the bomb" from slip as encouragement to his bowlers not to neglect their bouncer. But here his plan was more pre-determined and obvious. The bowler was Ian Austin, the rotund all-rounder known as either Bully or Oscar, whose ascent to England one-day colours was no doubt aided by the habitual assertions of David Lloyd, one-time England coach and opener, and now Sky TV commentator, that, "He bowls gun-barrel straight."

But that was not working for him at Liverpool as Morris and I built a solid start on a sluggish pitch. So Fairbrother made a point of telling everyone within earshot that he wanted Austin to bowl a bouncer at Morris. He spent an age deliberately placing a man back at deep square leg just for that purpose, all the time grinning at his ex-Young England colleague. Austin duly delivered the short ball and Morris' response was something in between a hook and a fend, which betrayed his indecision and confusion, and only ended up in wicketkeeper Warren Hegg's trusty gloves.

I was surprised that Morris had fallen for such a telegraphed ploy.

I eventually reached my hundred, Glen Chapple bowling one 'proper' ball, before some filthy declaration bowling set up an intriguing match, which Waqar settled with a devastating seven-wicket burst as Lancashire were skittled for 51.

But still none of these happenings are the most memorable recollection of that season's trip to the north-west. That honour goes to Darren Thomas and involves a tale oft-repeated in after-dinner speeches and sports forum answers since. But it is worth relating again, for it is in no way apocryphal or embellished. It is traditional on Glamorgan away trips for there to be a team meal on one of the evenings, at which a 'dick of the week' award is made, the recipient being ordered to wear a particular shirt. A combination of reticence and sense has more often than not precluded my winning this, but I was fortunate that the occasion on which I went from Lord's to Cardiff in Alan Butcher's car with Colin Metson's car keys in my pocket was pre-'shirt'. It was also pre-mobile phones, for those wondering!

And on another occasion when I did win it, I was required to wear my own Sunday League shirt with name emblazoned across the back. Unfortunately, there were some Somerset second-eleven players in the same Birmingham restaurant, and as I was in the process of explaining to one of them in the toilets what it was all about, Tony Cottey burst in to exclaim, "Don't listen to him, he always wears that!" I don't, but apparently there are people who do. It is rumoured that Dermot Reeve was especially keen to show off his new England playing shirt when he returned from the World Cup in 1995.

Anyway, one person is designated to organise a venue for this meal. On this occasion it was Thomas. Don't ask why, because I do not think it would be unfair or unkind to report that he has a tendency to be a little scatter-brained. It is to his credit that he sought help in his little task, for without it we may not have eaten at all. His aid was the receptionist at the hotel, who, unfortunately for Thomas, possessed a strong Scouse accent. She sorted it for him, and attempted to tell him all about the place.

Thomas merrily announced to the team that everything was arranged, taxis and all. "It's called Maissez-vous, must be French, I suppose." We were all surprised. Team meals are normally taken in an American-style burger place, such as TGI Fridays. So the taxis arrived on the evening and whisked us away. After some time, it became apparent that none of the drivers were entirely sure where this establishment was. Eventually our man said, "That's it over there, I think." It was no cosy French restaurant. It turned out to be a Beefeater... with a Mersey view!

My two most valuable innings in 1997 were my twin centuries (the only occasion on which I ever achieved this feat) at Abergavenny against Northamptonshire. This guided us to victory in a match that Morris missed because of a twisted ankle sustained in pre-match kick-about, and in which Maynard could not bat in the second innings because he had dislocated a finger. I felt pretty good about myself and my form at that stage – a purple patch, if ever there was one; and it was characterised by my complete lack of dread about batting. I had the runs in the bank, and the fear of failure was notably lacking. I was not willing it to rain, unlike Northamptonshire's Alan Fordham, who was in his final season of first-class cricket before becoming one of what seemed at the time like a flood of former players acceding to a position within the EWCB corridors of power. At mid-on, he was continually glancing at the clouds gathering over the nearby Sugar Loaf Mountain, and on the second day, when rain did momentarily intervene, was the first to joyously announce, "Come on the Duke (of Spain)" as it approached. The Glamorgan players prefer to confuse the English umpires with Welsh shouts of "Bwrw glaw."

Indeed, we were fortunate with the elements on the final day. As I left Abergavenny to travel to Neath to watch their rugby match against Cardiff, I was no more than 10 miles away on the Heads of the Valleys road when the heavens opened, prompting me to detour to Steve Watkin's Cimla residence to borrow a jacket. I'm probably the only Glamorgan player who would have done that. My scruffiness and Watkin's dress sense both merit equal notoriety.

Further evidence of my positive frame of mind had come earlier against Sussex at Swansea on a damp wicket. I had arrived at St. Helens on the second morning not expecting to have to bat too soon, with us still having five wickets in hand. But a collapse meant we were fielding sooner than we had anticipated, and, before we knew it, Sussex were reeling with Waqar unplayable. Umpire Peter Willey turned to me at square leg and commented with a grimace that suggested that I might not fancy it on such a pitch, "You'll be batting again soon". But, for once, I did fancy it. Even from that early stage. My composed state of mind was reflected in an innings of 82 not out, which, coupled with my first innings 48, meant that individually I scored more in the match than the whole Sussex team, whose irresolute batting mustered only 54 and 67. Steve Watkin, who is not naturally effusive in his praise, commented that he thought my second effort was one of my best innings ever.

Sussex's capitulation on the Saturday morning completed an unusual hat-trick. For the third week running, a low score (our 31 against Middlesex, Lancashire's 51 and now Sussex's 67) meant that we were able to watch the British Lions in action against South Africa – a veritable Godsend for me, especially as Martin Johnson's men clinched the series with 'that Jeremy Guscott' drop goal. The media interest in the possibility of my playing for England was enormous, mostly beyond my comprehension. In truth, I never thought that the selectors would pick me. During mid-August the chairman of selectors, David Graveney, came to Worcester to see our Championship match there.

That was my first chat with anyone from the hierarchy and I was at pains to stress that I had changed as a batsman, that I no longer ran everything down to third man. He said that he knew that, and that all I could do was keep scoring runs. It was a particularly difficult match for me, in that my uncle had died of cancer the week before and the funeral was on the last scheduled day of the match. I was still hoping to make it if circumstances allowed.

As it was, we were batting on that day, in what turned out to be a forlorn pursuit of Worcestershire's 374. My father urged me to make a century if I could not make the obsequies and I did – my fifth of the summer, but we lost the match in a rather gung-ho chase. My family has never been given to excessive shows of emotion but my father could not hold back the tears when, during the traditional celebration of the life of his brother Gwyn, at his favourite Cross Inn at Aylburton, he was told that I had made a hundred. He might have been pretty proud too, when I hit those winning runs at Taunton. But he wasn't there. He had decided that the game would no doubt run into a fourth day and that he would travel then to witness the final rites. My wife-to-be, Jane, made a late decision to rush down the M5, but my parents decided that it was too late and missed it. And by now I wanted them there! For me the final confirmation that we had achieved something special came the next day. Cardiff were playing Harlequins at the Arms Park, and, after the game, I met up with Rory Jenkins, a friend from Cambridge who enjoyed a decent rugby career with Harlequins, Wasps and Swansea. As we shared a beer, a team mate of his approached us. "Ah, Fester, meet Steve," said Rory.

"Pleased to meet you," he said. "Congratulations on the win yesterday – first time for 28 years." Now, if Keith Wood, the former Ireland hooker, knew about it, then that was good enough for me. In fact, Wood was keen to celebrate the success with me then, but the Harlequins bus was about to leave. "Come up to London for the return game and we'll have a few beers then," he said. Unfortunately, I didn't. I wonder if he remembers. I doubt it. But if he does, I wouldn't mind celebrating that win some time with one of the more inspirational sportsmen I've ever seen. Not that there was any lack of celebration. There was my wedding to Jane for a start, which took place exactly a week after our triumph. I can't say it attracted a lucrative offer from *Hello!* magazine, but it did receive more media interest than it might have ordinarily, with most of the Glamorgan players there, as well as Mike Atherton and rugby luminaries such as former Wales fly halves Jonathan Davies and Gareth Davies, who were present because of Jane's job as physiotherapist to Cardiff RFC.

But there was one rather annoying postscript to the 1997 season. One of those regular dreams had been to appear in the crowd of the prestigious BBC Sports Personality of the Year

Awards in London. That and every sportsman's fantasy of appearing on the BBC's *A Question of Sport*. Now, I have never achieved sufficient fame or standing to merit the latter, but at the end of 1997, Glamorgan did receive two invitations for the former, as the Championship-winning county quite rightly does every year.

Captain Maynard was away wintering in New Zealand. So who do you think went? Hugh Davies, the chairman of the cricket committee and Tony Dilloway, the director of marketing. That's who. Decent enough blokes, but how many runs did they score or how many wickets did they take? No player was even considered. Now that rankles.

CHAPTER TWO

THE ACID TEST

I am not sure what quality certain young players possess that sees them singled out as potential England cricketers. Whatever it is, it was missing in my case. Graham Saville, the Cambridge University and Combined Universities coach, told my father that he thought I would make a good county player. Others were not even convinced of that. One Gloucestershire youth coach thought I could not play spin, another that I was gun-shy against the quicker bowlers (I had broken a finger and was reluctant to play in a tour game in Sussex). And Alan Butcher told me, "Good players do not score as many runs down to third man as you do."

I think that it is fair to say that I was not one of the most aesthetically-pleasing batsmen to watch. Adjectives such as 'languid' and 'flowing' did not apply to my unique brand of batsmanship. Indeed, my Glamorgan team mate Steve Watkin once told me that England batsman Robin Smith had remarked to him on a tour to the West Indies in 1994: "Jeez, he's an ugly batsman, that James." He was right. Around that time I was awful.

At school I had been predominantly a leg-side player; basically a blocker, who could occupy the crease, mainly using the pace of the ball to deflect my runs. But when I got to university I became an over-eager theorist, a tinkerer. I thought that I needed to expand my range of shots and my proposed way of doing that was by bringing my top hand grip further round the front of the bat handle.

However, this was done without recognising the inherent lack of strength in my wrists, which are attached to quite the puniest (and hairiest) pair of forearms ever seen on a professional sportsman. Some concerted weight training over the years has considerably strengthened them, but at that stage they were pathetically weak and were unable to aid me in my deluded plans. The result was that I was unable to sufficiently control the face of the bat. It kept opening up and the ball kept sliding down to third man. I had always been a fairly adept late cutter of the ball, but now it was going into that region without me ever intending it to do so. Thus I became known as the greatest practitioner ever of the 'Fenner's drive', an intended cover drive that slips unwittingly off towards the third-man boundary.

The situation reached its nadir during a match for Cambridge against Northamptonshire in 1990. *Wisden* records that I scored 39, before being lbw to my former Glamorgan colleague Greg Thomas, but what it does not say is that I 'hit' four fours in one over from the distinctly quick Welshman, all of them going either through or over the slip cordon. It was embarrassing, prompting the amiable Thomas to utter through clenched teeth: "Are we playing by different rules today?" I can think of many other fast bowlers who might have put it slightly differently.

Mike Atherton was watching, en route to Lord's to play for the MCC in the season's pipe opener against the champion county Worcestershire. "Well played, Bradman," he said at lunch just after that over. I am not sure that Atherton ever really altered his opinion after that day. Such were my technical inadequacies at that stage in my career that, from then on, I faced an unending battle to convince people that I had changed.

In 1996 when I scored a double century at Worksop, I was

met by David Lloyd, then England coach, in the tea room. "Athers has just been on the phone," he said. "Wants to know why they haven't got a third man." Charles Randall of *The Daily Telegraph* said to me later: "You were really unlucky with England, you know. I reckon that the selectors, even your mate Athers, thought it was impossible for someone to have improved that much." Of course, I had dreamt about playing for England. I had enacted my debut on the lawn at Lydney. But did I ever really believe it would happen? I was in Zimbabwe in 1990 on an evening out with the future captain and mainstay of Zimbabwean cricket, Andy Flower, when he asked me what my ambitions were in cricket. "To play for England," I said instantly. But I knew that it was a long way off. Miles away.

In the end, I went back to my old school, Monmouth, to see my coach and mentor Graham 'Budgie' Burgess, the former Somerset player. "What have they done to you?" was his astonished reaction upon seeing me bat.

"It's my fault, Budge (sic), no one else's," I mumbled.

We went back to basics. And I think that, over the years, I did change. I might not have convinced everyone, but I certainly got people talking. I kept overhearing professionals saying the same thing. "It's incredible how he has improved" – commentator Mark Nicholas, the former Hampshire captain, speaking to Matthew Maynard; Worcestershire and England wicketkeeper Steve Rhodes to Maynard; umpire Barry Dudleston to a Middlesex fielder. All conversations I was not meant to hear, but highly encouraging and satisfying ones.

So it came to be after all those years of struggle that my annus mirabilis of 1997 meant that, for the first time in my entire career, the announcement of the winter touring parties held some appeal for me. It was the first time I had ever been in serious contention. And the last, as it turned out. I did not honestly think that I would be included in the senior party to go to the West Indies, but there were some glimmers of hope. Atherton was still captain, and I had spoken to him a few weeks before, ostensibly to ascertain whether he would be attending my wedding at the end of the season, but no doubt subconsciously fishing for information. "I reckon you've got a chance," he said.

A couple of seasons before, Atherton had invited me, among a host of England stars and some old Cambridge pals, to play in a charity game in Chelsea for him. He put us all up in the Hilton opposite Lord's, and it just happened that, on that same evening, he was meeting with the selectors to pick the winter touring party.

Ray Illingworth was chairman of selectors then, and was in the bar with Atherton. As they left to go off to make their decisions, I, fuelled by much Dutch courage, shouted: "Hey Athers, tell Illy I can't make it this winter," in the certain knowledge that Mr Illingworth would not have the faintest idea who I was.

On the day in 1997 that the touring parties were announced, Colin Metson was having a benefit six-a-side at St. Fagans in Cardiff. I had pulled out of the match because of a dislocated finger, but I had agreed to meet the press there, whatever happened. I listened to the radio in the spare room at home. I was on the A tour, not the big one. It was not the news I wanted. I drove to St. Fagans, rehearsing what I was going to say. It was obviously big news in Wales, because all the local media had been pushing for me. My exclusion was a prime chance for them to have another go at the England selectors for omitting Glamorgan players, more because of the county they play for than their playing talents. But I did not want to fuel that argument. I dead-batted all the questions just as I would have done in my schoolboy blocking days, but inside I was disappointed. I thought it was then or never.

I still think that being given the vice-captaincy of the A tour to Sri Lanka and Kenya was a sop. Sure, I was proud to go on my first (and last) international tour, but there was still the lingering feeling that if I was not to be selected then, it was never going to happen. There was talk of being on standby should someone be injured in the Caribbean, but I felt deflated. All the Glamorgan boys were very supportive and Duncan Fletcher made an interesting comment. "Don't worry about the vice-captaincy thing. If I were you, I wouldn't get too involved. Just concentrate on your own game and make sure you get the runs," he said.

I actually think the England selectors have a very hard job. There are too many cricketers to pick from in this country and therefore it must be difficult to decide which ones will cut the mustard at the top level. Sustained success for a county does not necessarily mean a player can do it in Test matches, but as county cricket is the only barometer, it cannot be ignored. I think that in Wales it is an easy line to trot out: "Our players do not get picked because they play for an unfashionable county." Two players of yesteryear, Alan Jones and Don Shepherd, certainly have cause for grievance. Neither got an official cap, although Jones did play against the Rest of the World in 1970, receiving a cap and blazer before the match was demoted in status. He scored a remarkable 36,049 first-class runs while Shepherd took 2,218 first-class wickets.

Jones helped a lot in my formative years with Glamorgan, and when I was eventually selected for England, I wrote to him to thank him. But I was embarrassed because I knew that I was nowhere near the player that he was; that people would never talk in the hushed, reverential tones that they still use today when discussing the left-hander from Swansea. He truly is a Glamorgan legend, as is Shepherd.

Of the more recent players, Steve Watkin has been the one to receive the rawest of deals from the England selectors. Three caps were a meagre reward for years of consistent success. I think that there was very little to choose between him and Angus Fraser. Their first-class records are remarkably similar – Watkin 902 wickets at 27.92 and Fraser 879 wickets at 27.40 – and yet Fraser played 43 more Tests than Watkin. What is more, England won two of the three Tests in which Watkin played. He did go on the West Indies tour in the winter of 1993/94 and Atherton confided in me some time afterwards that he had made a mistake in preferring Alan Igglesden to Watkin in the first Test of that trip. Not that that will be of any consolation to Watkin, for, save a couple of One-Day Internationals, his tour, and indeed, international career, was over.

Critics have suggested that Watkin disappeared in the heat of the battle, citing the 2000 Benson & Hedges final, when he bowled an uncharacteristically erratic opening spell, as an example. But I have never seen that in him. The reason why he bowled poorly in that game was the fact that he was given the West Indies tour match off in the week before, as well as what would have been a timely dress-rehearsal in a Sunday League game at Lord's the previous Sunday. He was the type of bowler who needed to bowl lots of overs to establish his rhythm.

The A tour to Kenya and Sri Lanka was not a successful one for me, nor especially enjoyable. It began in a damp Nairobi where I missed out badly in a three-day game against a moderate Kenya side, where Leicestershire batsman Darren Maddy filled his boots with a double hundred. Early on in Sri Lanka, Jane phoned me and announced that she was pregnant, later becoming ill enough with morning sickness to be admitted to hospital. So my mind was maybe not as much on the job in hand as it might have been, especially when a bomb blast in Kandy, where we were due to play an unofficial Test, threw the whole tour into doubt.

Prince Charles was due to visit the country as well, and there was talk of that being cancelled, so there was a good deal of discussion and debate as to what we should do. I just expressed the view that we should follow the advice of the British High Commission. They knew more than we did. But I would not have been distraught if we had abandoned the trip. Maddy had seemingly jumped ahead of me in the queue of aspiring Test batsmen (skipper Nick Knight was also having a modest tour) and I wanted to be at home with my pregnant wife. As it was, the itinerary was altered slightly so that we avoided Kandy and I was dropped for the final Test at Moratuwa, a desperately disappointing blow, which, I thought, signalled the end of any chance of representing the full England team. It was not done in the most subtle circumstances either. I had been part of the tour selection committee all along, but now was curiously not invited to a meeting. Knight appeared at my door some time later to say that they had decided to give an opportunity to some of the younger batsmen (Owais Shah had just arrived from the U-19 World Cup).

I'm sure that it was not Knight's decision. It was down to the two England selectors, Mike Gatting and Graham Gooch, who were coach and manager of the tour respectively. It was interesting working with these two on the trip. I knew Gatting reasonably well from county cricket, and thought him friendly and helpful, whilst I had barely spoken to Gooch before. When he played county cricket, it seemed that the brutal excellence of his play rendered him a little aloof, often unaware of the identities of the youngsters he was facing. But by the end of the trip, I felt much more comfortable dealing with Gooch than I did with Gatting. I marvelled at Gooch's work ethic, even in retirement. He was up early every morning to put himself through the most rigorous of fitness sessions. If there was no gym or suitable running venue available, we would often pass him on the stairs on the way down to breakfast as he did a punishing series of climbs up and down the hotel. Gatting did not join him. His reputation is more for eating than running, and he lived up to this by spending every spare minute arranging meals and team evenings out. I spent a lot of time with Gooch, practising and training, and found his methods stimulating and rewarding. He is a thoughtful man, too. I was most touched when he made a special point of seeking me out for some comforting words at Cardiff in 2003 soon after I had had my final knee operation.

Unfortunately, I did not enjoy Gatting's style of coaching. I disliked his habit of chiding the players on the field while he was sitting on the balcony. "What was he saying about me when I was out there?" I wondered. His relatively unsuccessful tenure at Middlesex, jumping straight from being a player, has probably revealed that coaching is not to be his future, but that should not detract from his engaging conviviality. He belonged to an era in cricket where tales were told and lessons learnt between teams in the bar after the game, and has therefore always been the first to try to make a youngster who is fresh into the game feel at home with a word of advice or a pint to make acquaintance.

In my first year at Cambridge, he was busily doing this in the Salisbury Arms when he was rudely interrupted by an anti-apartheid supporter, who objected to his presence as skipper of the rebel tour to South Africa, branding him 'a racist pig' and throwing a drink all over him. It was clearly a set up, because this happened at 9pm and, without any difficulty, the story was plastered across the front pages of *The Sun* newspaper the next day.

I think I took Duncan Fletcher's advice all too literally. I was an awful vice-captain to Knight, rarely offering advice and, on the one occasion when he left the field to have a discussion with the British High Commissioner, I could not wait for him to return. I left the same two bowlers on for half an hour and barely changed the field. The most animated I became on the whole tour was on the last evening when we were attempting to track down a recording of the England versus Wales rugby match, which had taken place earlier in the day. But, thankfully, I began the 1998 county season in decent form, recording a double century against Northamptonshire. It obviously impressed Gooch, who appeared at our next game at Lord's to talk to me. "Should have got a few more," I said to him in all seriousness. I had played a tired shot to the off spin of Graeme Swann, not long after the break during which Adrian Shaw had mentioned to me that history beckoned (Emrys Davies' Glamorgan record of 287). I hadn't deliberately meant to, but I was parodying the famous Gooch phrase that permeates county cricket. "Never got enough, youngster" in that easily-imitable high-pitched Essex drawl.

Playing for England seemed as distant a dream as ever, but in less than three weeks' time it would become a nerve-racking reality. On June 17 I was at Sophia Gardens watching the rain fall as we attempted to begin a Championship match against Leicestershire. The forecast was poor so I badgered Adrian Dale into going across the road to the National Sports Centre to do some weights. Suddenly, Mike Fatkin, Glamorgan's chief executive, and Matthew Maynard, the captain, appeared at the door.

"David Graveney has been on the phone," said Fatkin. "Mark Butcher is injured and they want you up at Lord's as cover."

"I'd better be off, then" was the best I could come up with. Dale joked about being left to train on his own and that I should remember my roots. I was in a daze. I returned to the dressing room where there were congratulations aplenty, with only Owen Parkin, who was probably trying to be funny, unhelpfully pointing out: "Oh my God – 28,000 people watching, and Allan Donald steaming in. Your arse will be going!" He was right, but it was not what I wanted to hear at that time. There was an embargo on the news until 12 noon. So when Rob Freeman, then of the *South Wales Argus*, phoned me in a panic because he had not received my weekly column, I could (and probably should have, considering how good that paper has been to me) have provided him with a major scoop for his later evening editions. But I didn't. And not long after, he phoned. "What's this story on the wires? Why didn't you tell me?"

Next came an uncomfortable moment as I saw Darren Maddy, who must also have been in contention. He hadn't heard the news, so I thought it best to tell him. He must have been gutted inside but he shook my hand and even hugged me. I went home to pack some stuff and the BBC Wales crew came round, even interviewing my now heavily-pregnant wife, Jane. When I arrived at the hotel in Swiss Cottage, Robert Croft was there to meet me and most of the players were milling around. I arranged to go out for a meal with Croft, Mike Atherton and Angus Fraser. As I went up in the lift, I met David Lloyd, the coach, who said: "Have they told you whether you're playing or not? I think you will be, because Butch is really struggling with his thumb."

I was a little confused as to why the coach was not telling me whether I was playing, but anyway thought it best if I prepared as if I was going to play. I was tired. I had a long soak in the bath. I had played a lot of cricket over the preceding weeks. I kept saying to myself: "You've faced Donald before. You can do it again." But I was not convinced. Did I really want to play for England? That may seem like a daft question, but it did occur to me. I am not sure if everyone who plays county cricket aspires to the highest level. They might trot out the familiar clichés when asked, but what about when it came to the crunch?

County cricket can be a comfortable existence, with some public-ity but not too much. Test cricket is completely different – a harsh environment, and not just on the field. The exposure can be frightening and the media glare baleful. Like me, I reckon most dream of batting for England but dread what Geoffrey Boycott and the other TV experts might be saying about their technique. Did I want it? Could I handle it? Other Glamorgan players hadn't managed it. Maybe I was another country bumpkin who couldn't cope with the 'big city' atmosphere? All these bewildering thoughts and questions were whizzing around inside my head. But eventually, after much deliberation, my inner man, amidst a whirl of emotions, resolved that I had nothing to lose and, even if I did fail, it would not matter. Not exactly full of confidence, then.

I went for a meal and unexpectedly ordered a bottle of Budweiser to accompany it. This was most unusual for me and reflected my nervous disposition. Some of the others ordered beer, too (not from nerves, I'm sure) and this did not go unnoticed by a member of the public, who immediately reported it to *The Daily Mail*. Unsurprisingly, he did not recognise me and my name did not appear amongst the miscreants. The only piece of advice I can recall came from Atherton, and in this he presaged his later and much-publicised disparagement of county cricket. "Remember, this is not that piddly county cricket. Don't try any quick singles to Rhodes." It was tongue-in-cheek, but he was clearly recalling from Cambridge my obvious eagerness to get off the mark. Ironically, I received this message the next day from Hugh Morris.

Jamer,
Many congratulations – thoroughly deserved. I'll be running every one with you! I only hope Athers can run as fast as your old opening partner!
All the best,
Banners (He was thus nicknamed after the TV detective Banacek.)

Morris was not the most fleet of foot between the wickets. Mind you, neither was Atherton.

It is my biggest regret about my time with England that I was never involved in the build-up to a Test. If I had netted with the team two days before the Test, it would have helped me to settle in. I would have been able to size up the situation and handle it a little better. Some people reckon that it is better if you have no time to think about such things but I hold the opposite view. I wanted that extra time.

Thankfully, it was raining as I drove to Lord's on my own on the morning of June 18, so that assuaged my fears a little. That old habit again – the moment of truth was likely to be delayed.

There were numerous faxes and good luck cards awaiting me in the dressing room. But where the hell did I change? Whenever a youngster comes into the Glamorgan side, the old sweats normally allow him to find a space before joyfully exclaiming something like, "Oww, Matthew Maynard has been changing there for 50 years."

I didn't quite have that problem, as everyone's kit was in situ after the previous couple of days' practice. But where could I sneak in? There was precious little room. There were a lot of players there, because Jack Russell and Graeme Hick had also been called up late to cover for injuries. I dithered for a while and then was mightily relieved by the soothing Yorkshire accent of Chris Silverwood, who eventually missed out on the final eleven.

"Come next to me, Jamo."

"Thanks, Spoons."

Mark Butcher arrived. I watched him like a hawk. He looked fit to me – well, I suppose he would, because he had a thumb injury. He wasn't likely to be limping now, was he? But my thinking was not rational at this stage. The rain continued. And the faxes kept on coming. I was overwhelmed. School friends I had not even spoken to since leaving sent their best. And I wasn't even sure of playing. Butcher went to the indoor nets to try out his thumb. I waited on the balcony for him to reappear.

It did not take long. I spied him walking back dejectedly. This was it. He was out. I was in. Confirmation came from skipper Alec Stewart. "You're in. Good luck."

The dark clouds lifted and the warming up began. Simon Hughes, the former Middlesex and Durham seamer, whose last years of cricket coincided with my most awkward of technical times, grabbed me for a live TV interview. It was a change not to be cursed by him. He asked what it was like to have two Welshmen (Croft being the other) playing together in a Test at Lord's. I panicked a little because I was, of course, born in Lydney. I told him my father would not be happy with that contention and declared myself an Englishman. In a flash I realised I might have ostracised myself from all those loyal Glamorgan fans who had so pushed for my elevation. I had much more pressing worries, but suddenly that statement consumed my world. Thankfully, I managed to clear my mind and the comment passed relatively unnoticed (though one or two team mates noted it).

There were congratulations from the other players, none more animated than Jack Russell, who in the end was not required. He grabbed the three lions on my sweater and barked (excuse the pun), "They can never take them away from you." As if mindful of some mild embarrassment (it was more surprise really) on my part, he quickly qualified his actions with, "Don't worry, I do that to everyone." And there was a fax from Monmouth School: *Euge! Super lunam praeceptores puerique!* I did not bother showing that to Dean Headley, England's Darren Thomas, but if I had, I'm sure he would have told me that it translated as: Bravo! The masters and pupils are over the moon! Stewart won the toss and inserted the South Africans – a wise move, in my mind. Again the moment of truth was being delayed. The ball moved around in the overcast conditions. Early wickets fell, and then I became embroiled in a moment of controversy. I was fielding at short leg (as good a place to hide as any) and Dominic Cork bowled a ball to Daryll Cullinan, which he clipped off his toes. The ball hit me and then bounced up off the ground near my right foot into my hands. To some it looked as if the ball had hit me on the boot and bounced up for an unlikely catch. Cork was adamant it had. I knew it had not, but as the umpires were consulted I lacked the courage to contradict my colleague's conviction. Atherton was at slip and knew it was not right. "You've been in this game five minutes and already you're cheating," he joked.

Later, Cork hatched a plan that, as he ran up for the fourth ball of an over to Hansie Cronje, I would retreat backwards (surreptitiously, and against the spirit of the game) from square leg towards the boundary to hopefully catch his misdirected hook shot to the inevitable bouncer. But as I did so, the non-striker Jonty Rhodes spotted what I was up to and stopped Cork (quite rightly, too) amidst some acrimony. What was I doing? I should never have got embroiled in Cork's gamesmanship, but my naivety rendered me more like a teenage tyro than a 30-year-old county cricketer of some experience. I apologised to Rhodes at the next break and watched him score a superb century. I had to laugh in 2003 when Cork became involved in a cheating controversy with Australian Brad Hodge. Cork lamented that the game was becoming ever more akin to football with its sharp practices and its failure to uphold the spirit of the game. From anyone else it might have been a valid point.

That night, my mobile phone was bombarded with calls, mostly full of well-meaning felicitations ahead of my maiden Test innings the next day. There was a cheeky request for tickets from Gary Martin, the former Zimbabwean cricketer, whom I had not spoken to for four years. Out of the woodwork and all that! I went to my room, which I shared with Jane, and did not see another member of the team until the morning. This was to continue for the whole game. It was something I was unused to at Glamorgan, where all but the captain, coach, overseas player and the odd senior player, share rooms. I can understand that most Test cricketers play all year round and need their privacy and down time, but for me it was not what I wanted. I wanted to feel part of this England side. I did not.

It was not that any of the players were aloof – some were naturally friendlier than others – but it was just what they were used to. And, anyway, they had their own games to consider. The most intriguing to observe was Graham Thorpe, who sat in one of the armchairs near the balcony doors, twiddling with his row of Kookaburra bats, immersed in an introspection that bordered on brooding self-absorption. The only time he really spoke to me was when he cast a repugnant look at the plates of 'refuelling' food, which arrived after play – slices of pizza topped with chilli con carne – and muttered: "Carbohydrates? Huh…"

More faxes awaited me on the second morning including one from the Wales rugby team, who were in South Africa. That made me proud. Earlier, I had pronounced myself English, but I felt Welsh then. The South African first innings continued well into the second afternoon after the rain breaks of the first day, and eventually we got down to Allan Donald batting at number 10. I was back in at short leg as Dean Headley steamed in at Donald. The England fast bowlers were working on the theory that their South African counterparts were going to dish out plenty of 'chin music', as the West Indians so love to call it, so they would get their retaliation in first. So Headley bounced Donald mercilessly. With each one, Donald became more incensed. And so did I, quaking in my boots at short leg as I contemplated my first Test innings against a highly-charged Donald. "For Christ's sake, Dean, pitch it up," I was thinking. I wanted to shout it out.

Donald survived, despite taking some body blows, but his partner, Paul Adams, did not, so I ran off to prepare for an innings I thought would never come. I wrote a diary piece for the *Wisden Cricket Monthly* the following month and it is worth recalling my thoughts then. "Although I wouldn't tell him to his face, there is no one I would rather have walked through the Long Room with on my debut than the former Downing College defender (I saw him score a cracking own-goal once)."

Atherton asked me whether I wanted to take first ball. I was resolute in my insistence in doing so. Subsequently, Atherton has praised Marcus Trescothick for his confident insouciance on this subject. So I had failed an early test. I always preferred to take first ball; a superstition eased by my long-time partner, Hugh Morris' liking for being number two. Although, with experience, I became less concerned about it, initiated by Matthew Elliott's arrival at Glamorgan, after which we used to take it in turns. And, ironically, that is what myself and my erstwhile university colleague ended up doing here.

There were 14 overs left in the day and I was remarkably relaxed as I jumped out on to the Lord's turf with Atherton. It was a proud moment, and without being supercilious, I bet it was greeted by quite a few people saying: "I know him. I once got pissed with him in Swansea/Cambridge/Lydney/Harare." Delete as appropriate. I know that a group of Zimbabwean friends crowded around the TV in the Harare Sports Club to watch; Craig Wishart, the Zimbab-wean cricketer, apparently urging me to keep my head still as Donald pounded in.

Donald's first ball flew wildly down the leg side. But it got me thinking: "That was quick." A furtive glance at the speedometer confirmed my suspicions – 90mph. I soon opened my international account thanks to Australian umpire Darrell Hair, who took pity on me and gave me a run for a ball that clearly thumped against my arm guard.

Glamorgan were batting against Leicestershire at the time and a cheer went around the ground as I got off the mark, apparently prompting their voluble wicketkeeper, Paul Nixon, to comment, "I bet it was down to third man." I now faced Shaun Pollock, who very kindly treated me to two juicy leg-stump half-volleys, which I gratefully dispatched to the square-leg boundary. There was much applause, and I felt good. A third leg stump delivery should have been sent on its way too, but I succeeded only in finding wide mid on. Next ball, I scrambled a single.

Atherton then departed for a duck, getting squared up by Pollock and being caught in the gully. Later he asked me what I thought of his dismissal and I just stated the bleeding obvious: "You got squared up, mate." However, interestingly, he thought he had tried to stay too side on, and then had to overcompensate. It was the end of the over and Nasser Hussain arrived, looking fiercely determined. We said nothing. He stayed at the other end, and just nodded his head, as if to say, "Come on."

I remember as Donald ran in, I was thinking to myself: "I wonder if I'll hook, if it is short." It is such an instinctive thing. This ball, though, was not short enough for hooking, just short of a length, in fact, but it bounced and jagged back towards my body, coming down the famous Lord's slope. All I could do was glove it down the leg side. The ball made significant contact with my glove and I turned, half expecting it to have been well out of the reach of wicketkeeper Mark Boucher, who was having an indifferent tour.

He seemed to drop as many as he caught, exemplified by his spilling a much simpler chance off Stewart later that evening. But this one he caught. And quite spectacularly, too. He leapt high to his left to pouch it, much to the delight of Donald, who roared triumphantly down the wicket, arms outstretched as if mimicking an aeroplane. I did not hesitate in walking. It seemed the obvious thing to do. There were some comments the next day in the dressing room, questioning whether I should have walked. But Stewart soon silenced that by saying that was the way I played, and that should be it. However, he seemed determined that I should wear a chest guard in the second innings because he felt sure that the South Africans would target me in that area again. I had never done so before and was reluctant to do so now. The ones I had previously tried on had been cumbersome and uncomfortable. But Stewart and some others were insistent.

Donald later wrote in his autobiography, *White Lightning*: "We were pleasantly surprised that England had picked Steve James to replace the injured Mark Butcher, because Lord's was a very difficult place for an England player to win his first cap. At our team meeting the night before, I said to the boys, 'Steve James will be filling his pants. He's come out of the blue at short notice; he's in unfamiliar territory with all the pressure on him. What's more, he likes the ball on leg side, and also wide on the off. We've got to be at him all the time and deny him his favourite scoring areas.' That's exactly what we did, and the poor bloke looked out of his class." Hmm, thanks Mr. Donald. What I do know is that I had faced him before in county cricket with some degree of success, but this was different. He bowled at least a yard quicker here.

We were three wickets down at the close of the second day and I hoped that we would bat well enough on the third to avoid the follow on. I did not really fancy that on my debut.

But it was not to be. Early on that third afternoon, the South Africans invited us to bat again after we were out for 110. Just before that, Atherton and I found ourselves in the toilets at the same time. "Are you okay?" he enquired, maybe sensing some unease. "Can I take first ball this time, as I hate being on a pair?" he added. Who was I to argue? I would have preferred to have taken first, but was not about to complain. But hang on, where was that famous strength of character from the former England skipper? I thought it was a rare moment of weakness from him, especially when one considers his later observations about Trescothick. Robert Croft kindly lent me his chest guard, and, for the only time in my career, I wore one. I looked and felt fat – as if that mattered. Atherton was indebted to umpire Hair for getting off his dreaded pair; a ball from Donald striking him on his backside before skirting off to the boundary, with Hair declining to signal leg byes. We joked in the middle of the wicket. "Off 'em, off your arse," I said.

As I prepared to face Pollock, I made the mistake of suddenly beginning to think of my first innings' leg-side boundaries. I thought how nice it would be to do that again. As a result, I squared myself up too much and Pollock's second ball was a decent leg cutter pitched on a good length. Because of my poor position, I edged it to second slip where a future team mate, Jacques Kallis, eagerly snapped it up in his fly-paper mitts. I was crestfallen and was embarrassed to walk through a deafeningly-quiet Long Room. There were none of the 'bad lucks' of the first innings.

It was a Saturday and the players of Lydney CC had gone to great lengths to ensure that a TV was in the clubhouse so that they could watch their former player bat. Sadly, before they could adjust the picture on the portable, I was gone. And, I thought, I was gone forever from Test cricket. Back to that diary piece in *The Cricketer*: "Alas, the Test initiation of this late developer was not destined to be a successful one. I honestly felt that I got two fairly decent deliveries. I would love another chance, because I don't think anyone, whoever they are, can get used to Test cricket in one match. There is a lot to get used to – the intensity of everything, the media scrutiny and all that goes with it. It tells its own tale that I, normally the most voracious of eaters, did not make it up to the dining-room, which Nancy made so famous, until the final day."

I returned to Glamorgan, a chastened, even embarrassed man. The media already seemed to be suggesting that I was a one-cap wonder, and I had no reason to disagree with them. I played for Glamorgan at Trent Bridge against Nottinghamshire but, on the second morning, as I drove to the ground with Matthew Maynard, I received a call on my mobile from David Graveney, the chairman of selectors. He said: "They've decided to go for a left hand/right hand combination, so Nick Knight is coming in." He went on to trot out the usual flannel about continuing to score runs and keeping myself in contention. I didn't question anything. I just said, "Thanks for letting me know," and put the phone down. By saying 'they', either Graveney was not brave enough to say himself that he did not consider me worthy, or he was absolving himself from the decision. I was gutted, because I presumed that Butcher would have regained fitness and he would play. But this was different.

If I was good enough to have been given the chance at Lord's then I was worth an opportunity now at Old Trafford. I had failed at Lord's, but surely my form over the previous seasons warranted a second bite. It was a classic case of the inconsistency that blighted England selection in those days.

Things improved considerably under the regime of Duncan Fletcher and Nasser Hussain, but this was poor and mirrored the treatment meted out to the Gloucestershire left-armer Mike Smith in 1997, when he was picked for one Test at Headingley against Australia. He did not open the bowling, which is when he is most effective with his late swing, and saw Matthew Elliott (who went on to make 199) dropped at slip by Graham Thorpe when he was on only 29. He was never picked again.

I scored a hundred later in the day, having received a thoughtful fax from Mike Atherton on Warwickshire County Cricket Club notepaper.

Dear Jamer,

Just heard the Test team and I wanted to drop you a line to commiserate.

Try not to be disheartened: in the time that I have played, of all the batsmen making their debuts only Thorpie made a success first time around. Everybody else took a game or two to find their feet, and I am sure that given a run you will find success at the higher level.

It would be easy to be disheartened after just one game, but experience says that continued good form at county level and the door is always ajar given an injury/loss of form to those in possession.

So keep going!

Speak to you soon

Athers

After I was out, there was something of a media scrum at the bottom of the stairs down from the changing rooms at Trent Bridge. Initially, I said that I did not want to speak to them. I feared that I might say something which I might later regret. But I was assured that there would be nothing controversial. Indeed there wasn't, apart from Simon Wilde, then of *The Times,* the next day using an aside of mine when I said, "Well, they would say that" when asked if the selectors had told me I was still in their thoughts.

It didn't come out too well, so I asked Edward Bevan, the BBC Wales cricket correspondent to phone Graveney, whom he knew well, to smooth things over. Unfortunately, when Bevan had finished, he forgot to turn his phone off and proceeded to vociferously berate Graveney and his co-selectors for their decision not to re-select me. Graveney heard it all and hasn't let Bevan forget it in a hurry!

A few days later, Alec Stewart gave me a courtesy call, assuring me that if I continued to score runs I would be considered. It was nothing more than that. I did not know it at the time, but I was the 589th player to be capped by England. Nowadays that number would be on my playing shirt – an admirable initiative. A few days after returning from Lord's, I spotted a lad walking through Cardiff city centre wearing an England cricket shirt. It was exactly the same as mine. I wanted to rush up to him and shake him: "I've worked my socks off for years to earn one of them." I grew up in the pre-replica shirt age. I always wanted a white rugby shirt with a red rose on it. But my mother always told me that only those good enough to play for England received one of those.

I suppose now is as good a time as any to come clean on my nationality. When England play rugby, I support them vehemently... even against Wales. I'm afraid to say that to all those wonderful Welsh supporters who have adopted me as one of their own. I do feel Welsh in many other respects, and will always support Wales against anyone else but England. But with rugby it is different and I can't pretend to be something I am not. I was born in England and have always supported them, my father taking me to Twickenham from an early age. I spent too many unhappy hours at Monmouth School fending off the banter in the late seventies and early eighties, when Wales were ritually slaughtering England, to change that.

On the morning of November 22, 2003 I sat wearing my England rugby shirt (my Welsh wife, Jane, bought me that because she, too, knew that there was no changing me) cheering England on to becoming world champions. Apologies to the Welsh for that.

I had more or less resigned myself to being a one-cap wonder, until one remarkable day later that summer in 1998. It was Wednesday, August 26 and I was due to play in a benefit match for Steve Watkin at Tondu Cricket Club. Jane was not due to give birth until late September, but suddenly that morning, at the ungodly hour of 6.45, she woke me to announce, "My waters have broken. Come on – we've got to go to the hospital."

"Just hang on while I get a coffee," I countered – a typically selfish and thoughtless reply. But we were off anyway. The nurses checked out Jane and said that she would have to stay in. I phoned Watkin to tell him the bad news – I knew that he was already struggling to raise a side, but it was not a bad excuse after all. As we waited for what seemed like many an hour, there was a message from one of the nurses that I should phone Glamorgan. I thought little of it, assuming that they were enquiring about Jane and the impending birth. So I did not reply for a while. Not long after, Jane suddenly said: "You should phone them. You never know, Atherton might be injured and they might want you for England." My reply was sarcastic – I had had one late call-up, and certainly did not expect another. But there had been speculation in the press that Atherton was struggling with his long-standing back injury, so I made the call. And sure enough Jane was right (wives always are, aren't they?). Atherton was struggling, and the England selectors wanted me to go up to the Oval to cover.

I phoned Mike Fatkin, the Glamorgan chief executive, and David Graveney to explain the situation. Both told me to take my time and phone later. I went back to Jane and had one of those conversations you never imagine that you will have. She was showing no signs of going into labour, but was brilliantly supportive – you've got to go and play. Her only caveat was that I should stay as long as possible before making the trip.

I made all the necessary calls and began the long wait. Sadly, by about 8pm, nothing was happening, so I had to bid farewell (and it was a tearful one – you try telling your wife that you won't be there for the birth of your first child). My head was all over the place. I had no idea how to reach the team's hotel, which was in Chelsea, so I kept in constant touch with Brian Murgatroyd, the EWCB's media liaison officer at the time. Brian is a Welshman, who began his career with the *South Wales Argus*, and a life-long Glamorgan supporter, so it was nice to keep hearing a familiar voice, even if his sense of direction is hopeless!

I had been surprised when I'd first played in June how protective he had to be of the players, and how, in turn, the players were so reluctant to speak to the press, especially at the end of the day's play. He had sheepishly sidled up to me towards the end of the Lord's Test and asked if there was any chance of my having a quiet word with Paul Abbandonato, then reporting for the *Wales On Sunday*. It was as if he fully expected me to refuse. But I was doing no such thing.

At Glamorgan, we always had a very good rapport with the media and, whenever we could, we helped them, because we hoped they would help us, too. This was clearly not the case in the England dressing room. Most players seemed to treat journalists with disdain. Mind you, they had probably had a few more brickbats hurled at them than we had at Glamorgan. Generally, the Welsh press was reasonably kind to us, which could be a mixed blessing. I know that I could be very sensitive to any criticism that came my way, but I also know that there were occasions when I recognised that the criticism was correct and it actually inspired me to prove the writer wrong. And at times I think some of the over-zealous championing of Welsh players' England claims in the national media might have been a little detrimental, because it was seen as too blindly partisan.

But the England players' attitude smacked of double standards to me. Many of them were very happy to pick up lucrative contracts for their weekly columns, which, in the majority of cases, were ghosted. Atherton, Angus Fraser and myself (and lately Ed Smith and Andrew Strauss) are the only ones I have known write their own stuff for the nationals.

Eventually, I found the hotel and went straight to my room. As at Lord's, I was unsure as to whether I would be playing in a Test match the following day. But there was no time to fret. Too many other things were concerning me. And anyway, Sri Lanka did not have anyone quick to worry me. Muttiah Muralitharan may be an exceptional bowler, but he is not going to physically harm you.

I awoke early and immediately phoned my in-laws to see if

there had been any news regarding Jane. There had not. So I went to breakfast, where coach Lloyd and captain Stewart were already seated – Stewart, as usual, surrounded by his many vitamin pills and health drinks.

I nervously suggested to Lloyd that I did not have the foggiest idea how to get to the Oval from the hotel, so he kindly agreed to travel with me. On the way, he told me that Atherton was really struggling with his back and that I should ready myself to play. Again, the coach did not really know. He asked if I wanted to watch a video he had compiled of the Sri Lankan bowlers but I politely declined. I had faced them all, either when I played for Mashonaland Country Districts against them in Zimbabwe in 1994 or during the A tour there in 1998.

It took Atherton little more than five minutes of stiff limbering up to announce that he was unfit. "Are you in the right state of mind to play?" asked Stewart. "Of course I am," I said, rather unconvincingly. Steve Bull, the team psychologist, made the comment, "Your first Test is for acclimatisation, the second is for performing." Fair enough, but what if your wife is about to deliver your first child? "You're not going to win father of year," said Ian Salisbury, the leg spinner whose career reached its nadir later in the game as shouts of "Get him off" rang around the ground only moments after he had been introduced to the attack on a turning wicket.

Arjuna Ranatunga won the toss and, surprisingly, inserted us. My partner this time was to be Mark Butcher. Time to see if the words of the Glamorgan fans' ditty – 'Stephen James, superstar, scores more runs than Mark Butch...ar' – were true. Despite everything, I batted reasonably well that morning. Butcher went early, edging to slip (he kept berating the TV producers later in the day, "Stop showing it from that angle – it looks as if I pushed at it") and I was joined by Graeme Hick, who had not been having the most productive of international summers. His three Test innings against South Africa had yielded nine runs.

Robert Croft was rightly miffed to be made twelfth man on a pitch that was more Colombo than London, and he came on with the drinks after an hour and joked with Hick: "Got a nose bleed yet?" in reference to Hick's extended stay at the crease.

I reached lunch on 34 not out, and Darren Gough said at the interval: "This makes the selection for Australia interesting." The tour party was to be revealed at the end of the game. I wish that he had not said that. Not that he meant any malice, he never does. And I think he rated me. I met him in the car park at Sophia Gardens in 1997 after he had dismissed me for nought in a NatWest Trophy match. "I'll see you next week, I reckon," he said in reference to the Fifth Test against Australia at Trent Bridge. Sadly, he did not. But this set me thinking a little too much – thinking of what people must make of my being 34 not out at lunch in a Test match. What it meant to all my supporters and family. Only 16 to a Test 50.

And so all this proved a little premature, as I only added two more to my tally after lunch, playing a little too positively against Muralitharan, Sri Lanka's only real strike weapon. I came down the wicket looking to hit him wide of mid on, but failed to spot his over spinner (thankfully, then not as dangerous as his 'other' ball – the 'doosra' – which he has since controversially developed) and only succeeded in giving a gentle return catch. It was a tame dismissal, and one I have rued ever since. I was well set on a plumb batting wicket and, apart from Muralitharan (whose action was the source of constant conversation in the England dressing room throughout the game, Lloyd going public with some concerns over it and landing himself in hot water), there was little threat.

My knock had obviously not impressed the watching media. Christopher Martin-Jenkins, then with *The Daily Telegraph* and a writer for whom I have a lot of respect, observed: "While his wife, Jane, expecting their first child, was in the final stages of labour in Cardiff, James was seeing the shine off the new ball with a fair amount of luck but familiar watchfulness and determination. A lack of foot movement seemed to confirm, sadly, that Mike Atherton's substitute, and former university partner, will always struggle against the best bowling at the highest level."

He continued: "A decisive hook when Wickremasinghe strayed for once from his usual full length was the most satisfying of James's three fours but his on-side play generally was more convincing than his off-side, especially against the slower bowlers." County bowlers around the country will surely not concur. I did not generally favour the 'man's side' as the leg side is known in the game. An arc between extra cover and third man (very fine) is where you will find that the majority of my runs were scored. It is interesting to me that this impression was garnered that day. CMJ is usually a most keen-eyed observer, so maybe it was my nerves that betrayed my normal style.

Atherton and Nasser Hussain – missing after undergoing a groin operation – went for lunch on the King's Road and returned moaning about how all the batsmen were filling their boots against this friendly attack after they had had to fend off the pace of Donald and Pollock all summer. They were jesting, but I could sense that there was some seriousness in their comments. At tea, Graveney called me into the physio's room and said that if I wanted to I could return to Cardiff to be with Jane. To be perfectly honest, I hadn't really thought about it at that stage. I thought that I was there for the duration and had resigned myself to missing the birth. I wanted to stay until the end of the day's play though and did so, clapping in Hick who was unbeaten on 107, before rushing off to Paddington for a train back to Cardiff.

My father-in-law, David Parker, met me at the station at 10.30pm and said we should hurry because Jane had been having contractions for two hours. So, dressed in my England blazer and slacks, off I went to the University of Wales Hospital. When I arrived, Jane was in the delivery suite. "Get in here; get that blazer off and help me," she said in between puffs of gas and air. I couldn't believe that she didn't ask how many I'd scored! Apparently she had been unable to get to a TV all day and did not have a clue what had been happening up in London. And, mimicking the scene in my favourite *Only Fools and Horses* programme when Del Boy's son is born, I took a puff of the gas and air too – lucky I wasn't drugs-tested when I returned to the Oval.

It is difficult to express my emotions that night. That may sound clichéd but it was an unreal experience. All my life I always ensured that I had the required number of hours of sleep before a match and here I was staying up all night during a Test! Eventually, at 4.40am, Bethan Amy James was born, weighing 7lbs 6oz – a healthy weight given that she was a month premature. She was jaundiced though, and looked incredibly yellow, so she had to be put into an incubator to be given ultraviolet treatment.

She could not open her eyes either, but the nurses kept reassuring us that it was probably because the birth had been so swift. Myself and Jane thought differently. We knew something was wrong. And indeed there was. Bethan was born with a syndrome called Blepharoptosis Epicanthus, which has manifested itself only in the ptosis part – in other words, she has droopy eyelids. She has had one operation to suspend her eyelids and will have another soon to take a muscle graft from her leg and place it in her eyelids.

But that August morning I held Bethan and was thankful that I had been there to see the birth. Then it was time to get back to London, still dressed in my England issue uniform, the beige chinos with smatterings of blood on them from the birth. I caught the 8am train and was hoping to grab some sleep on the journey, but unfortunately I met Ricky Needham, once chairman of the Glamorgan cricket committee. Not that he's a bad bloke, far from it, but it was bad timing. He beckoned me into first class and sweet-talked the ticket collector into allowing this second-class citizen a touch of luxury, as well as talking to me all the way up to London! Oh, for some slumber! I arrived after the start time, which was a curious feeling. There was much good will, with the Sri Lankan team sending me champagne and everyone asking after my young daughter. Hick and John Crawley were forging a formidable partnership (Crawley also went on to make a century) so I decided to head into the physio's room and have a lie down. Wayne Morton, the England physio, woke me at lunch time – the only occasion on which I ever properly slept during a match in my professional career. Many others cannot lay claim to such a solitary instance.

We had to field for less than a session on that second day so it was not too onerous for me, but I was mighty glad to see my hotel bed that night. A good night's rest and then some serious leather chasing the next day. Sri Lanka compiled a mammoth 591, despite Fraser's urgings of "Let's get one for Bethan Amy". And, late on the fourth day, it was our turn to bat again – 146 in arrears and only survival on our minds.

It will surprise readers who knew me well when I was younger that I had to restrain my natural inclinations. There were 42 overs bowled at us on that fourth day. I ended up 20 not out! It was just like the late-eighties when Simon Hughes, in his *Independent* column, named me as one of the three best blockers in the county game.

Talk about a grind. At the end of the day, coach David Lloyd said that maybe we were being a little bit too negative in our approach, and he may well have had a point. But it was bloody hard work, especially against Muralitharan, on a wicket which must have made him feel at home. I was wary of my over-positive demise in the first innings, but probably went too far towards the other end of the scale with my watchfulness. I got myself into such a negative frame of mind that when Sanath Jayasuriya entered the attack with his most unthreatening left-arm spin, I was unable to dominate him as I undoubtedly should have done. And, when the seamers returned for a quick blast, my slovenly footwork and tired arms, not to mention dulled mind, meant that I was unable to force the ball anywhere but third man. A most inopportune reversion to type.

Mahela Jayawardene, that most fluent and attractive of Sri Lanka's young batsmen, whose acquaintance I had made during the A tour, walked past me as the tourists left the ground. "We don't want any trouble from you tomorrow, now." He need not have fretted. I survived a further 11 overs on that final morning, adding just five more to my total before succumbing to Muralitharan, caught at silly point off my glove. I walked before the umpire was required to make a decision. Paul Rees, then of the *Wales On Sunday*, later said to me that he thought it strange but typical of me that I should walk when there was every likelihood that it was my last Test innings. I had thought the night before about the fact that it was likely to be my final bat at this level, but I just walked out of habit. It was an obvious glove, anyway.

My reaction in the dressing room was unusual. I felt no great disappointment. No real anger, as I so often did when out. In my younger years I would often scream loudly once inside the sanctity of the dressing room; often cursing what I perceived as the cruel injustice of the game I was attempting to play, or uttering a ridiculously flippant "I'm retiring" after a low score. I was known to hurl my equipment in a rage and to abuse spectators who taunted me as I walked off. The groundstaff at Cardiff (who were once housed in a tiny room at the bottom of the stairs to our changing room) never let me forget how, in 1997 against Hampshire, I screamed at them as I walked past their room having been dismissed by a ball that bounced wickedly off a length.

The standard of pitches was often the source of my post-innings ire. But only once can I recall being unhappy with my team mates. It was a match against Warwickshire in 2000, where Nick Knight scored a huge double century to bat us out of the game. In reply, myself and our new overseas batsman, Matthew Elliott, scored centuries. My innings stretched into a third day when a relatively small number of runs were required to avoid the follow on, but our lower order reacted timidly to the challenge and, when I fell, I knew that we would have to bat again that day. I felt annoyed that, after all my efforts, I should have to go out again. I was seething. I dumped my bat, helmet and gloves into my coffin and stomped out towards the shower area, which is behind the dressing rooms at Edgbaston. "F****g c***" I bellowed, carefully leaving out the 's' to create the impression that I was berating myself when, in fact, I was railing at the tail. It was silly because I should have done the job myself (I only added one run that morning to my overnight 165) and it was no surprise when I was dismissed for nought second time around.

But there at the Oval, there were no tantrums, just quiet contemplation. It was as if I was relieved that it was all over. I sat there for a long time, watching Graeme Hick writing letters to potential donors to his upcoming benefit year, and Alec Stewart desperately urging the genial dressing room attendant, Ray, to find him some chocolate. Ben Hollioake, whose life was to be so tragically cut short in a car crash in 2002, was clearly unhappy with his leg-before decision. His "Don't they [the umpires] realise that they are messing with people's careers?" being resonant of Mark Ramprakash's outburst at Darrell Hair on my debut, which resulted in the then Middlesex batsman being fined. Hollioake wisely vented his fury inside the confines of the dressing room.

The touring parties for the winter were to be announced the following day and, while I did not think that I had much chance of going to Australia with the full team, I had been buoyed by weekend predictions in the newspapers that I might be captain of the A tour to Zimbabwe and South Africa. I thought that my considerable experience of Zimbabwe might help me. Dean Riddle, England's fitness adviser, was flitting around the dressing room, so I thought I would pick his brains on some training techniques. We talked for a while and then I asked him what sort of training he thought I should be doing in the remaining couple of weeks of the county season. "Those guys going on tour will need to keep in shape for the fitness tests at the end of the season. As for you, well..." He paused. His face said it all. He was embarrassed. I did not question him further, and made my excuses to move elsewhere. What a way to find out.

It was not Riddle's fault. From my little contact with him, he seemed like a decent bloke who was doing a good job with England, having been appointed as their first ever full-time fitness consultant, with all the accompanying cynicism. We duly lost the game and I drove back to Wales with Paul Morris, a friend from Lydney who was good enough to listen to my gripes as well as my anxieties about being a father. I had almost forgotten about that. I did not listen to the touring teams being announced the next morning. I did not need to. It was nappies and sleepless nights for me.

For someone so young, Bethan has already spent so much time in hospital. And in 2002 she gave us an almighty scare. She has always suffered from constipation, but, in the June of that year, it became so bad that she was admitted to hospital. Unfortunately the enema given to her to relieve this produced an adverse reaction, resulting in her potassium levels dropping so alarmingly that she was rushed to the High Dependency Unit (HDU). None of the muscles in her body were functioning properly. Her stomach shut down completely and there were worries about her heart. I was playing at Lord's against Middlesex and initially Jane had said things were okay. But when her mother phoned me to say that Bethan's condition had deteriorated markedly, I left immediately to go back to Cardiff, finding it difficult to speak to any of my team mates as I departed, for fear of bursting into tears. Jane describes that day as the worst of her life, and she still thinks about it regularly, recalling the moment when Bethan went limp in her arms. Jane thought she had lost her. At the time I was on a train on the way back from London, knowing the situation was serious, but without understanding its full severity.

In most other occupations, I would have sped back home immediately when Bethan was admitted to hospital, but such is the nature of professional sport, Jane had not wanted to alarm me in the middle of a match. To think that I might have been too late. What I do know is that walking into the HDU and seeing Bethan connected to all manner of wires, drips and ECG (electro-cardiogram) monitors was the scariest moment of my life. Any parent who has experienced serious difficulties with their child will know what myself and Jane were going through. There were other parents in that unit walking around looking as ashen-faced as we were. Nobody spoke. The air was full of panic and foreboding. For over a week Bethan, who amazed us all with her bravery and resilience, underwent treatment to stabilise her condition. Thank God that, having undergone minor surgery, she made a full recovery. Naturally I missed the incredible C&G Trophy against Surrey at the Oval in which Glamorgan failed by just 9 runs in chasing Surrey's world record 438. I left the decision to miss the match until the last minute, but there was no way I could have played. Not in that state. However, I did keep in touch with what was happening through Ceefax and I could not believe what I was seeing.

With all fears alleviated, I was able to captain Wales to victory over England in the first match of its kind, despite having picked up a bug while staying in the hospital. I scored 83 not out, batting with the freedom of a man relieved after Bethan's recovery, and I felt like a Welshman, until... I was overlooked for the man of the match for a proper Welshman, Robert Croft, who took 2-36 and made 30 with the bat. The adjudicators must have known that I supported England at rugby.

CHAPTER THREE

ABOUT A BOY

F or most cricketers the story of their first century is a joyous one, even if it can become rather tediously bland when recounted in an autobiography. Mine is slightly different. I wished desperately that I hadn't scored it. For the record, it came aged 12 for Monmouth School Bantams against Brightlands, then a preparatory school in Newnham, Gloucestershire. It took so long that we had to bat on after tea, the normal time for a change of innings. I had crawled to 97 not out by the interval when my father – who was only there because I had forgotten my socks – had to leave to go and close his sports shop.

I duly reached the milestone and we all trooped off to continue a match that had momentarily been hijacked by personal ambition. I was embarrassed by the furore, especially as I overheard some of the opposition's parents complaining about the protracted length of our, especially my, innings. Once it had happened, I felt genuine fear. The tradition then was for every centurion to be honoured by the headmaster by dint of the presentation of a new cricket bat in front of the whole school during Monday morning assembly. My customary seat – among my Hereford housemates – was at the very back of the hall. So that meant that I would have to walk the length of the hall – it was probably little more than 30m but seemed like 300

– with more than 500 people gawping at this small boy with a basin hair-cut, wondering who on earth he was. And back again to my seat. This terrifying thought began to overtake me as I took my place in the field at Brightlands. It consumed my whole weekend. "Why had I not got out in the nineties?" I kept asking myself.

I caught the number 40 bus as usual that Monday morning at 7.40am from Lydney, and sat on my own. There were very few of us going to the public school from the Forest of Dean in those days – my sister, Karen, was but I was never going to be seen sitting next to a girl – and even fewer came close to matching my preoccupation with sport. My solitude gave me time to daydream, but not that day. I was just shaking with trepidation, my brow furrowed. "Maybe they will leave it till tomorrow," was one escape clause in my mind, uncannily reminiscent of my later procrastinations over batting. But they didn't. I somehow survived the ordeal, making my way up to the stage to receive my new bat from Mr. Bomford, the headmaster, without tripping up along the way. But I didn't score another hundred for three years. Could have been technical incompetence. Might have been fear.

However, once I did reach that landmark again I have to admit that I began to like the experience. In fact, my six centuries in one term prompted a rethink on the liberal distribution of bats. I had quite a selection then – and, remember, my father owned a sports shop – including a Slazenger V12, which was apparently a Viv Richards cast-off. Finally the rule was changed so that a bat was only presented for a pupil's maiden century.

I did not initially want to go to public school, but my father and uncle had gone to Monmouth, which was renowned for its rugby. All my mates were in Lydney and I wanted to be like them and progress to the local comprehensive. Many family discussions (arguments, more like) ensued until I was talked around. It did not help that all my mates in Lydney had got wind of what they deemed my 'defection'. All the usual jokes and ribaldry abounded, with them being especially obsessed with the fact that I would have to wear slippers at this curious establishment I was off to. I tried to reason with them that I was, in fact, going to be a day boy (which inevitably brought howls of "gay boy") and therefore would not require slippers like the boarders, but it was to no avail. I was too posh for them and that was that.

I was soon to discover that Monmouth, whilst being an excellent seat of learning, is anything but posh. It is an incredibly down-to-earth public school – a "fee-paying comprehensive" my mischievous Sherborne-educated Swansea University housemate, Mark Bryant, used to contend. But I realised that I would have to win my hometown mates back by sporting prowess, and there was plenty of opportunity for that at Monmouth. Rugby ruled (under the expert but sometimes blinkered supervision of Rod Sealy) despite the presence of a cricket professional in the late 'Sonny' Avery, the former Essex opener. His time at the school finished at the end of my first year, but he left me with some sage words of advice, which eventually served me well in the professional game. "If you are going to go down the wicket, go to attack, not defend." Habitual sallying down the wicket was clearly not a feature of my game, but, when I did so, it was with a positive intent.

His departure opened the door for the arrival of Graham Burgess in his stead; the single most influential event in my cricketing life. He became my coach and mentor, despite his initial misgivings that I was too bashful and was not really interested in the wealth of cricketing knowledge and experience he was attempting to impart.

I think the turning point came one lunchtime when he 'caught' or rather found me in the squash courts. I had persuaded a friend to throw tennis balls at me in order to groove some shots. Burgess seemed surprised and delighted in equal measure at my assiduity. From then on, a strong relationship and friendship developed, only once descending into any level of disagreement when Burgess became enraged that I missed a fitness session before the school tour of Sri Lanka in 1985.

Those who have become accustomed to my obsessive attitude to physical fitness will be surprised to read that I was a most reluctant trainer during my schooldays, a significant amount of body fat being increased by frequent, furtive trips to Tommy Jones' grocers up St. Mary's Street for sweets and biscuits.

Every Wednesday, Sealy used to supervise a gruelling circuits session, during which he used to masochistically scream, "It's money in the bank" or "You won't beat Millfield on Saturday if you don't finish this". But on this occasion he had invited a local fitness fanatic to work his perverse pleasure upon the first fifteen. Burgess had also invited him to do the same immediately afterwards for the squad who were off on tour. Despite being captain, I thought that one session was enough, and left immediately. Burgess did not catch up with me until the following day when he tore into me and reminded me of my responsibilities.

There have been some decisions I have palpably disagreed with since Burgess became a first class umpire – he once adjudged me caught behind at Middlesbrough when the ball struck my foot – but that was not one of them. I was wrong. Even at that early stage of my career it made me realise how much Burgess had done for me. His technical expertise had been readily passed on at all hours. On Sunday afternoons in the winter I would practise from two until eight, first with a carefully selected group of the keener school pupils and then, after a cup of tea at Burgess' school-side house, with Lydney Cricket Club.

I would listen in awe as Burgess recounted his tales of county cricket, of Viv (Richards), Ian (Botham) and Joel (Garner) – always referred to by their proper Christian names, rather than any matey nicknames, out of respect rather than any distance from his team mates. There were some useful cricketers at Monmouth. There was Gareth A. Davies, now a freelance sports writer for *The Daily Telegraph*, an all-rounder who thought he was Imran Khan with his black flowing locks and high bounding bowling action. He was an astute captain though, with a real passion for the game and an unbending self-belief. He recently interviewed England batsman Michael Vaughan and taunted him with, "I'd love to bowl at you on a club wicket." It is probably of little consolation to Vaughan that Davies tells me that every time I speak to him, reasoning that my knee problems are a direct result of constantly being hit on the pads by his in-swinger.

Equally passionate was Roger Clitheroe, a Lancastrian whose reverence for Mike Atherton outstrips my admiration, and who went on to win a Cambridge Blue for his cussed batting and neat wicket-keeping. And there were the Kear twins, Mike and Tony, from Usk, who were ultra-competitive and utterly committed to their home-town club. Mike was the more talented, as a dashing left-hand batsman and lively seam bowler. His career was blighted by a broken leg, sustained during rugby practice. He was never the same cricketer after that. But because of his natural size and strength he was always one step ahead of me, being plucked out of a chemistry lesson in the third form to make his first-eleven debut. And he made an appearance for Glamorgan seconds on his home ground the year before I made my debut there in 1985.

But I found these experiences immensely inspirational, really focusing my mind. Mike scored quite a few centuries in his latter years at the school and every one would strengthen my resolve to emulate him. It was healthy competition. We were fortunate to have Peter Anthony (who later did sterling service on my benefit committee) as our master in charge of cricket – 'a lovely man', in the words of my unnaturally-effusive father. The only other person I know to have received the same compliment is David Morgan, now chairman of the England and Wales Cricket Board and formerly chairman of Glamorgan.

Both judgements are spot on, despite the fact that Anthony dropped me from his Colts rugby fifteen for "not getting involved enough". It was a salutary lesson for me, as I had to face the ridicule of my Lydney mates when I arrived there one Saturday afternoon to watch the town's first fifteen play at a time when I was usually playing at school. I was still struggling to earn their full respect, but a vital recognition soon softened their stance. I was selected for the Welsh Schools U15 side. I was an international cricketer, even if it was for a foreign country. I still felt thoroughly English then.

Around this time I developed a lasting friendship with Adrian Knox, a lavishly-talented sportsman from Bream, near Lydney. My parents took him under their wing and he became their second son, spending more time at our home than he did at his own. He really should have played for England Schools against me at Neath that year, after scoring more runs than anyone else in the regional trials. His character, as well as his uncomplicated batting, may have been a little rough around the edges, but it was an outrageous decision by a typically cliquey organisation. Most people in Lydney will tell you that Knox was a more talented batsman than me at that age. Even though I suspected that he did not possess the dedication or commitment to make the grade, how could those selectors reach that decision? What was the point in having the trials? Knox was an excellent rugby player – as hard as nails – who dabbled briefly at first-class level with Gloucester. If he had converted to hooker early in his career, he may well have scaled greater heights. He is the archetype of the loveable rogue, with an uncanny habit of landing himself in the hottest water. I gladly organised tickets for him during my Test match at the Oval and, after play on the third day, Dominic Cork approached me with a worried frown. "There's a rough-looking skinhead outside who reckons he's your mate."

"That's my best man," I said proudly to general astonishment. Knox had been partaking of the extensive hospitality then available to players' families and friends. In other words, he had been drinking free beer all day. Unfortunately, this led him to trouble that night. He eventually fell asleep in a shop doorway, and when the local constabulary awoke him to move him along, he reacted badly. He was inevitably charged, and I was required to provide a glowing character reference. Thankfully, after a protracted case, he was reprieved.

When Knox was my best man in 1997 it is the only occasion on which I have seen him truly nervous. His speech had been carefully scripted with the aid of my father but, despite frequent rehearsals, the image of Knox anxiously reciting his lines on the lawn of the New House Country Hotel in Thornhill, Cardiff, only minutes before the big moment, is an enduring one. I think that it was the presence of some of the more famous sporting celebrities that unnerved him, but, in typical Knox fashion, he was soon treating them all like life-long friends, bending Atherton's ear at the bar until some ungodly hour and then tickling everyone at breakfast with his deafeningly loud and rustic "Mornin', Athurrs" when the England skipper appeared.

I am not sure whether Atherton recalled that this was the same person who had also once commandeered the phone for 20 minutes when I was down from university and attempting a serious conversation about cricket. Knox thought he was, too, but his inebriated state dictated otherwise. "Sorry about that," I said afterwards, to which Atherton replied: "Ah, don't worry. I get idiots like that pestering me all the time."

Knox is very proud of the fact that he hails from Bream, which Foresters reckon is the biggest village in Britain. "That makes you the biggest village idiot in Britain then," once countered Colin Henderson, another friend, who idolises Graeme Hick and who, because of his unquenchable desire to cadge as much kit as possible from any first-class sportsman, is known as "the friend of the stars". Henderson followed my career closely and faithfully, and was himself a decent rugby player and cricketer (so he tells me) whose bowling was characterised by a remarkable stutter in a long, curving run.

My father once said to Graham Burgess, who spent quite a few seasons opening the batting with me for Lydney (it did not improve my running between the wickets) while still coaching at Monmouth: "Henderson's not the worst bowler in the world, mind."

"No, but he's in the f***ing frame," came the classic Burgess reply.

I suppose I should point out that Henderson did once bowl me in a mid-week league match, earning himself substantial bragging rights. I suppose I should be glad that someone should want to boast about being able to dismiss me. Professionals do not usually indulge in such braggadocio, not in public at least – even though I have been known to reply "runs" when asked what a particular bowler is bowling – but I did read once of one who has done so about me. And although it is not without good reason it is a little unusual. This is what I wrote about it in *The Sunday Telegraph* in September 2003.

When Martin Bicknell snared Herschelle Gibbs in the first over of his Test return at Headingley last month, I'll wager that I was not the only county batsman who heaved a huge sigh of relief. "It's not just me then," I thought to myself, in recollection not only of the frequency, but also the ease, with which my wicket has been taken by Bicknell, a bowler who, until this year, was only considered good enough to have played two Tests. In my mind the torment which he has caused me did not stack up. For someone with the same number of Test caps as me, he was exerting an incontrovertible hold. A record of 982 first-class victims at 24.58 is mightily impressive but it was the brusqueness with which his international claims had been rejected which confused me, just as much as his skyward glance just before delivery.

So it was with much glee that I witnessed his reappearance on the international stage. It assuaged some nagging fears about my judgement, for I had always ranked him as a skilful and thoughtful bowler, who swings the ball both ways and exacts more bounce than you might expect.

And his re-emergence was a shot in the arm for the much-maligned county game, where labels, often ill-judged, too easily stick. In Bicknell's case it was his pace – or lack of it – which was, apparently, his international undoing.

Indeed, it is true that he is slow for an opening bowler, not like the genuinely quick men who induce stomach-churning night-before jitters, but nonetheless he is, as his Surrey colleagues are so quick to point out when you play against him, high class, and he took 10 wickets at 28 apiece in his two comeback Tests.

However, I must admit that it was with more than a little trepidation that I contacted him this week. We have never really got on. While I have always recognised that Bicknell is a model pupil from the Angus Fraser school of niggardly metronomic bowling, I have also thought that he must have qualified with a distinction in grumpiness and lamentation, such is his on-field persona. Now, one conversation is not going to completely alter my perception but I reckon I'm relenting.

"I'll talk as long as we can talk about me getting you out," he told me jocularly, but not without a touch of the chilling certainty of a lion stalking his prey. "You and Darren Maddy [of Leicestershire], regular as clockwork," he added, not boastfully, but matter-of-factly.

When last year, I had first read of Bicknell mentioning myself and

Maddy by name in such a context, my professional pride was pricked. "How dare he say that?" I thought. "I'm sure I've scored some runs off him." But swift communication with Glamorgan's statistician brought unwelcome news. Bicknell has dismissed me more times than any other bowler in first-class cricket. QED.

Better change the subject. Talking of reaction to comments, was he not a little miffed at Michael Vaughan's remarks about county cricket after the Headingley Test, which might have implied that he did not have the mental toughness required for Test cricket. "I was surprised, but I don't think they were aimed at me," he said, "rather an observation on how players from other countries like Australia and South Africa mature more quickly as cricketers and people. All that happened in that game was that we missed a great opportunity."

And anyway, Bicknell is a staunch defender of the county game: "I hate people knocking county cricket all the time. There are a lot of good players playing a lot of good cricket. Everyone knows that it is a big jump up to Test cricket but I think the problem goes deeper than county cricket – to the way in which we have grown up. Some 12 Championship games a season would be ideal, but how do we get there? And would the culture change so quickly that the extra practice time would be used beneficially? I'm not sure it would."

But what of his time now that he has missed out on the winter tour party? "David Graveney phoned me and told me to keep fit, but, even though I was just starting to feel comfortable in the environment, I'm realistic enough to realise that my bowling would not be suited to the pitches of Bangladesh and Sri Lanka."

Surely there must be some regret at the time lost in the wilderness? "I wish I was five years younger, certainly, but I've played for England again, and there are a lot of good cricketers who've never played at all."

And, despite the romantic return, is this the end now? "If it is, it's nice that I've done well in my last Test, at my home ground, with my reputation intact, leaving people thinking that I'm a good bowler." This "bunny" is not doubting that.

Once, at the Oval, I lamented, "Bloody Bicknell does me all the time" within earshot of Duncan Fletcher. Come the second innings, Fletcher grabbed me, placing his hands on my shoulders, which was rare, and eye-balled me. "You've got to win this mental battle with Bicknell." I didn't.

I know Bicknell did not rate me particularly ("Just pitch it up outside off stump and he's mine" is something I've known him to say) and the above conversation did nothing to change that. And we often exchanged choice words, not least in our last clash in 2001 when I cut him for four. "Some people never change," he snarled. As so often happens, I was too slow with my riposte. I would have loved to have said, "Yes, I still hit it down to third man and you're still a twat." He's probably a decent bloke off the field and he did conduct the interview without hesitation or reluctance, but, as I've already said, I generally found it difficult to separate players' characters on and off the field. Just as, at times, I found it hard to distinguish between trying to impress my friends back in Lydney and the advancement of my cricket career. I'm talking drinking here.

Peer pressure can be repressively overbearing, especially for someone as insecure as me, a public schoolboy desperate to be accepted in his hometown. After cricket at Lydney it was not too bad because there was some excellent talk, mainly the stories of Burgess and a Lydney stalwart called Rob 'Basher' Brain, a club cricket legend if that is not an oxymoron. If Glamorgan's MCC Spirit of Cricket Awards in 2001 and 2002 were anything to do with me, then the county has much to thank Brain for, because he inspired me with his ability to effect thoroughly dominating performances with good grace and a sense of fair play.

But as for rugby's social side – wow. The drinking began as soon after the 4.30pm final whistle as possible (no isotonic rehydration here) and continued until you dropped. I was like a Nationwide Conference footballer trying to ply his trade in the Premier League. It was too much for me. As in everything else in my life, I tried hard but it was no good. Embarrassment normally ensued and a stinking hangover always did.

I enjoyed it, revelling in the absurd machismo of being one of the 'rugby boys', but it was not long before I realised that I had to be a little bit different if I was to become a professional sportsman. All my mates were good sportsmen but I wanted to be a notch above.

My professional team mates might be astonished to read that I even used to over-indulge the night before I was playing cricket – club cricket, that is. I pride myself on the fact that I never batted in a first-class match with a hangover – fielded a few times, yes, but never batted. I bet there are few others who can lay claim to that.

But here I was, getting riotously drunk before performing on a Saturday. Once, after the Lydney Rugby Club presentation evening, I had to drive the next morning to play for Glamorgan Colts at Ynystawe. I was in no state. I phoned coach Alan Jones to say that I had food poisoning. I had to stop three or four times on the M4 to be sick and made it to the ground only ten minutes before the scheduled start. I only managed nine that day. Now, there is a surprise.

I am intensely proud of my Lydney roots. Just mention the Bledisloe Cup between the Australian and New Zealand rugby teams and I will puff my chest out and announce that Lord Bledisloe hails from Lydney and was Governor-General in New Zealand when the teams first competed. But I needed to break away from the local, narrow-minded approach to life if I was to succeed.

The unending cycle of middling-quality sport followed by heavy inebriation had to be broken. I had won over my mates through my sport, but now it was time to move on. This process could not be done in an instant, though. It had begun in my last term at Monmouth when I had to make the difficult decision of which county to join. My father had played a lot for Gloucestershire seconds, and had spent much time liaising with the county club when the first eleven had played matches at Lydney (the only other ground, I believe, apart from Canterbury, to have hosted first-class cricket in England with a tree well inside the outfield), where he was groundsman for a time.

He was very friendly with Graham Wiltshire, one of the club coaches. The previous summer I had spent time with Wiltshire, playing for the county U-19s under his guidance, staying in the dressing rooms at the County Ground, Bristol, and eating bacon butties for breakfast before beating all-comers when we won the Hilda Overy Trophy. Now, in 1985, Wiltshire wanted me to make my second team debut at Lydney. But the match was immediately prior to my A-levels and I resisted the temptation. I felt that I was only being asked because it was on my home ground, a placating move for the locals.

All the while, Glamorgan were expressing considerable interest. David Lewis, the leg-spinner from Cardiff, was chairman of cricket. I faced him when the MCC side visited Monmouth and, despite my nerves-induced inability to hit him off the square before rain intervened, he told me he wanted to sign me. The TCCB (Test and County Cricket Board) rulings at the time decreed that if a county wanted to talk to a player born in another county they had to write to that county and allow them a 14-day period in which to determine their course of action, if any. As fate would have it, on the 13th day of that period I played for Monmouth School against Gloucestershire Etceteras, which was basically a second eleven. They included a particularly grumpy Tony Wright, who moped about the outfield mumbling, "Why do I have to play against this lot?"

I narrowly missed a century, and thought I played reasonably well in the circumstances – a view clearly not shared by future captain and coach Wright, or John Shepherd, the former Kent and West Indies all-rounder, who was in charge of the second eleven. My father was most upset that Shepherd did not even have the courtesy to congratulate me, a Gloucestershire boy after all, on my innings. Clearly irritated, he spoke to Wiltshire, who was also there. "We're going to speak to Glamorgan after tomorrow," he said. Wiltshire seemed to think that because of their friendship I would choose Gloucestershire.

"I can't do anything about it, because the chairman of cricket, Don Stone, is away," said Wiltshire.

My father decided to ring the late Ron Nicholls, a stalwart opening batsman and then on the cricket committee at Gloucestershire. He was terribly upset by the situation. Minutes later, the chairman of the club, Don Perry, was on the phone. And very soon this letter arrived, addressed to my father.

11 July 1985
Dear Peter,
Further to your discussions with our Chairman Don Perry, I can confirm that Gloucestershire would like to offer Stephen a summer contract for the County. We understand that Stephen is likely to be available from late July until early September.

As our Chairman explained we should pay Stephen a gross wage of £100 per week during this period and he would be responsible for his own accommodation or travelling to the County Ground.

We should pay him an overnight allowance and travelling expenses incurred for away matches and we should provide him with his club sweaters and shirts.

If Stephen wishes to live in Bristol we should be pleased to help him find accommodation and I do hope that he decides to play for Gloucestershire.

I look forward to seeing you again soon.
Yours sincerely
D. G. Collier
Secretary

I had made my mind up, though. Glamorgan it was. For one thing, I had abhorred the attitude of the Gloucestershire team I had just played against. And anyway, they did not seem to be a Gloucestershire side to me. Where were the members of that successful, home-grown under-19 team from the previous year? This lot seemed like a nomadic group, thrown together from distant parts of the country. I had played in a benefit match at Lydney the previous year against the first eleven, and I had heard Andy Brassington and David Graveney whispering about me. "They reckon this lad can play – but he's going back to everything. He doesn't look much cop to me." I wonder whether Graveney recalled that day when he was later deliberating over my England credentials.

As a lad I had watched the likes of Mike Proctor, Zaheer Abbas and Sadiq Mohammad from afar with a modicum of support for the county, but no great, lasting attachment. There was that history O-level project on the Grace family, but that was more a declaration of my love for cricket than any emotional longing to play for Gloucestershire. The shifting of county boundaries has meant that Gloucestershire's home is in Avon. The Forest of Dean, and Lydney, is the other side of the River Severn and, for me, a million miles away. There was no history of Gloucestershire cricketers coming from Lydney.

I had played against the Glamorgan seconds that season too. Glamorgan cricket may not have been in the finest fettle then, but moves were being made to produce their own cricketers; to identify local potential and back it all the way. They saw me as part of that because I had come through with the Welsh Schools. I liked what I saw. The camaraderie was apparent and the togetherness and humour genuine, Welsh even. My path to becoming a fully adopted Welshman took a steep upward turn with the receiving of this letter:

15 July 1985
Dear Stephen,
I was delighted to hear from David Lewis (Chairman of Cricket)
this morning that you have agreed to join Glamorgan. I am writing
to confirm the terms of our offer which are as follows:
For each of the four seasons, including 1985, Glamorgan will pay
you the sum of £500, and £60 for each week of the season for which
you are with us. Salaries are normally paid monthly in arrears.
We will also look after your accommodation in Cardiff while you
are with the club.
You will be expected to pay the cost of your travel from your
accommodation to home matches and practice at Sophia Gardens,
but we would expect you to be accommodated very close to the ground
in any case.
I confirm that you have been selected to play for Glamorgan II v
Somerset at Usk on Wednesday, and that you are required to report
to the ground by 9.45am at the latest. I would point out also that
Second XI Players are required to wear a blazer and tie to the
ground on each day of the match (or a sports jacket if you do not have
a blazer).
I would like to wish you every success in your career with
Glamorgan, and hope that we have a happy and long association and
that, above all else, you enjoy your cricket with us.
Very best wishes.
Yours sincerely
Philip Carling
Secretary

Wiltshire has never forgiven my father. But my father was
behind me all the way. He knew Glamorgan was the sage
choice. Gloucestershire were only reacting. Glamorgan had
been pro-active. They wanted me. Gloucestershire seemed more
concerned about the bad press they would receive if I slipped
through the net.

I often took delight in ribbing Jack Russell that we were the only two Gloucestershire-born players on the field when we met. And he has said that when I did well, it was often mentioned in the Bristol dressing room that I was a local boy. By coincidence, one of the players in that under-19 side with me was David Russell, Jack's brother, who died tragically in an accident. I like Russell, with all his eccentricity. He used to try to eyeball me when I batted, but I could not help myself laughing. He is so small and physically unimposing that I found it hard to do anything else. He and Robert Croft often enjoyed some good banter, Croft once really winding him up with "We know where you live, Jack" as he walked into bat. It is well known that Russell is a most intensely private man who does not even want his team mates to know his address.

There is a story, maybe apocryphal, that he once wanted some of the painters at the County Ground to do some work for him at home, so he blindfolded them and piled them into his car, before doing the same on the return journey. *Barking?* was a most apposite title for his autobiography.

Russell is a very fit man, who has prolonged his career by adopt-ing the latest trends in physiology, causing hilarity in 2002 at Cheltenham when he was noticed in the showers with his head perched over the top of a wheelie bin full of ice, dutifully undergoing the required recovery technique. "Boys, boys, there's a dog in the bin," was Croft's observation.

By the happiest of coincidences, my first century for Glamorgan seconds was at Lydney against Gloucestershire. It may have been a turgid effort, spanning four sessions in a successful bid to save the game, but it was a seminal moment for me, prompting some comical reaction at the end from the watching Lydney regulars: "Get back owt thurr, Jamurrr, we 'avunt 'ad 'ur money's wurth."

Unsurprisingly, Gloucestershire were not impressed. I overheard (I am a champion eavesdropper) a fellow called

Jonathan Addison, another wannabee from a distant county (Staffordshire, in fact) who, to be fair, did score 151 in that game, telling an assembled group what he thought of me, the gist of it being, "We kept bowling him half-volleys and he couldn't hit them for four. He'll never make it." Addison played one first-class match.

CHAPTER FOUR

CAMBRIDGE BLUES

"You won't end up sweeping the roads." That was my father's typically frank assessment of my future prospects if I decided to supplement my three years of university education at Swansea with a further spell at Cambridge. It was ironic that I was contemplating further studying when I had not wanted to go to Swansea in the first place (the second time my parents had needed to persuade me to attend an academic establishment). I had had my first taste of the life as a professional cricketer in the summer after leaving Monmouth School, and had enjoyed it. "Why can't I just carry on with it?" was my naïve take on the perceived immortality of a professional sportsman. "You need to get something behind you," was my father's rather less memorable but, all the same, very sensible advice.

And, while researching for this book, deep in a wardrobe I found a tattered scrap of paper with my arachnidan scrawl on it. It recalled a conversation my father and I had had with Peter Roebuck after a dinner at Millfield School at which he had spoken. "Bloody awful speaker," I remember my father saying, "tried to tell a load of lewd jokes we'd all heard before, when what we really wanted him to tell us was why (Viv) Richards, (Joel) Garner and (Ian) Botham had left Somerset." But this is what I had written down after talking to him afterwards.

Roebuck: It is the stance of any man of dignity to try to be able to dictate to one's employer, not let them dictate to you. Getting a degree allows this to happen. At the moment he could easily say to Somerset that he is not content and will go away and easily find a career in journalism or law. While at Cambridge he made most of his cricketing cock-ups but without them really being noticed. When he played on summer contracts, there was less pressure. If you play full time at a young age there is a lot of pressure on you – Gary Palmer (son of umpire Ken, and an unfulfilled talent) *is an example of one affected by this. He has just advised Ricky Bartlett* (another wasted talent) *to take up his place at Swansea University. He has decided against it. It will be the worst decision of his life.*

Roebuck had already had a profound effect on me with his diary of the 1983 season, *It Never Rains*. At such a youthful and blissfully ignorant age I could not comprehend his mental anguishes with the game, but I liked his descriptive turn of phrase. And his portrayal of county cricket was alluring. That was what I wanted to do. And I dare say I subconsciously vowed to write a book one day, too. Both Roebuck and my father were right about university then, even if my first degree subject was Classics, not an obviously career-pointing qualification.

I don't really know why I had chosen Latin and Greek for my A- level subjects (along with Maths). I think it was for the simple reason that I mildly enjoyed them as opposed to the turgidity of some of the other subjects. And I could burgle an academic prize at the annual Speech Day. No one else did both Latin and Greek. I still did not relish the attention of a public presentation, but I was permitted to choose Mike Brearley's *The Art of Captaincy* as my reward.

At Swansea I was among the original batch of students to be offered sports scholarships. This included future Wales rugby internationals David Bryant and David Evans, as well as

Gloucester's Great Britain swimmer Duncan Rolley. I think that Glamorgan may have exerted some influence in my case. I had wanted to go to Oxford, to the former college of my Classics teacher, Mr. Dennis-Jones, but I was under the misapprehension that my turning up for interview with my Welsh Schools tie (a garish red thing) and blazer would warrant a place. What about those wonderful, no doubt apocryphal, tales of rugby players going for interview and being thrown a book as they entered the room? If they caught it, they were in; if they also drop kicked it into the bin, they won a scholarship. Or so the story goes.

It was a disaster. I know that I should not use such an emotive word to describe such a relatively piffling experience but that was what it felt like. "They [the interviewers] said that they could not get anything out of you," was Mr. Dennis-Jones' pithy and almost embarrassed explanation. Too right they couldn't. I did not have the faintest idea of what they were talking about. Looking back I think what they were doing was bombarding me with a host of long, complex words, the meaning of which I was supposed to resolve through my Latin and Greek learning. But I did not twig that.

They began by asking, "Do you know anything about...", but soon they were saying "and of course you don't know anything about..." The only time I spoke with any conviction was when they took pity upon me and questioned me about my sport at the end. But by then it was too late. There was to be no Lincoln College, Oxford, for me.

I accepted Swansea's offer without hesitation. But in the meantime Rod Sealy, my Monmouth School rugby coach, had decided to take some action. "You're good enough to be a double Blue," he startled me with one day as we sauntered out to the 'Big Side' rugby pitch, where only the first team was permitted. This was in 1984 and we had just completed an unbeaten school season – the last Monmouth side to do so. And

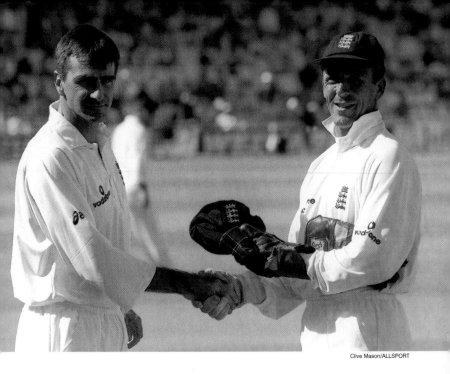

CAPPED: A proud moment (above), as I receive my England cap from Alec Stewart at Lord's in 1998, before the start of play in the Second Test against South Africa.

TRAPPED: Allan Donald celebrates after snaring me down the leg side for ten in the first innings.

IN AT THE DEATH: Walking out to bat with Hugh Morris at Taunton, 11 runs away from the 1997 County Championship. Nervous? Me?

CARRIED AWAY: The beginning of the post-match celebrations.

CHEER LEADER: Waqar Younis is at the centre of our salute to the fans (above).

GLORY DAY: A moment to hold on to (right).

HOT SHOT: A hook for four in my second Test match against Sri Lanka at The Oval in 1998.

OVER AND OUT: Walking (and I did walk) back to the pavillion [facing page] after my last innings in Test cricket, caught Jayawardene, bowled Muralitharan, for 25.

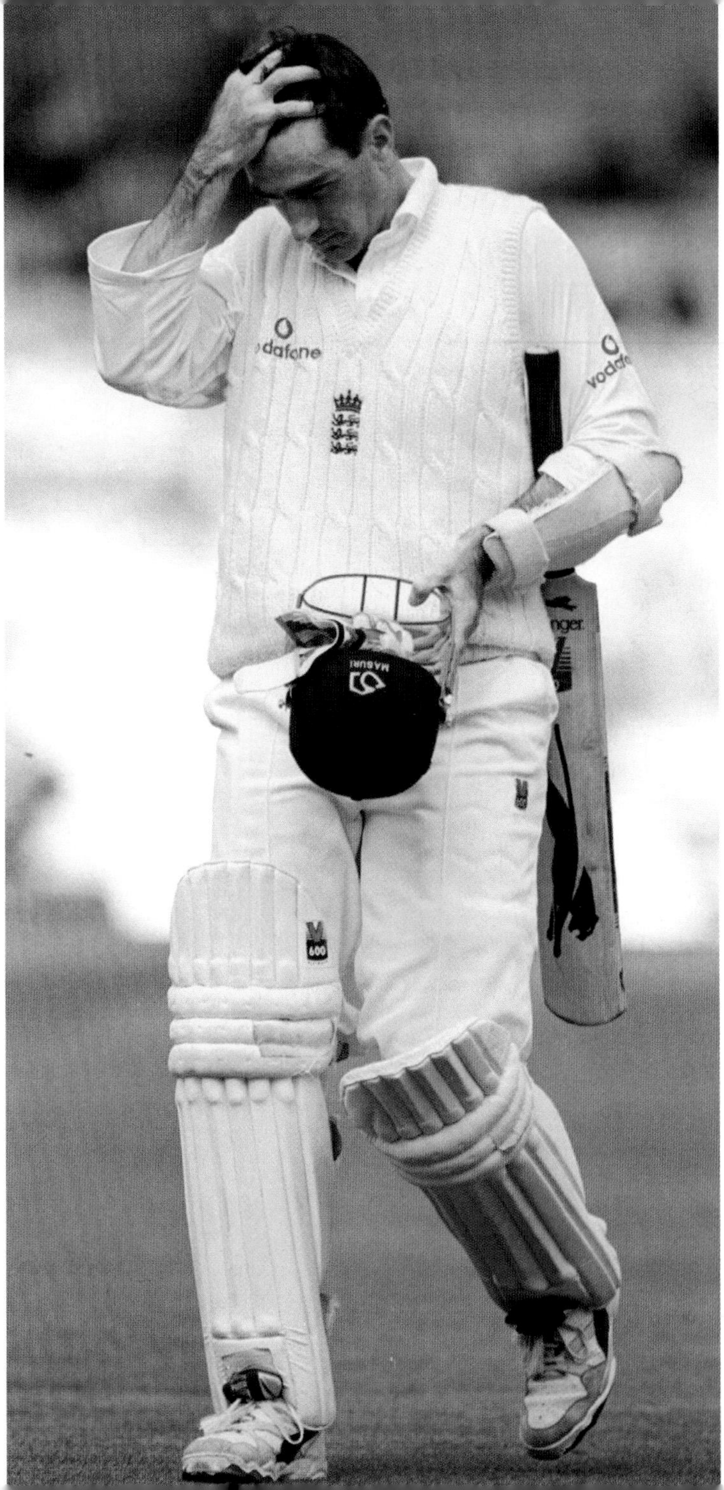

Lawrence Griffiths/ALLSPORT

SPOT THE FORESTER: That's me (above), second left, front row, with the rest of the Monmouth school under-12 team.

LYDNEY DAYS: On tour with Lydney CC (above), in the late Eighties.

FENNERS FINALE: A hundred versus New Zealand on my last day at Cambridge (right).

CANN THE MAN: Michael James Cann, who lit up the days in the Second Eleven.

"IF I WERE YOU..." A word of advice for future England captain Mike Atherton during our days at Cambridge University (below).

FLOWER ARRANGING:
Grant (right) and Andy (left) organising yet another night out with Alistair Campbell in Zimbabwe.

BOAT PEOPLE:
Relaxing with Adrian Dale on the Zambezi river (above) and at the helm (left) on Lake Kariba – clearly born to be skipper!

with all due respect to all the other worthy sports deemed sufficiently weighty to merit a full Blue, double Blue has only ever meant rugby and cricket to me.

Sealy had got in touch with Tony Jorden, old Monmothian, double Cambridge Blue and former England full back. I had an appointment with a Dr. C. Kolbert in Magdalene College, Cambridge. My father drove me up. Four long hours. Kolbert was, let us say, renowned for his sympathy towards sportsmen, especially rugby players. The rugby coach, Tony Rodgers, was there too. No sign of anyone connected with the cricket though.

"We've heard good things about you. You can either take a gap year and come up in a year, or go to Swansea and then come up. We will sort something out for you," said Kolbert. It all seemed so simple and without stress after the intellectual traumas of Oxford. But I had committed myself to Swansea. And I knew that if I did take a gap year, I would never want to return to my books. So Swansea it was. And it will be of little surprise to anyone to read that my three years there were something of a 'treading water' process. It was not that I did not have a good time. I had far too good a time. I was still struggling to shed the less disciplined habits of my Lydney upbringing. It was not quite a case of Dylan Thomas' 'graveyard of ambition' but at Swansea my cricket stagnated. Drinking and rugby took over. And both improved.

Swansea did spring a surprise and win the UAU (Universities Athletic Union) cricket final against Durham, thanks to an Adrian Dale hundred, but in general, despite the enthusiasm of the director of sport, the former Swansea RFC coach, Stan Addicott, there was no cricketing tradition and therefore no infrastructure. It was hoped that the close proximity of the Neath indoor nets, where Glamorgan practised, might prove beneficial. But the most productive practices were held on a Wednesday evening. And Wednesday afternoon was when the university played most of their rugby matches. And then we went for 'team bonding' afterwards.

So, in my final year at Swansea, came decision time. Was I to ring Dr. Kolbert? I wanted to. For once, I did not require a coaxing, sage parental hand to guide me into a bastion of academia. It was mainly because I could foresee a glorious oasis of first-class rugby and cricket. First, I had to ask Glamorgan. I still wanted to be a cricketer, after all. Tony Lewis, himself a double Blue, was chairman.

Lewis has always been someone whom I have held in the highest regard. There are all the obvious reasons for this, and it could be said that I have followed his lead (albeit very much a poor man's effort) in many aspects of my career, not least a battle with chronic knee injuries. But for me as an impressionable youngster, there was one particular detail about Tony Lewis' life that earned my instant respect, nay even reverence. He had played full back for Gloucester RFC. Forget about the fact that he captained Glamorgan and England, even that he was full back in the Varsity match (he was third choice after all), and also played for Neath and briefly Pontypool. He wore the Cherry and White number 15 shirt. Now that was something. In my little world, and beyond too, you had to be good to play rugby for Gloucester. Only the very best players from Lydney made the trek up the A48 to try their luck. And some very good players did not make the grade up there.

Kingsholm, their small but hostile ground, was a place of awe and worship. I played there a couple of times for Lydney in the traditional Boxing Day clash, once ending up in Gloucester Royal Infirmary with concussion after I had ill-advisedly attempted to tackle their rampaging, and famously tough flanker, Bobby Fowke, with my head. I was sitting there, still in my treasured black and white hooped jersey, when the doctor entered with the brain scans. "We couldn't find anything in there, but you are from Lydney, so that's to be expected."

I did manage an appearance for Gloucestershire against Cornwall there, when a wag from the legendary Shed chided me, "Get stuck in, you big poofta." But Lewis, while stationed at nearby RAF Innsworth, had played as a regular in front of those fanatical, vociferous and no-nonsense 'Shedheads'. He was a man to whom I should listen.

"As chairman I would say no because I want you to play full time for Glamorgan. But personally I would unequivocally say yes. It is too good an opportunity to miss."

The call to Dr. Kolbert was made. "Just apply to Hughes Hall for the one-year PGCE (post graduate certificate in education) in Classics," he said, implying that once a college had accepted me I could easily change subjects. I did not really want to teach. I was accepted. My rugby had got me in. I phoned Hughes Hall to ask if I could change my subject to Land Economy, thereby securing a second year, but also the stigma of the degree that has become famed for its synonymity with hulking, rather dull rugby players. I doubt if I did a great deal to alter that perception, but I had a whale of a time. And I passed my examinations, too. A second Desmond (Tutu – 2:2) to go with the one I achieved at Swansea.

I immersed myself in the whole Cambridge experience, even if my college – as a former all-women teaching establishment, but most conveniently situated right next to Fenners – was considered to be in a different world from the more traditional ones. I was acutely aware that my admission had been through the back door and, while I was not being as financially subsidised as some of the more celebrated rugby players, I recognised that I was privileged.

I bought a push bike, a racing model rather than an old-style one with a basket on the front, and cycled to lectures. I even found time to write a few essays, albeit with the considerable assistance of some 'hand-me-downs' from ex-rugby players. It was blatant plagiarism, but I was pushed for time, or I thought

I was. Sport did not prevent me from whiling away many an hour, with a coffee and a rock cake, in the 'Grad Pad', a tall, modern building near the River Cam only open to graduates; its enduring attraction for me being its possession of every single daily newspaper. In the company of Simon Bryant (brother of my former Swansea housemate, Mark), a craggy, under-rated blindside flanker from Bridgend, I eagerly devoured every single bit of sports reporting, especially the clever and irreverent wit of an emerging Martin Johnson, a fellow Monmothian, in *The Independent*. A seed was sown.

A debut for the LX Club (the university's rugby second team) against London Welsh Druids presaged some bench appearances for the university team, which was especially strong in my time in Fenland. There were two future British Lions in Welshman Mike Hall and Scotsman Rob Wainwright, as well as three future Scottish internationals, Andy MacDonald, Cameron Glasgow and Simon Holmes, one English in Richard Pool-Jones, and one Welsh in Adrian Davies.

Those were the times when it was considered a prudent career move for an aspiring rugby player to go to Cambridge. The fixture list was demanding, and the media coverage extensive. There were frequent trips to Wales to meet Cardiff, Bridgend, Llanelli and Neath, as well as matches in England against the likes of Leicester, Northampton, Harlequins and Rosslyn Park.

For some reason, and I do not think that it was my local knowledge, I seemed to regularly qualify for the Welsh away matches. My first full match for the Blues was some baptism. I played at full back against Llanelli at a damp Stradey Park, in direct opposition to the quite brilliant Jonathan Davies, who was playing his first-ever match at full back in what turned out to be one of his final matches in union before heading north to Rugby League. In Davies' favoured outside half position that night was a former Glamorgan Colts colleague, Colin Stephens, who thankfully spared me too many testing up-and-unders. But there was one terrifying moment when Davies displayed his electrifying pace off the mark. I thought I had him covered before he stepped off his right foot and was away from me like a thief in the night.

Next came an unforgettable evening at the Gnoll in Neath when I made my first appearance at scrum half, deputising for the resting captain, Mark Hancock, in an otherwise full-strength side on its last run out before the Varsity match. It was brutal. As our coach pulled up in mid-afternoon outside the Castle Hotel, locals were shouting "They're going to kill you."

Indeed they tried to. Cambridge had already seen off Cardiff and Bridgend that term, so the formidable Neath side sensed a match on their hands, or maybe a one-sided fight. The first thing to say about Neath is that they were as fit as maggots; a side way ahead of its time under coach Ron Waldron, who spent many hours of torture on the impossibly-steep climbs around Gnoll Park. But that night they acted like the psychopathic, skin-headed bunch of animals that they were often accused of being. It was student bashing of the most gratuitous kind.

Just two feet in front of me, Rob Wainwright was rendered unconscious by a punch of murderous intent from flanker Lyn Jones. It will not surprise anyone that I did not intervene. Jones was also a fast bowler who terrorised anyone playing against his side, Cwmavon, and many years later, when he appeared for Glamorgan in a benefit match for Steve Barwick, confessed to me "I wouldn't have done that if I'd known Wainwright was a boxer."

Indeed, he was a heavyweight boxing Blue, but it mattered little that night. Andy MacDonald was ruled out of the Varsity match and only luck (and a cover-up on the extent of Wainwright's injury) prevented others from befalling the same, cruel fate. For me, there was humiliation at the hands of Andy

Booth, the Wales B international who would consign me to bench duties in my second year at Cambridge.

It was the era before neutral touch judges, whose sightings can now be brought to the attention of the referee. So, as the two packs of forwards set themselves for a scrummage on our 22-metre line, I bent down, awaiting the customary tap of the hand from hooker Jim Ashworth on the loose head prop's shoulder to indicate he wanted the ball put in.

As I was doing this, Booth must have spotted that the referee had gone around to the other side of the scrummage to keep an eye on any potential shenanigans arising there. He quickly flipped the ball out of my hands – very much as Leicester and England flanker Neil Back so controversially did to Munster scrum half Peter Stringer in the 2002 European Cup final – straight underneath the feet of his own second row. Out the ball went and across the Neath back line, with me in hot pursuit of Booth, shouting: "You cocky little w***er, I'm going to have you."

Thankfully, I did not catch him. Simon Bryant, my faithful ally, who moments earlier had saved me from almost certain death by boot, dragging me on to the right side of a ruck after I had lain admiring a rare tackle on prop Jeremy Pugh, then proffered some uncharacteristically sensible advice. "Leave it. They'll kill you." I was disappointed with Booth though, because only that year I had played in the same Swansea University side as him, and I did not expect such public belittlement.

The following Monday morning I waited in my room at 18 Clarendon Street. Normally I could not get out of there quick enough of a morning, as it was owned by an eccentric old gentleman, whose constant prancing around in a silk dressing gown unsurprisingly led me to believe that he was not heterosexual. But now I waited. Rugby Blues are awarded by the captain. His decision is final. So it is also his task to cycle around all the various colleges and inform those players in contention whether they have achieved the then life-changing status of becoming a rugby Blue.

My only hope that morning was that Hancock might fall off his bicycle and injure himself, because he was a scrum half like me, and my other position of full back was already capably filled by my Hughes Hall colleague and future England squad member Alan Buzza. But I urgently awaited confirmation that I was to be on the bench. The blighter left me to last. He had begun at 7.30am and did not reach me until after 11.

"You knew you were on the bench, didn't you? No doubt about it," he said. Well, actually, there was considerable doubt. Russell Heap was a talented sportsman who went on to open the batting with me in my second year and he had played a number of games for the Blues during the term, beating me to a bench place for the prestigious Steele-Bodgers fixture. My sporadically-kept diary of that term tells me that was "a dark day".

All term I had spent many an hour lurking surreptitiously around outside the Ryder & Amies shop where the teams were posted, popping in and out of various newsagents and coffee shops before the arrival of the team sheet brought either joy or despair. So, in my eyes, it was not the fait accompli Hancock thought it to be. Nonetheless it was time to revel in the peculiar pre-Varsity match traditions. There was port and nuts at Downing College, where our president, Lord Butterfield, made the toast "God Damn Bloody Oxford." And 'Doc Dingle's feast' on the Sunday before the match, where the most gluttonous and piggish devouring took place under the façade of the sports nutritionists' favourite 'carbo-loading'.

Subsequent fitness training has taught me that our levels of conditioning were not what we imagined them to be. It was a commonly-accepted wisdom that the two university sides were the fittest rugby teams in the land. And, indeed, there were the legendary 'Doc Turner' runs to be often endured at 7.30am. Dr. Mike Turner, a fellow of Peterhouse College, was a fanatical athlete who became manager of the Great Britain Olympic Squad. He was a genteel, mild-mannered man who turned into a sadistic disciplinarian when he began his 40-minute fartlek (speedplay) runs.

But, as with most rugby clubs at the time, and this is remarkable given the physical demands of the sport, there was no formalised weight training. True, some of the more assiduous members of the squad did embark on their own programmes, but generally, even though we may have been fitter than most sides then, we were light years behind the athletes of today's professional age. And we probably had as much time to train as they do now. I did not become a rugby Blue in 1988. Nor in 1989, when at least I came a little closer. Booth, who was being violently sick at regular intervals, told the trainer: "Tell Jamer to warm up. I'm coming off."

I made my way from the Twickenham stand where the replacements sat – we were not substitutes; we required the doctor's agreement to replace an injury victim – whipped off my tracksuit, and stood in the tunnel, with the lights of the TV cameras glaring in my face. "Just pass everything," I was telling myself in a vain attempt to suppress spiralling nerves, as I waited for what seemed like an age. Then came the news. It may even have been welcome then, given my timid state, but later, and most certainly now, it is desperately disappointing: "He's not coming off." No rugby Blue, then.

I had come across Mike Atherton in the Emmanuel College bar in my first term. "You do want to play cricket, don't you?" he enquired. "It's one of the reasons I'm here," I said, a little in awe and also very impressed that the Lancashire batsman had recognised me. I had made the briefest of appearances at a Combined Universities trial the year before – caught behind second ball for nought – and I reckoned the last time our paths had crossed before that was an England v. Wales under-19 schools international at Pontardulais.

Cricket at Cambridge was markedly different from the rugby. At rugby we generally competed, even with the best sides. At cricket we palpably did not. There was Atherton, myself, Jonathan Atkinson and Rob Turner, who went on to play regularly as professionals. But the rest were club cricketers at best, all joyously able to declare themselves first-class cricketers when they were anything but.

Even Turner, who has kept wicket and batted with such distinction for Somerset, was not certain that he wanted to be a professional then. And neither his performances, nor his work ethic, suggested that he would. He often seemed distant and unfocused, prompting me to chivvy him in the 1990 Varsity match at Lord's when his hesitant innings was not aiding us in a difficult chase: "Do you want to win this game or not?"

But he has improved immeasurably, overcoming the handicap of being an unusually large man for a wicketkeeper to reach the cusp of England recognition. He even developed a harder edge to his naturally reticent personality to become a typically chirpy and sometimes aggressive voice behind the stumps. "I've decided that my team mates will be my friends and I am not too bothered about anyone else," he remarked to me when I once mentioned to him that he was not among the most popular opponents among some of the Glamorgan players. Not that there was much sledging going on at Cambridge, from either side. The cricket was all a little too civilised and perfunctory; a form of glorified net practice. Now and again, the professionals would lose patience with my annoying occupation of the crease. Middlesex's Phil Tufnell once remarked: "I can't wait to play Glamorgan this year. They must be crap if you can get a game for them."

There may just have been the odd expletive in there too, as there most certainly was the day when Tufnell lost control of the ball as he bowled to our flame-haired Scotsman, Geoff Dyer. I was at the non-strikers end as the ball trickled to a standstill at square leg. In my mind, I was urging Dyer to leave the ball alone, because I knew the furore it would cause if he hit it. Another professional would not have entertained the thought, but Dyer was blissfully ignorant of such protocol and could not resist walking over and swatting the ball for four, as you are entitled to do in the laws. Tufnell, in his considerable rage, bowled a beamer the next ball, which Dyer nonchalantly ran off the face for a further four.

But, despite our frequent ineptitude, we had some real fun and I was privileged to befriend some wonderful characters. There was Richard 'Pumper' Pyman, a charming and aristocratic Harrovian, who bowled accurate medium pacers with a quirky, windmill action off the wrong foot. The professionals did not relish facing him on the slow, seaming tracks at Fenners. I would not have done so either; my only proper confrontation with him, mercifully, coming on a Sophia Gardens belter when he played for Dorset in the NatWest Trophy. He did bowl me in the charity match, which Atherton arranged in Chelsea, but I did have the distraction of George Best staggering from the hospitality tent to a waiting taxi – a journey of no more than 50 yards, but one that involved at least five stops.

Pyman would greet me each morning with, "Ah, Jamo my dear boy" but not before he had bellowed, "Mornin' Cap'n Willatt, sir" in mock military tone. This was directed at Jon Willatt, who was my opening partner in my first year; Atherton was batting at number three, because he realised that Gehan Mendis and Graeme Fowler were established as an opening pair at Lancashire and first drop was his most likely route into the side. Willatt was a left-handed front-footed blocker, who had resigned from the Army to return to mature education, and was the only one in the side who did not snigger when our three-day fixture against the Combined Services was referred to as a match against the Combined 'Filth'.

There were some wonderfully laid-back fixtures away from the maulings by the counties; against the likes of the Cryptics, the Free Foresters, the MCC and, of course, our old boys team, the Quidnuncs. I used these to experiment with new shots and to try to express myself a little more as a batsman; a little too much, apparently, for the Reverend Andrew Wingfield-Digby, a one-time England cricket team chaplain, who bowled the most infuriating 'dobbing' medium-pacers for the Free Foresters. I could see no way of scoring off him other than some hits over the top and the blatant lack of respect clearly irked the vicar. So, when he had the loudest of leg before appeals turned down, I was astounded to hear language most unbecoming of the clergy.

You would never have found Jon Willatt indulging in such behaviour. Despite his military background and muscular stature, I found him quite the gentlest person with whom I had played sport. Indeed, his admirable sense of sportsmanship stretched so far that he once walked against Leicestershire when no one appealed. The opposition, as well as me at the other end ("Come back, Jon, you might get away with it still," I was muttering under my breath) were aghast at such probity. Atherton soon followed leg before, essaying a drive. He immediately repaired to the nets to hit some drives against the bowling machine. I could hear the old professionals, David Gower and Peter Willey, whispering at slip: "Ain't no good practising hitting half volleys when you don't get them in the middle."

Jonathan Agnew, whose on-field persona of persistent moaner was the antithesis of his joyfully-articulate role as the voice of *Test Match Special*, was becoming increasingly frustrated with the sluggishness of the pitch. "I could face Jeff Thomson on here without any pads on," he whined.

There was a myriad of future professions within our squad: doctors, lawyers, vets, stock brokers, even a vintner and a couple of future professional rugby players in Buzza and Rory Jenkins. Given Buzza's robust physique, and his reputation for Wasps and then Rotherham as one of the most recklessly-hard tacklers on a rugby field, one would have assumed that he would have either bowled very quickly or hit monstrously huge sixes. He did neither. Instead, the smiling Cornishman bowled the most impossibly slow, tempting, left-arm spin, which confounded many a professional who was never quite sure what to do with such superficially easy offerings. And, charged with the unenviable task of attempting to blend this batch of misfits into some sort of cricket team, was our coach, Graham Saville, the former Essex batsman, whose constant swearing and use of cockney rhyming slang always brought a levity to the gravest of situations. He encouraged us to go to him for advice rather than him foisting anything upon us.

Only once can I recall him approaching me unsolicited. It was during my second year, when my technical travails were reaching crisis point. "We need to forget about this fitness lark for a minute and concentrate on basic technique," he said, before embarking on a bowling machine session that very nearly resulted in a premature and painful end for me. Saville had decided that I needed to work on my playing of spin, especially when advancing down the wicket to drive straight. So he dutifully adjusted the machine to a slow, loopy speed and I proceeded to practise coming down the wicket, often slicing the ball 'inside out' through extra cover when it should have been driven back past the machine. As I began advancing to the next one, I heard – certainly did not see – something whizzing past my nose. I saw the yellow ball rebounding off the back netting as I hit the ground in panic.

"This machine is f**king f**ked," was Saville's priceless observation, echoing a similar dose of expletives in the Welsh cult film *Twin Town*, where the character Fatty Lewis (played by Glamorgan die-hard supporter Huw Ceredig) falls off a ladder and breaks his leg. "Fatty's leg is f**king f**ked," his work-mate, Chip, later observes. Thus can overworked Glamorgan bowlers often be heard muttering at the end of a day: "I'm Fatty's leg." And thus the title of this book.

The fun-loving Saville revelled in the fines sessions at the end of a day's play, in which petty but humorous offences were punished. These included 'sliding doors' – the ball bisecting two sprawling fielders; 'Sprake' – an outrageous fielding howler (named after the former Leeds United goalkeeper, Gary Sprake, who was renowned for his spectacular mistakes); and 'Taff of the day' – always me until the quixotically-named David Shufflebotham from Neath arrived. I was also regularly fined for a 'strop' as I took the cricket a lot more seriously than most, resulting in Pyman dubbing me 'the dour professional'.

I was called a few other things by my new team mates too, Dougie No Mates being a particular favourite. It was not as though I was friendless – this moniker was the result of a casual comment after a social arrangement fell through. I had arranged to meet Russell Heap and a few other friends in the Prince Regent public house opposite Downing College. I did not dither when they were not there and decided to head back alongside Parker's Piece, where I used to jog most mornings, to Hughes Hall, mindful of not wanting to sit alone in a pub looking distinctly sad. When I spoke to Heap the next day he apologised for their non-attendance. They had not even got near the Prince Regent. "Did you wait around long?" he asked.

"Who do you think I am? Dougie No Mates?" I replied in a flash.

I am not sure why I said Dougie, because I think the more common name used for this nickname at the time was Norman. But that was it. Dougie I was. I even appear as D.N.M. James on the official Blues photograph of 1989. On that same photograph Mike Atherton's school is listed as Westward Ho! rather than Manchester Grammar, R.J. Turner becomes R. St. J. Turner, and there is a G. de W. Saville, of Eton and Trinity College, as coach. Monmouth School, who wanted a copy as a proud reminder of their latest Blue, were so disgusted by the defacement that they sent the photograph back. In truth, it was little more than a puerile prank, but in another way it was like some subconscious return to a university version of the days of Gentlemen and Players. All those with a connection to the professional game were ridiculed, except for J.C.M. Atkinson of Millfield and Downing. Atkinson was the tall, blond-haired and handsome cricketer who strode out of Millfield, where his late father, Colin, was then headmaster, and straight into the Somerset first eleven, where his father was also president, smiting mighty sixes on his debut. As a schoolboy he bowled faster than anyone I saw at that age, and he swung the ball too. But at Cambridge his cricket deteriorated dramatically to the point where he could not bowl at all, and his innings were reduced to flighty cameos, which promised much but delivered little. Let us say his social life was hectic. He drank the most ridiculous amounts of alcohol, and became immersed in the Rah element of the university – the posher end of the market, where the alumni of only the very best public schools congregated.

The Rah factor did for me in my quest to succeed Atherton as skipper of the side in my second year. Myself and Atkinson put ourselves forward as contenders, to be voted upon by the Blues eleven on the second evening of the three-day Varsity match at Lord's. I am not the most natural of leaders but this was something I really wanted to do. I felt that I was the best man for the job. But the Rahs did not. Maybe they were worried about my perceived 'dourness' and my obsessive practice and training. Maybe it was because I was a graduate and not considered a bona fide Cambridge student. But the vote went against me.

I had already batted twice in the match and the weather forecast for the final day was dismal, but I do not think it would have mattered anyway. It was time to drown my sorrows. "If you drop a catch tomorrow, you'll be in serious trouble," warned my room mate, Atherton. Bollocks to it. They said to me that they all thought that the added responsibility would help Atkinson and rekindle his marvellous natural talent. But it seemed obvious to me that he had little intention of becoming a full-time cricketer and that his situation was irretrievable. Somerset did make a forlorn attempt, but his swift exit from the game validated my thoughts.

His relationship with Atherton intrigued me. I thought Atkinson was a little jealous of the former Manchester Grammar School boy, and at times he tried to deprecate him with disparaging comments, often mimicking his northern accent, which he reckoned to be similar to Orville, the green-feathered duck friend of ventriloquist Keith Harris.

But Atherton was too strong to be affected and just used to urge Atkinson to "run in as fast as you can" at him in the indoor nets, in order to replicate the sharpness he knew he required for first- class cricket. Atkinson, not a spiteful individual, quite often attempted humorous ways of belittling me, delighting in calling me Dougie, and aping my odd habit of curling my bottom lip over my top one, when unsure about something. And he often used to accompany this facial contortion with a monotone rendering of "But they're first-class runs" – an off-the-cuff comment, totally at variance with my later stance on the subject, which I made during that first Varsity match, when being consoled by fellow opener Heap about my lack of runs in the fixture. I often wonder who Atherton voted for. Pyman apologised to me half-way through the following season: "We got it wrong." But I was already getting used to disappointment.

That season was a remarkable one for the Combined Universities side, which played in the Benson & Hedges Cup. In my three years at Swansea, I had never come remotely close to making the side, but now, among the inner sanctum at Cambridge, I was a shoo-in, although Atherton did warn Atkinson and me when we all stayed together during pre-season training at Fenners: "You'll both almost definitely play, but we could do with you scoring a few runs to make it easier."

It wasn't a bad squad:

M.A. Atherton – Capt (Cambridge University and Lancashire)

S.P. James (Cambridge University and Glamorgan)

M.A. Crawley (Oxford University and Lancashire – later Nottinghamshire)

N. Hussain (Durham University and Essex)

J.I. Longley (Durham University and Kent – later Durham)

J.C.M. Atkinson (Cambridge University and Somerset)

M.P. Speight (Durham University and Sussex – also later Durham)

A. Dale (Swansea University and Glamorgan)

C.M. Tolley (Loughborough University and Worcestershire – later Nottinghamshire)

J. Boiling (Durham University and Surrey – later Durham)

A.R. Hansford (Surrey University and Sussex)

T.J.G. O'Gorman (Durham University and Derbyshire)

And, just as the famous Barbarians rugby team always include one uncapped player, so we had one player who did not go on to play first-class cricket – Treherne Parker of Swansea University, who did play some second eleven cricket for Essex.

The other teams in our group that year were Surrey, Middlesex, Worcestershire and Gloucestershire. We defeated Surrey at Fenners in the first game – a rain-reduced 37-over affair in which off-spinner James Boiling mystified his home county with the miserly figures of 3-9 from his 8 overs. A heavy defeat then followed against Middlesex at The Parks, Oxford, where Mike Gatting lorded over us with an instructional century. But if our first victory might have had an element of fortune about it, the next, against Worcestershire at New Road, had no such thing. Our successes were based on a useful batting line-up, which was supplemented by an accurate attack, albeit lacking pace, which whipped through their overs at a frantic rate.

This was amply illustrated in the Worcestershire match, where we got through an incredible 47 overs in the two and a quarter hours before lunch. Adrian Dale was only just starting to make a name for himself with his canny medium pace, and that day he snared Ian Botham for nought, caught behind off a wide half volley. But once the considerable celebrations were under way, that delivery quickly became something much more akin to a devastating, unplayable leg cutter. He even pleaded with the boorish bouncer of the local nightspot, Tramps, "But I got Ian Botham out for nought today," when we were refused entry.

We should have beaten Gloucestershire at Bristol, but some lusty late hitting from Courtney Walsh saved the home side. We had done enough to qualify as the second placed side in our group – the first student side to do so. The quarter final was to be against Somerset at Taunton on May 31. Now that was a problem. I had a statistics preliminary examination on that day. But it was only a preliminary. Nasser Hussain and Martin Speight had final examinations at Durham. That would surely be more problematical. Not so. Despite all the plaintive protestations of myself and my supportive college, the Cambridge authorities insisted that I sat the exam at the appointed time. The previous year they had come to the aid of Mike Hall when he requested dispensation to go on the Wales rugby tour to New Zealand. And in the 1970s, Alastair Hignell, a double Blue who played cricket for Gloucestershire, had had his examinations postponed in order to tour Australia with England and had been met by an examiner at Heathrow.

But that was rugby. The goal-posts were firmly in place for that. They did not even exist for cricket. Questions were already being raised about Oxford and Cambridge's right to first-class status and Durham was rightly touted as being much more deserving.

"What happens if I just don't turn up for the exam?" I asked my tutor, Dr. Raffan.

"You will be sent down," came the stern reply.

I seriously considered it. However, all the advice I received, including that of Atherton, was that it was not worth it. Hussain and Speight were allowed to sit their examination a day early and travel to Taunton with a minder. I had to sit mine on the morning of the match and listen agonisingly to the final stages of the match on the radio in my room. We lost by 3 runs. Atherton and Saville telephoned me as soon as the game had finished. "We would have won if you had been here," they said. It was a nice thing to say, but may or may not have been true. It was the bigger picture that needed to be considered. *Wisden* faithfully captured the mood:

"But the problems Cambridge have in attracting cricketing students were never better illustrated than when James was not permitted to play in the quarter-final at Taunton because it clashed with a preliminary examination paper. At the same time two members of the side, from Durham, were allowed to take their finals early in order to play. It is this sort of attitude by senior members of the University that encourages those who would like to see an end to what they believe is the privileged position enjoyed by Oxford and Cambridge in English cricket".

It was a disgraceful decision. From then on, I thought that first- class cricket at Cambridge was on borrowed time. Therefore, I am absolutely astounded that, as I write in 2004, not only have Oxford and Cambridge got first-class status but also Durham and Loughborough. This slavish adherence to tradition is a damaging anachronism in the modern game. I know that I can easily be accused of hypocrisy, because I took full advantage of my time at Cambridge, and my success there did in some way help my county career. Indeed, I would not change a day of it. But I do believe, without being arrogant, that I would have succeeded in county cricket without having gone to Cambridge.

Equally, I do not believe that I would be able to spend five years at university in this modern, cut-throat age of cricket. County staffs are much smaller, and expectations all the greater, often without the bedding-in time players such as myself were permitted. I say it with a heavy heart, but it is time for this tradition to end. I do not mind the EWCB spending money on their University Centres of Excellence. That makes sense. But any matches they play should not be deemed first class. Let the counties play them as a warm-up for the season, but do not allow mediocre players to boost their averages against inferior opposition.

It is ridiculous that runs and wickets against the students should count in the first-class averages. Some players even secure new contracts because of such performances, which lend an unrealistic look to their end-of-season returns. I know, because I have been there. I did not secure a contract because of it, but in 1994 a century against each of the universities propelled my season's average from a distinctly modest 30 in the Championship to a passable 38. But I was not fooled. I knew that was not good enough, just as I knew that all the runs I was scoring for Cambridge meant little when I got back to Glamorgan. Indeed, I worried that I might be 'found out' on the quicker pitches of county cricket. Fenners was unresponsively slow and, when the quicker bowlers pitched short, I was able to hook and pull with comfort. Those were not shots that I had played before and I fretted that I would struggle when the fast men tested me. Indeed, that Combined Universities match at Bristol is a case in point. Earlier in the season, when Gloucestershire had visited Fenners, I had hooked the extremely rapid David 'Syd' Lawrence, with his arcing run up, arms and legs pumping like pistons, for a couple of fours. Atherton said that night: "You were brave today, but he may be after you on a quicker pitch." I could not sleep the night before that game in Bristol, even though bouncers were not permitted in one-day cricket in those days. He could still pepper my chest if he felt so inclined. Either Lawrence didn't recognise me or he felt chastened. I suppose it was the former. He hardly bowled a short ball, which was most rare for him.

Once I established myself as a regular run-getter in the Glamorgan first eleven I had no desire to play against the universities. Indeed, my name does not appear after 1996, except in warm-up matches that were not first class.

In one of those, a one-day match at Oxford, I scored a hundred, before advancing down the wicket and deliberately missing a delivery from their excitable young off spinner, whose wild yelps of delight at my intentional demise revealed a less than discerning eye for the yawning gap in expectations of amateur and professional. Mostly, my runs for Cambridge were garnered at Fenners against attacks resting their most potent weapons, especially after the first couple of games when the counties had completed their practice. But there were two stand-out innings, which I can lay claim to as being properly 'first class'.

Firstly, there was a 151 not out in my first year against a Warwickshire attack, which boasted West Indian Tony Merrick, future England internationals Tim Munton and Joey Benjamin, as well as Paul Smith and Adrian Pierson. I consider that my maiden century because my only previous one had been tortuously slow, for Glamorgan against Oxford in 1987 in my second first-class innings. I am glad that it was not my debut. I would not have liked to have been in the record books as having made a century on debut – against Oxford. Mike Powell is. And it was a double to boot. I have ribbed him mercilessly about it. He will never be able to expunge the 'double on debut' bit from the records, but he has the ability to better that career best, falling agonisingly short in 2003 with 198 against Durham. Cricketers who end their careers with a best against a university are normally either under-achievers or simply not good enough. Powell falls into neither category.

Then there was my final innings at Fenners, 131 not out to win the game for an Oxbridge side against New Zealand. The tourists' pace attack was not particularly threatening without the resting Sir Richard Hadlee (some of the students were joking that we were playing the Kiwi equivalent of the Club Cricket Conference) but they did have John Bracewell as their premier spinner on a turning pitch, and he had been causing England some problems in the Test series with his aggressive off-stump line and his voluble nature. Not that I impressed Kiwi wicketkeeper Adam Parore. "Must be your first one," he remarked, as some unusually enthusiastic applause rang around Fenners for my century. The cool answer would have been just "No". But I added an uncharacteristically boastful rider: "My seventh."

The upshot of the success of the 1989 Combined Universities side was that we won some prize money. Decent money, too. But, as this was the first time this had happened, nobody knew what to do with it. So after some deliberation it was decided to send us on a celebratory tour to Barbados. And some celebration it was. The cricket was appalling, but the drinking was long and hard, with Adrian Dale belying his slender frame to surprise everyone with his stamina and unquenchable thirst. Atherton, too, let his hair down. His image can be rather ascetic in such matters, but he was known in some circles as 'Iron

Mike', not because of some pugilistic likening to Mike Tyson, but rather because of a surprising ability to quaff multiple ales of a night and then be right as rain to open the batting the following morning. So when he awoke on the second morning to announce that he had "thrown a wild cat or two" during the night – you don't need to be a genius to work what this was a northern euphemism for – I knew that this was going to be more like a Lydney cricket tour than the British Universities (which was how we were known).

Atherton had made his Test debut that summer, but had been pipped for a winter tour place in the West Indies by Nasser Hussain (given his teetotal tendencies, it was just as well that Hussain did not make our trip). But Atherton was in demand from the Caribbean media. And suddenly, the presence one morning of their most famous commentator almost caused me enormous embarrassment. I awoke hazily in the apartment, which Atherton and a couple of other tourists were sharing, to hear the famous voice of Tony Cozier downstairs. It was too good a chance to miss to meet such a well-known figure, so I arose unsteadily and staggered down the stairs, all the time cursing the local beer, Banks, which was now causing me to feel so unwell. I spotted Atherton on the balcony, sitting with a white chap. "Where's Tony?" I thought. "I'm sure I heard him. Who's this other chap?" Luckily for me, before I could make a complete fool of myself, Cozier spoke. It was him. The concept of a white Bajan hit me like a thunderclap, snapping me out of my alcoholic stupor. Tony Cozier was not black. "Pleased to meet you," I said with great relief. My only defence, other than a hangover, is that I had only heard him on the radio.

There was no tour the following year. The Combined Universities did manage one victory in the Benson & Hedges Cup but those dizzy heights of 1989 were not to be revisited. That solitary success came against a dispirited and strife-torn Yorkshire at Headingley. I scored 63. But when I tell you that I was dropped six – yes six – times, you will begin to realise that this was an innings of which I am not proud. In fact, I was thoroughly embarrassed. Normally when a batsman is playing poorly, the end is swift and relatively painless. But this was torture. I was almost trying to get myself out by the end of it. My technique was in tatters. "Look at his pick up," fast bowler Paul Jarvis kept saying to his team mates. The face of my bat was opening alarmingly as it reached its peak, which was also somewhere in the line of third slip rather than straight back behind me.

If Jarvis was not sufficiently riled by his inability to dismiss such a technically incompetent player, then Adrian Dale soon had him foaming at the mouth with "I thought you were quick." Jarvis was then bowling what captain Martyn Moxon wanted to be the last over of his spell. "I want another one at him (pointing at Dale). I'm going to knock his head off," raged Jarvis, as Moxon had to forcibly drag him away. At least the jovial Arnie Sidebottom was able to see the funny side of it, as he continually rubbed my shirt saying, "Can I have some of your luck, please son."

Without wishing this tome to become some personal eulogy to the man and him claiming royalties, I must say that it was extremely beneficial playing alongside Mike Atherton. I marvelled at his mental strength and the burning intensity he brought to his innings, but also his ability to switch off and even share a joke between deliveries. I also learnt from his dedication to his physical fitness. That may sound strange, because many will recall Atherton as being a most unenthusiastic trainer in his later playing days, but this disinclination was entirely down to his back problems. Through necessity, Pilates and swimming became his only training.

At Cambridge he set the example by running every morning before breakfast in the winter months, leading weekly fitness sessions for the squad on top of that, and then by running four laps of the Fenners outfield before play in the summer. He did, though, give me one piece of poor advice. At the time I was, on the insistence of my rugby playing mates, Bryant and MacDonald, ("You've got to sort that chest out – and those arms, well…"), toying with the idea of a weight-training programme. Atherton emphatically advised against it, reiterating the commonly-held misconception that weight training will bulk you up unnecessarily. "It will affect your timing," he said. But, in a note he later sent me with a training schedule in it, he did say that he had been told by the England fitness advisers to do some because he was a "weakling".

I wish that I had not listened to him. For when I did eventually begin – firstly under the guidance of Malcolm Jarvis, a Zimbab-wean left-arm bowler and Harare gym owner, and then with Steve Davies, a prison warder involved with Cardiff RFC – my career took a distinct upward turn. As well as giving me strength, it gave me confidence. Still not enough cricketers use weight training. As captain of Glamorgan, I was constantly trying to convert the players, but, with the notable exception of my training partner, Mike Powell, few would.

It was interesting to see how Atherton was viewed amongst his university contemporaries. He had not, of course, played for England by then, but it was almost universally agreed that he would, from the ubiquitous references to the FEC acronym (whose translation of Future England Captain suited the press, but in fact the E meant educated, with two swear-words either side) to a tourist guide I stumbled upon soon after arriving in Cambridge. Under the famous alumni of Downing College was one M. Atherton, cricketer. He hadn't even left. Despite this premature fame, he was very popular, the rugby players in particular enjoying his frequent inebriated attempts to demonstrate his tackling ability. He and Andy MacDonald were like a double act sometimes; the 6ft 8inch second row eager to show his prowess as a quick bowler while Atherton was more interested in a vain attempt to bring the mighty Scot to the floor. Once their horse play was abruptly ended by a tap on Atherton's shoulder. It was Lord Butterfield, master of Downing College and president of the Cricket Club as well as the Rugby Club. "Is this any way for the captain of cricket to behave?"

On the field, it was difficult to assess Atherton as a skipper at Cambridge because we were never competitive enough for him to assert himself; the bowlers rarely good enough to execute any plan. He certainly became used to losing, and I incurred his considerable wrath by suggesting in a column in *The Western Mail* that his failure as captain in Zimbabwe in 1996 was in no small part due to his knowing of little else as a leader. "You know things are bad when even your mates start having a go at you," he gloomily remarked.

Atherton was not afraid to back his judgement and make some bold decisions. He had one novel solution to our bowling problems at Cambridge. A bearded graduate called Mike Mullins had taken five wickets on his debut against Glamorgan but had done little thereafter, and was a strange, reclusive character who did not really fit in with the rest of the team. Atherton wanted him out, but there were no ready-made replacements in the Crusaders (the second team). But at the back of his mind he recalled how sharply Roger Clitheroe, my old school mucker and ostensibly a wicketkeeper, had turned his off-spinners with a rubber composition ball on the matting in the winter indoor nets. So he gave Clitheroe a chance in a couple of the jazz-hat fixtures to see what he could do.

"That's crap," said Richard Bate, christened the 'smoking doughnut' by coach Saville for a rather obvious weakness for cigarettes and sweet food, and a former Blue then captaining the Crusaders. The experiment naturally failed, forcing Atherton into the equally contentious decision of handing David Shufflebotham his first-class debut in the Varsity match, when my former Welsh Schools colleague had made himself unavailable for most of the term. "You have to promise me you will play next year," said Atherton, aware of the impending controversy. If these were early signs of the stubbornness that characterised Atherton's career then the Clitheroe saga revealed an unusually outlandish side to our Mancunian leader. If only he had been so eager to include another Monmouth schoolboy when he was captain of England! He may well have been. I don't really know. I have never fully broached the subject. He was keen to publicise my talents at the end of the Australian series in 1997 by saying "and Steve James has been scoring a stack of runs for Glamorgan" when the press questioned him about the possible composition of the West Indies tour party.

And at the start of that summer he told me that he had pushed for my selection in an England A versus the Rest trial match at Birmingham. But the selectors preferred Jason Laney of Hampshire – galling for me, given his subsequent early parting from the game through a combination of inconsistency and insouciance.

Even though the third man predilection may never have totally left his mind, I think Atherton rated me to some extent. He would giggle when imparting compliments from others. My debut for Cambridge was coincidentally against Glamorgan – the only time in my career I have been out hit wicket. Having pulled a Steve Watkin long hop (he says it was all planned) for four, I dislodged a bail with my foot. Atherton returned from tossing up with Hugh Morris to say: "He thinks you're a gutsy player." And so? Nothing more, nothing less. A giggle and he was away.

He did recommend me to Lancashire in the early 1990s when I was struggling to break the Morris/Butcher axis at the top of the Glamorgan order. "He would have made a good signing for us," he wrote in my benefit brochure. I doubt it. I'm a Taff, aren't I? At least where cricket is concerned.

CHAPTER FIVE

DINKY DOS

Michael James Cann. The name may not be familiar to a lot of Glamorgan cricket followers, let alone cricket watchers in general. But it instantly springs to my mind when I recall my early days at Glamorgan. And it invariably brings a smile to my face. Cann was a left-handed opening batsman who bowled some occasional off-spin for Glamorgan between 1983 and 1991. He was a gutsy player, especially adept against the quicker bowlers, but only appeared in 36 first-class matches with a modest batting average of 25. But he was much more than a modest cricketer. He was a real character, the type you do not come across often. The stories about him are endless and enduring, still recounted in the Glamorgan dressing room when I was involved, some 12 years after his release from the staff.

There is an oft-used description of someone being blessed with "genius that borders on madness". It would be an exaggeration to say that Cann was the classic example, but he was a gifted, intelligent individual who seemed unusually prone to lapse into acts of madcap hilarity.

He was born and bred in one of the rougher areas of Cardiff but managed to compartmentalise the distractions of a disturbed family life so successfully that he achieved an excellent biochemistry degree from Swansea University. His last year of study in west Wales coincided with my first, and, even though it was obvious then that we were going to be rivals for the same place in the Glamorgan side, he was very helpful and friendly, especially when it came to recommending the cheapest (which invariably meant the most heavily-populated) watering holes.

I will begin at North Perrott, a picturesque ground near Crewkerne in Somerset. Glamorgan second eleven were playing their Somerset counterparts in a three-day match. It was the game in which Cann and I set a Glamorgan second eleven record for the first wicket – 302 – against some weak bowling. And it was also my first sighting of a young chap called Mark Lathwell. He was the shy, tubby boy from Devon whose wristy stroke-play immediately impressed, especially his ability to whip seemingly respectable, straight, short-of-a-length balls wide of mid-on for four. He went on, somewhat reluctantly, to play twice for England, but his career finished unnecessarily early due to a combination of ennui and recalcitrance on his part, and inflexibly poor man-management on the part of Somerset.

The fun began that day when captain and coach John Steele brought Cann on to bowl. He was a talented spinner, who could give the ball a real rip, but he was famously unpredictable and temperamental. The pitch was beginning to turn, and our strong position meant that Cann's introduction to the attack could be greeted with an attacking field. I was at silly point and there were men stationed at slip, leg slip and short leg. We all crouched down and waited as Cann began his run up. And we waited. Nothing. We all looked to see Cann returning to his mark. He had lost his run up. We crouched again and waited. Again nothing. A grin came across the face of our Cornish wicketkeeper, Martin Roberts. Cann had lost his run up again. It was only three or four paces anyway. When it happened a third time, I was not even watching the batsman, as I should have been. My eyes, like everyone else's on the field, were on Cann. He had developed a serious case of the 'yips', that curious psychological affliction, which mainly besets golfers, rendering them unable to perform what was previously a simple and grooved task. In cricket it seems mainly to affect left-arm spinners – someone once did a study as to why that was, but I didn't understand it – who suddenly cannot pitch their flighted deliveries on the cut strip. It happened to Surrey's Keith Medlycott on an England A tour of Pakistan and Sri Lanka in 1990/91, when his assortment of head-high full tosses and double bouncers to Mark Ramprakash in a practice match left him in tears. He never recovered from that, despite the patience and understanding of his county, and it was sad to see him in Pretoria on Glamorgan's pre-season tour of 1996 playing club cricket solely as a batsman. He could bowl off one pace in the nets but, when faced with the wide, open spaces of the middle, the demons returned.

Thankfully, he was cutting his coaching teeth out there – the previous year he had been coaching the Northern Transvaal B side while I was in charge of the Zimbabwe B side ("us coaches are getting younger," he said) – and has recently finished a highly-successful spell as coach of Surrey.

Ravi Shastri, while at Glamorgan, was also struck down by this mental torment, spending hours with bowling adviser Don Shepherd, to attempt to remedy the problem. He never fully recovered from it. And here was Cann, unable even to begin his run up. He did not know which foot to put in front of the other. He stuttered and stopped, stuttered and stopped. The grins on the fielders' faces turned to smiles, and, finally, to hysterical laughter.

Cann might have expected some sympathy, but second team cricket is a harsh, unforgiving and cynical place. Cann knew that. He had indulged in his fair share of banter and ridicule. But he lost it. "John, look at all those f***ers laughing. That's it; I'm never bowling another ball for Glamorgan." It did not appear that he could, even if he tried, but he did eventually manage to propel some sort of delivery down the other end.

From then on, his bowling could only be classed in the 'partnership breaking' category – in other words, it could only be used as a last resort or as an alternative in the last over at the end of a session. And when he did capture a wicket, he let everyone know about it. "He's only gone and f*****g got him," he would exclaim, before embarking on a celebratory lap of the square. Now it is the County Ground, Bristol. The last over before lunch and Steele turns to Cann to bowl at Paul Romaines, the experienced Gloucestershire batsman with the delightful nickname of 'Human' (remains: come on, speed up), playing out time at the end of his career.

Cann bowled five waist-high full tosses, which were all deposited for fours by a startled but grateful Romaines, again with all of us in an increasing state of merriment. The sixth was exactly what Cann had been striving for – a perfectly-flighted and pitched off-break on off stump, turning a little towards middle. Romaines smashed it over mid-wicket for six, before walking off, leaving a bewildered Cann open-mouthed. "Never again, John. I'm never bowling for this club again."

Accidents seemed to follow Cann around. Once, at Panteg, he was fielding at long on when a six was hit way over his head. He gleefully signalled the fact, taking his cap off with both arms theatrically aloft, only for the ball to strike a tree and rebound on to the back of his head, knocking him to the ground. On another occasion at Usk he fell foul of one of his own on-pitch jokes. He was fielding at mid off. It is sometimes considered a jolly jape for the slip fielders to continually hurl the ball skywards for the fielder in that position, with his proximity to the bowler, to catch. What the recipient sometimes does is pretend not to be looking, prompting exasperated shouts of 'Canny' or whoever, before the fielder calmly turns and catches it.

This time, Cann had tired of fielding all these high balls, or rather his sore hands had, and had decided to turn his back completely on the slip men. But they, led by the plummy-voiced Stephen Henderson, the ex-Worcestershire and Cambridge University batsman, who had a brief flirtation with Glamorgan from 1983 to 1985, thought that Cann was playing up. So Henderson hurled the ball high towards Cann, who was not looking. Last second cries of 'Canny' were to no avail as the ball came down with considerable velocity and clattered him on the head, knocking him unconscious.

A visit to the hospital followed, and the subsequent X-rays and tests revealed that Cann had had a shotgun pellet in his cheek since childhood. "I thought that I felt something," Cann observed, in reference to the 'shooting'. Cann once twisted his ankle at the same Usk ground, suddenly bursting into tears and screaming, "I hate pain."

One of his many peculiar habits was to keep his white inner batting gloves on while smoking one of his preferred Benson & Hedges cigarettes after he had been dismissed. He was a strange sight, sitting cross-legged, considering his innings. More often than not, he would eventually utter something comic after a period of introspection. Once, at Old Trafford, he perished by playing an awfully injudicious hook shot early on against Paul Allott, the former England seam bowler. He returned to his spot in the corner of the dressing room and adopted his contemplative stance. He lit his cigarette and puffed. We waited and waited for an utterance. The cigarette was little more than a stub when he eventually announced, "A word of advice for you boys." Everyone turned towards him. He had a captive audience. "Never hook the new ball."

Cann played his club cricket for Cardiff in the Western League, following in the prolific foot steps of Hugh Morris – the only other Cardiff-born-and-bred Glamorgan player of recent times. But for a short while he was required to turn out for the Glamorgan Colts in the South Wales Cricket Association. This concept, which nurtured the likes of myself,

Adrian Dale, Steve Watkin, Tony Cottey, Robert Croft and Adrian Shaw, had begun in 1986; the archaic and inflexible governing body stipulating that we had to start life in Division Two.

We fell under the tutelage of Jim Pressdee, a former Glamorgan all-rounder who had emigrated to South Africa. He was a harsh task-master, being especially critical of my inadequacies in the fielding department, and regularly keeping me behind for extra practice. And so, every Saturday, we were required to attend Neath indoor nets for practice at 9.30am. The games started at 2pm. There were obvious flaws to this intensive routine, not least the fact that the hard, generally true, surface we practised on inside was a million miles away from the slow, soft, soggy pitches we usually encountered in the afternoons.

These practices were particularly hard work for those of the team on the full-time Glamorgan staff, who would often have played a three-day game finishing on the Friday, sometimes travelling a long distance late that evening. But Pressdee instilled a discipline in us that was not to be forgotten, preaching the basics to us over and over again and then making us practise them until they came naturally. He was particularly keen that we ran well between the wickets, often enacting middle wicket sessions where we would run every single ball so that we became aware what was possible if both partners were willing. Myself and Adrian Dale were the openers in that team and it is no coincidence that, as soon as we reached the first team, we developed a reputation as excellent runners between the wickets. Pressdee's sessions opened our eyes.

I saw him in 2002 when he returned on holiday to Swansea, and the first thing he said to me was, "Still running hard between the wickets?" Too right I was. I don't think I would have had a first class career without doing it. I wasn't nicknamed 'The Run Thief' for nothing. And I heard Dermot

Reeve say once on TV that he thought that I had based my early career solely around running between the wickets and had developed the confidence from that to develop a range of shots. He may well be right, because I enjoyed some unexpectedly heady success in one-day cricket early in career, almost exclusively because of my scampering between the wickets. I was either playing the ball down in front of me with 'soft' hands and scurrying a single, or was nudging it to third man or fine leg and hurrying back for two.

My running and turning technique was unique and self-taught. I turned in a circle, staying mostly upright, rather than getting low and pushing in and out. And I did not call for a second run until I had completed my turn – something my partner had to get used to, because he had to make sure that he had made his turn, too. I know Mike Atherton (who I thought was a rather reluctant runner between the wickets) was not particularly enamoured with my technique, leading to a heated mid-pitch 'discussion' when we were batting for Cambridge against the MCC. I had swept the off-spinner to deep square leg and Atherton, on not hearing a quick call for a second, had not turned ready to do so, only to suddenly find me haring back for it. "As long as you're f***ing all right," was the gist of his comment.

If Pressdee had had the benefit of a qualified sports scientist, who knows what I might have been able to achieve? This is a subject that my friend Scyld Berry of *The Sunday Telegraph* is forever raising with me, questioning whether cricketers are actually taught how to run and turn between the wickets. They are not – or they were not when I was at that learning stage. I don't blame Pressdee, or Graham Burgess, or any of my other coaches. It is just that there was not that attention to detail in those days. The same was true of throwing technique. I was never taught how to throw properly. And it showed. I had a powder-puff arm, which was only effective from short range when I could adopt an under-arm flick. One thing that Pressdee did teach well was to value one's wicket. In those Saturday morning practices, if you were dismissed in the net, that was it. You were out. End of net. Inevitably this led to humour, and back to Michael Cann and his side-kick, left-arm spinner Phil North. North and Cann had made the long journey back from Yorkshire one Friday evening and had risen early the next morning for Pressdee's practice. North had been short of form with the bat, so, unusually, had asked the coach to have a knock early on.

He was a talented striker of the ball, but there was a suspicion that he did not 'fancy' the quick stuff. And indoors at Neath you receive plenty of short balls. Indeed you do at most indoor schools, where the quickness of the surface excites the fast bowlers. They tend to bowl shorter and shorter, not least because if they do pitch the ball up, it is usually hammered back past them by thankful batsmen.

Heavy use over the years had rendered the Neath surface slightly uneven as well as quick, so North may not have been totally confident as he walked out of the dingy, dark changing rooms at the back of the indoor school, pushing aside the thick white tarpaulin sheet that acts as a sight screen at the back. But he might have hoped for a slightly longer hit than what he got. One ball. It had taken him over four hours to drive back from Yorkshire, and over an hour to get from Newport to Neath. As the ball shattered his stumps, he looked to Pressdee, hoping for some sympathy. "Out you come, then," the coach growled.

As luck would have it, Cann was already prepared to bat. "In you go, Canny," Pressdee shouted, while following a cursing North out into the changing rooms. Cann walked down the net, and, as he approached the crease, his mischievous side took over. He decided to rattle the metal spring-loaded stumps with his hands, creating the same noise as there had been moments earlier when North had been bowled. It attracted much laughter from the rest of us but not from Pressdee, who came storming out of the back. "Right, you're out as well, Canny."

And, sadly for Cann, he was out of Glamorgan by the end of the 1991 season, released along with Ian Smith, Simon Dennis, Mark Davies, Geoff Holmes, Martin Roberts and John Derrick in a clear-out instigated by Tony Lewis. His belief was that only players who were likely to feature regularly in first-team cricket should remain.

Cann's last match was against Northamptonshire at Ammanford. He strode jauntily to the wicket. Umpire David Constant, polite as ever in inquiring which guard the batsman required, said to him: "What would you like, Michael?"

"A new three-year contract, please," replied Cann, before running down the wicket and carving his first ball from former Glamorgan fast bowler Greg Thomas over cover.

Cann probably made more of his name for himself in South African first-class cricket than he did in this country. After he left university, he spent most of his winters in the Republic, impressing especially for Griqualand West, based in Kimberley, in the B section of first-class cricket, and for the Impalas, a one-day team made up of players from the smaller provinces. He found love there, too, and returned one spring to announce that he was getting married. A stag do was therefore eagerly planned in Cardiff. It was during pre-season training. And as you would expect with Cann, it was an unforgettable night.

It culminated in the Philarmonic nightclub in St. Mary's Street, where an ever-so-slightly inebriated Cann was up on stage, stripped to his leopard-skin briefs, pretending to be Gary Glitter, as the rest of us adoringly screamed "Leader, Leader". Incredibly, at this point his wife-to-be walked into the bar, saw what was happening, removed her engagement ring, hurled it at Cann, and stormed out!

The wedding did go ahead, but, unsurprisingly, it did not last.

The following morning a whole group of us was late for

training. There was an almighty traffic jam around the Churchills Hotel area in Llandaff in Cardiff. Eventually, when we arrived near the scene, it was discovered that there was an abandoned car blocking the road. It was Cann's.

I enjoyed opening the batting with Cann, not least because it provided many moments of rare humour. Sometimes he would make paradoxical comments on the way to the crease, such as, "I'm going to look to leave a lot today," before flailing at his first delivery from wide of off stump. More often, his conflicting words were related to off-field activities. His predilection for a curry and a pint meant that he struggled to control his weight, and, at the end of every season, he would declare, "I'm going to get really fit this winter," only to return tubbier than before.

At Sittingbourne in Kent (we once turned up there to find that our hotel had closed down) in 1986, after we had been flayed to all parts by Graham Cowdrey in scoring 258, the pair of us had survived the few overs before the close. He said to me that he was going to get an early night, but I came down to the hotel bar later to find him drinking with a group of Germans. They seemed to be doing the paying and Cann the drinking; and he could be heard in his best German accent beseeching "More wine" at regular intervals.

Apparently it was a late one. Cann ran the mile to the ground the next morning in an attempt to sweat out the previous night's excesses, but it only resulted in him essaying an ugly heave at the first ball he received that morning from Kevin Masters. He was bowled. We subsided meekly and followed on, losing inside two days. Alan Jones was then in charge of the seconds (or dinky dos, as they are affectionately known on the circuit) and he held the mother of all inquisitions, which was interrupted by Masters entering the room to ask Matthew Maynard where they were to meet for a drink. Jones wanted us to go home that night, but he was persuaded that it might be best to stay for a little sorrow-drowning – a curious habit in cricketing circles, rewarding failure with a night out.

I'm not sure if Maynard did meet up with Masters, but he did with Laurie Potter, an ex-colleague from his short Kent career. He spent three seasons in the south-east when, amazingly, Glamorgan were not particularly enamoured with his abilities. Maynard nearly missed the bus the following morning, but awaiting him was some good news – his call-up to the first team. He duly made his first- class debut against Yorkshire at Swansea, and made a hundred too, going from 84 to his century in three successive deliveries from spinner Phil Carrick. A Glamorgan star was born.

Cann liked his banter, and whether it was picking up the phone and announcing, "Cardiff Morgue, you stab 'em, we slab 'em", or regaling us with tales of how he had been dismissed "pulling a half volley" in a weekend club game, he was an entertaining presence in the dressing room. Once, on a stinker of a pitch at Ebbw Vale, which had been damp but was now drying, we walked out to the middle for our second innings to be greeted by the inquisitive Mike Bore, Nottinghamshire's left-arm spinner and coach. "Who's facing?" he asked.

"Who's bowling?" retorted Cann. The opposition were planning to open with Bore and off-spinner Peter Such. They obviously wanted the left-arm spinner to bowl to me, and the off-spinner to bowl at Cann.

"Who's facing?"

"Who's bowling?"

This continued for some time, with the club umpires, whose sub-standard officiating so often devalues second team cricket, reluctant to intervene or make a decision. Eventually, Cann, as usual amid much drama, relented and agreed to take the first ball. Such fired one into Cann's pads and he tickled an easy single.

On another occasion we were batting on an equally untrustworthy pitch at Swansea against Sussex seconds. The ball was regularly rearing from a length at the batsman's head. And the bowler causing most problems was a chap called Andy Babington, a shaven-headed psychopathic fast bowler, with whom I endured something of a stormy relationship in my career. I actually scored my first runs in first-class cricket off him, at Hove in 1987, and from then on there developed a rabid mutual hatred. I'm not entirely sure why, but when he moved on to Gloucestershire later in his career, I asked one of his team mates. He told me that it was because Babington thought that I had got away with an edge behind off him in that maiden innings and had laughed about it with my batting partner. I cannot recall that happening.

Once, we met in a second team match at Bridgend. Before the game, I was wandering around outside the clubhouse when he arrived in his flash sports car, which he revved unnecessarily and skidded to a halt upon seeing me. (Not the only time a player has driven recklessly on that ground – a nameless but very short Glamorgan batsman was once fined for doing some wheel spins on the third team square there.) Babington's passenger later told me that he announced: "I'm going to f*****g kill that James today."

Indeed he attempted to. My innings was progressing serenely when Babington, in obvious frustration at not being able to dislodge me, suddenly unleashed a beamer, which, thankfully, was not that well directed, accompanied with a menacing glare and some choice words.

I was apoplectic. It was totally out of order and, again, the club umpires present did nothing (thankfully, a first-class umpire now stands alongside the learner in second team cricket). More words were exchanged, and Babington concluded by telling me that he going to "punch my lights out at tea time". He didn't. But I felt sufficiently strongly about the incident to complain to Gloucestershire's coach, Andy Stovold, reasoning that such a puerile action could easily have broken my arm and affected not only my season but my career. I don't think that any action was taken.

I seemed to attract this type of incident. A similar thing happened to me at Sleaford in Lincolnshire in a Cheltenham & Gloucester Trophy match in 2002 when their fast bowler, Simon Oakes, also bowled a beamer at me. He had thought that he had me caught behind the previous ball, and then delivered his yellow riposte with an accompanying "That's one all". His comment proved it was deliberate. Unsurprisingly, words were exchanged. To my enormous chagrin he snared me LBW soon afterwards, even though the game had already been virtually won. Wisden reports that it was an "ugly" end to the match. It could have been uglier. I called Oakes a few names as he came off the field, and one of his team mates was keen to get involved. Thankfully, matters calmed, and Oakes later came to our dressing room to apologise and shake my hand.

But back to Swansea. Cann survived the most vociferous of appeals for an inside edge off Babington. I thought that he had hit it and Babington was his usual enraged self. The next ball was a quick bouncer (a much more courageous response than a beamer) which clattered Cann full on his prized Glamorgan helmet, resplendent with daffodil painted on the front (we had to get our own done in those days, through a friend of Phil North), as he attempted to hook. This provoked another furious appeal for caught behind. But Cann went down like Frank Bruno on the end of one of Mike Tyson's haymakers, theatrically reeling backwards. Naturally, it took Cann some time to be dusted down and brought back to his feet. He went back to his stance, only to be disturbed by another of those delightful club umpires: "You're out." Nobody realised that the umpire had, indeed, upheld the appeal for caught behind. Cann had definitely not gloved it, but maybe it was a classic 'make up' decision by a nervy official.

"You're pulling the piss, aren't you?" replied Cann, in a tantrum which would, these days, warrant a hefty fine. But he had to go, and it was a few weeks before he did at last confess that he had inside-edged the delivery before. Cann was not a walker. Indeed few batsmen are, these days. I like to think that I was, although I am well aware that this statement will draw howls of disagreement from certain members of the Glamorgan dressing room.

The truth is that if I was 100% certain that I had hit the ball, I would walk. There were occasions when I was not sure and stood my ground. One example was a game against Yorkshire at Swansea in 2001 when I stood after a vehement appeal from the long-haired Ryan Sidebottom. Matthew Maynard was at the non-striker's end, and he thought that I had hit it, a view substantiated the following ball when I drove the left-armer through mid-off for four. Maynard has a specious theory that a boundary the following ball after a contentious appeal indicates that the batsman was out. Sidebottom did not have long to wait before capturing me, but his craven and predictable send off, profanely alluding to my being a cheat, irritated me and I waited for him at lunch time at the top of the pavilion steps to continue our spat. He wasn't interested, which is probably just as well, for it was pretty surly behaviour from me.

Only once in my professional career can I honestly declare that I did not walk when I was absolutely sure that I had hit the ball. And it taught me an important lesson. It was in a game against Lancashire seconds at Old Trafford in 1986. We were desperately striving to save the match on a turning pitch and I blatantly gloved a ball that turned and bounced from their off-spinner. It went to leg slip, but the umpire (another 'clubbie', as they are termed by the players) was unmoved. There followed the most fearful torrent of abuse I had ever encountered. Chief sledger was David Hughes, the all-rounder whose career looked over but was resuscitated soon after by the offer of the first-team captaincy. At one stage he shoulder-barged me as I attempted a single off his left-arm spin. The experience disturbed me, and, from then on, I vowed to walk.

I found second team cricket tough going at first. Given the recent shrinking of most county staffs and the proliferation of schoolboy trialists, it was certainly of a much higher standard then than it is today, with counties able to employ two overseas players but only play one in the first team at any one time. Thus I faced the likes of fast bowlers Allan Donald, Tony Merrick and Winston Benjamin, giving me valuable warning of what was to come when I stepped up a grade.

But it was not necessarily professional – in fact, it was anything but. There was much less emphasis on fitness and physical well-being then. There was no scientific fitness testing – just a quick weigh-in ("You've been having a good time," someone shouted as I stripped off to reveal a flabby abdomen after my first year at Swansea) and a three-mile run, which had to be completed in under 21 minutes. There was, however, a convenient short-cut, which many of the older players gladly accepted, even boasted about. Many players did not make the cut-off time.

John 'Ponty' Hopkins, the former Glamorgan opener, was always one. He might have made it one year though if his Glamorgan cap, which, peculiarly, was an omnipresent accessory for him on these treks, had not fallen off just before the end. There was no way he was leaving that precious item lying around, so its retrieval unfortunately meant that the 21 minutes had already elapsed by the time he huffed and puffed his way past the finishing line. Hopkins, a brave player who served Glamorgan well, was in the seconds when I started, short of runs and confidence. "Do you think I'm a good player?" he would ask fellow-struggler Alan Lewis Jones. "Yes, Ponty, and you're a good looking oke" (a South African colloquialism for bloke) Lewis Jones would retort, pre-empting

Hopkins' inevitable, laughing follow-up question about his looks. And another of Hopkins' strange habits extended to wearing his new batting boots out at night in order to wear the spikes down a bit so that they would not catch too much in the turf. There was no monitoring of diet or liquid intake, with alcohol at lunchtime on training days not discouraged. In fact, lunch at Headingley on match days was taken in blazers with bottles of beer available on every table. And second team away trips were a riot. I often wondered how any away team could be expected to win, given the ridiculous gallivanting that seemed obligatory.

The job of second team coach was mostly like that of a beleaguered school teacher on a field trip, with a variety of curfews imposed and duly broken, eventually forcing him to turn a blind eye to all but the most unruly behaviour. But I was fortunate to have two excellent coaches in my early years of professional cricket – John Steele and Alan Jones – who were founts of cricketing knowledge. They were also frequently exasperated by some of those extra-curricular activities, Jones once telling a young professional: "All you think about is beer and cock," in reference to his perceived obsession with his nocturnal activities.

Steele, whose brother David went on to the dizzier heights of representing England, was not a man given to frippery and frolic. His career had been hard work. He loved the game (and still does, as a first-class umpire) and its theories and intricacies. He was not lavishly talented but had made the most of what he had, becoming a determined, cussed batsman and a useful, low-slung, left-arm spinner, as well as a sure-fingered close catcher, especially at leg slip – "round corner," as he used to say.

His mannerisms are easily imitated, and still are by the older members of the Glamorgan squad who either played with him or were coached by him when he was in charge of the second eleven. I liked him as a coach because I could relate to him. I felt that I was experiencing similar struggles to those he had in his career – a limited batsman with a good temperament and immense determination. He liked to call us all 'youth' and his normally staid personality only came alive when in his car and his favoured Lionel Ritchie music was on, *Dancing on the Ceiling* being a particular rouser. He would fall asleep while you were driving but had the uncanny habit of opening one eye when you went above what he perceived as his speed limit. "Slow down, youth," he would caution. On another occasion, when I made a mess of parking his car in a hotel car park, expressionless, he said: "I think we're in the hedge, youth." Even now as an umpire he cannot resist going into the changing room, picking up a bat and rehearsing his unyielding maxim of "Play straight; leave wide", and, "Look, leave".

The good thing for me in my formative years at Glamorgan was that I always felt rated by the coaching staff. There was even a hint of special treatment, with my abiding by a different set of rules for petrol expenses from everyone else. And there was an empathy between myself and Steele, and an even stronger bond between myself and Jones. As I have mentioned, he is a Glamorgan record holder with a bottomless well of knowledge and experience, which only the foolish would ignore. He was not naturally garrulous but what he did say was relevant and well worth listening to. The first piece of advice I garnered from him related to the playing of spinners. At this time I was still a cautious blocker, having temporarily forgotten 'Sonny' Avery's advice at Monmouth, and was increasingly struggling with quality spinners who placed fielders around the bat, often falling to bat/pad catches.

"Get down the wicket and hit them over the top," was Jones' rather surprising counsel, recalling to mind that of my first professional coach at Monmouth School, Avery. I had not seen Jones play first-class cricket, but I soon discovered that at the faintest sighting of a spinner, he would forsake his generally prosaic game plan, merrily dancing down the wicket and depositing him back over their head, often sending the ball flying into the Mumbles Road at his beloved home ground at St. Helens in Swansea. "You don't have to hit it that well [thank Christ for that, I thought]; just make sure that you can get it over mid-off or mid- on. Then, hopefully, the field will have to be put back and you can easily push the singles."

I surprised myself with how well I could do this – it improved more markedly after my conversion to weight training – as a method of avoiding 'dying in the hole', as the professionals like to describe bat/pad dismissals. Jones was at times ribbed (mostly out of his earshot) for his old-fashioned coaching methods – "head/leading shoulder" was a much-repeated mantra for the batsmen, while words were often not required for the bowlers; an exaggerated tilting of the head away from the vertical plane in which they are supposed to operate, with two fingers on an imaginary seam pointing down the leg side were sufficient to convey his impression that the bowler was falling away in his action. Or else it was a scream of "width" – more often than not followed by "Parky" (Owen Parkin) – to anyone allowing the batsman freedom outside his off stump. Parkin exasperated Jones more than most. Once, Jones thought that this most reluctant of trainers was cheating on his prescribed two-mile runs – one mile out of Sophia Gardens to a gate at the end of Pontcanna Fields, and back. So Jones hid in the bushes near the gate and, sure enough, caught Parkin turning round too soon.

Jones' fielding practices were regimented and less invigorating than many of today, but were what he knew from the benefits of repetitive drills inculcated by the likes of the intimidatingly peerless Wilf Wooller, whose passion for all things Glamorgan is a legacy never likely to disappear from Sophia Gardens. Indeed, his name can still be heard on the field today, with shouts of "Come on, Wilf" echoing around the field as elder statesman Matthew Maynard traipses after a ball. Wooller only ever really spoke to me once (in 1987), as old age had much diminished his role at the club by the time I joined. It was after I had just been adjudged leg-before on one of the old-style subterranean bouncing Cardiff pitches. "Now then, young James, you're a big, tall lad – for Christ's sake, use your height and get forward."

He scared me, even then. And so did Jones, not from any fearsome Woolleresque reputation, but by appearing for early morning practice with just his white inner gloves on and a bat in hand. "Now then, you boys, three lines," he would shout before launching steepling catches for what seemed like hours on end. Jones is not officially part of the Glamorgan coaching set-up now, but some of the younger players still seek him out for specialist batting coaching. Their tales of his pragmatic commonsense and devotion to the art of batting bring memories flooding back of hours spent with him in the nets; of his insistence on total respect for the bowler at all times, manifested in a quirky habit of referring to the ball in the feminine gender. "When she is out there [pointing to an imaginary spot outside off stump], leave her alone," he would say. I recall his exasperated cry of "You boys, heh" when his charges had been up to no good, and his enjoyment of a batsman successfully evading a bouncer in those wickedly-fast Neath nets. "Well played, Jamer," he would shout, even if, sometimes, I had only narrowly avoided serious injury (something I successfully managed in the nets until the pre-season of 2003, when an Alex Wharf bouncer sent me scurrying to hospital for six stitches in my cheekbone). I once incurred the wrath of Greg Thomas in such an instance when I had turned my head away. Thomas was then the quickest thing I had ever seen, even off a shortened run in those nets, sometimes lengthened by beginning it inside the back changing rooms when John Hopkins demonstrated his courage (heroic in my view) by urging Thomas to 'let me have it'. But Jones could be gullible. On a pre-season tour to Trinidad in 1990 he decided, for reasons still not apparent, to purchase a large steel drum from a band playing near a bar we frequented. They persuaded Jones to part with his money and then told him that his drum would be delivered the following day. Surprise, surprise nothing arrived. But then, out of the blue, early one morning the band players arrived at our accommodation, demanding just a little more money to take Jones to his drum. Wisely, he decided to take Dean Conway, our rugby-playing physiotherapist, as his minder, but again, inexplicably, there were given the slip. The lyrics of Lisa Stansfield's hit, *All Around the World*, were soon being altered in the Glamorgan dressing room to:

Been around the world I, I, I,
I can't find my drum
I don't know when and I don't know why
Why it's gone away
I don't know where it can be, my drum
But I'm gonna find it.

Second-team cricket could be a cynical environment, awash with moaning and back-biting; such is the nature of an environment in which the majority of players would rather not be.

Some of the banter was cruel and personal. Martin Roberts was a particular target, especially for Ian Smith, who would say to his face, "You can't keep f**king chickens." Roberts was not a natural gloveman, but an honest cricketer whose bottom-handed batting became particularly useful. Above all, he was a harmless, likeable person. But Smith probably never forgave him for scuppering a hat-trick at the Oval by dropping a dolly of a catch. The ball went through Roberts' gloves and hit him flush on the forehead. Players used to magnify Roberts' mistakes; once, at Usk, the keeper palmed a catch into the throat of first slip, John Hopkins, who staggered all the way to the sightscreen, holding his throat and screaming theatrically as if being strangled. And even the jocular Cann was not averse to delighting in nicknaming Roberts 'Chickens' in an environment where blame was usually placed anywhere but at the feet of the individual responsible.

Andrew Roseberry, brother of Mike and briefly on the Glamorgan staff, once ranted "Who the f**k is he to criticise my technique?" at coach Alan Jones. Well, actually, that was his job. And Roseberry's technique, with his liking for hitting most balls over extra cover, was most unconventional. When Roseberry was given a chance in the first team he returned to the seconds and lamented in his strong Geordie accent, "Paul Jarvis was steaming down the hill, and Banners [captain Hugh Morris] said 'Play positive'." Of course he did. That was what the situation demanded. But such statements are indicative of the mentality often employed in second team cricket, and indeed above, whereby the world is against you and it is never your fault that you have failed. I, too, took part in the blame game, often retreating to the dressing room after another low score to curse the pitch or umpire. Berating the standard of the pitch can have an unsettling effect on the other batsmen waiting their turn and I soon learned to temper such negativity, especially when Matthew Maynard mentioned it. "You're terrible at doing that," he said.

Cursing the umpire is an easy option in explaining away another cheap dismissal and one in which I indulged too often; one occasion in particular embarrasses me, when, during a bad trot, I was palpably leg before for a duck to Sussex's left-armer, Jason Lewry at Swansea. I made a big point of shaking my head in expressing my disappointment and walking off the field so slowly that it could have been said that I needed a JCB to get me off. Rain curtailed play not long afterwards and umpire

Allan A. Jones knocked on the Glamorgan dressing room door to announce, "I want to see young James." Quite rightfully, he gave me a serious bollocking. I deserved it. It was my fault; it was my ineptitude that had led to my dismissal, not his.

I am reminded of a comment by David Boon, who, at the end of his career, said that only once – a snorting leg cutter from Curtley Ambrose – had he felt that he could have done nothing more to have avoided dismissal. On all the other occasions it had been his failing. And he is right. Too often, batsmen look to blame others, or find excuses when they should look in the mirror. As I said earlier, batsmen's reactions to getting out have always intrigued me. And I mellowed considerably in this department, having been a bit of a screamer and bat-thrower in my earlier days. But I was not a dressing room-emptier like David Hemp, whose ranting and raving has also thankfully softened, nor a Nasser Hussain, who is the worst I have seen or heard. His intemperate tirade at the back of the Lord's dressing room during my Test debut, after being adjudged leg before to Lance Klusener, was a remarkable piece of sustained dummy-throwing. It was even worse than the antics of Mark Ramprakash, another of cricket's original brat pack (third member: Graham Thorpe) in the same game.

At least these players had fire in their bellies. I reckon that there were a number of cricketers with whom I played who didn't particularly enjoy playing cricket, certainly not professionally. Hugh 'Buck' Rogers, the gentle beanpole bowler from Chepstow, was one. After some hasty spells in the indoor nets he was hailed as the white Joel Garner, but within a couple of games, keeper Roberts realised that he should be standing up to the wicket – not something too many keepers contemplated doing to Garner! And when Rogers did not turn up at the Coldra roundabout near Newport to meet the team bus, that was the last straw.

Steve Bastien was another, I'm sure. He was a talented swing bowler from the Haringey Cricket College in London, which also produced Mark Alleyne and Keith Piper. He once took 12 wickets in a first-team match against Essex, but he did not relish the hard work of fast bowling. He was much more comfortable inside the dressing room, regaling the rest of us with stories of his batting, which involved a ridiculous stance with his backside sticking out awkwardly and a pick up that consisted of an impossibly extrav-agant 360-degree flourish. "See how I blade Boo-Boo, boy," he joyfully exclaimed, in his Dominican accent, after hitting Alleyne for six at Swansea. I'm sure Boo-Boo was first coined on Alleyne's debut for Gloucestershire at Lydney, with his larger brother, Steve, as Yogi. Bastien's "I wan't backing away, boy" after blatantly doing so against Waqar Younis at the Oval, was, however, more indicative of his effectiveness, indeed his courage, with the blade. Mind you, he soon put me in my place when I was moaning about the garish maroon blazers given to us for our tour of Cape Town in 1993. "What do you know about style and fash-onn?" he admonished. Of course, I should have remembered that the West Indian cricket blazers are of a similar hue, but we were being mistaken for bus drivers far too often for my liking.

There were times in those early years when I thought I'd be better off driving buses, such was my exasperation at my chosen career. I found the jump up to first-class cricket (or Championship cricket, rather) a large one, and my grappling with it reached its nadir in 1990. My final year at Cambridge had ended spectacularly, with match-winning hundreds against New Zealand and Sussex. My collection of 921 runs might have swelled to 1,000 for the first time in a university term since a certain J.M. Brearley, had rain not ruined the Varsity match. But the extent of my subsequent travails is revealed by the fact that it took me another 10 innings to reach exactly 1,000 runs for the season. I recorded a pair against Warwickshire at Edgbaston and two other ducks to finish with a Championship average of 1.66.

Byron Denning, our likeable scorer who sadly passed away in 2001, had mischievously decided to award an ornamental duck to the 'batsman' who recorded the most noughts that season. Glamorgan had the lengthiest of tails in those days – Metson, Watkin, Frost, Bastien, Dennis, Barwick were all less than brilliant with a bat in their hands – but I finished below them all in the averages. Denning had no doubt expected one of that motley crew to win his award, but instead I gate-crashed the party. Denning sheepishly awarded the duck to me at Worcester during the last game of the season. I could sense his unease and that he maybe did not want to do it at all, but there had been so much banter among the rabbits that it had to be done. I accepted it as graciously as I could. Inside, I was seething. I walked out of the back of the pavilion and smashed the duck in the nearest dustbin.

CHAPTER SIX

FOREIGN FIELDS

Strange as it might seem for an Englishman who has plied his trade in another country, but the issue that probably irked me more than any other during my county career was the still-continuing lunacy of county sides employing quite large numbers of foreign cricketers who cannot play for England, yet qualify domestically. They are the dreaded EU (European Union) players. This is what I wrote about them just before the start of my final season.

The Sunday Telegraph, **30 March 2003**
There is no point beating about the bush here because I feel strongly about this. There are too many players getting into county cricket through the back door.

By that I mean there is an ever-growing posse of players, mainly South Africans and Australians, who cannot represent England but have EU passports and therefore can ply their trade over here, and be classified as locals. This season there will be about 30 of them playing county cricket.

If it is not stopped soon, their increasing presence, allied to the decision to permit two bona fide overseas players per side this coming season, will make a mockery of the laudable and, let us not forget, costly efforts of the England and Wales Cricket Board to foster home-grown talent in this country.

In short, too much of the £1.3 million handed out to every county each season is being frittered away on players who cannot play for England. That cannot be right.

The winter signing of Australian Mark Harrity by Worcestershire has brought this problem into sharper focus.

The increase to two overseas players has certainly meant that only the most vigilant of observers has been able to stay abreast of all the comings and goings of foreign talent. As an ageing opening bat, I have had a particular eye on any incoming quick bowlers – the Shoaib Akhtar on-off affair at Hampshire has been a real teaser – but I was somewhat surprised to spy a snippet in the press sometime in February that Harrity had been signed.

Now I thought that my eagle eye had already detected that the Midlands county had secured the services of South Africans Nantie Hayward and Andrew Hall. Maybe one of these two had pulled out injured. But then it dawned on me – the dreaded EU scenario was rearing its ugly head.

Harrity had suddenly realised (as you do) that he was entitled to a British passport and therefore the chance of earning a decent salary as a pseudo-Pom.

But then another thought struck me. Surely I had seen that Harrity had appeared for South Australia during this latest Australian domestic campaign. And indeed he had, but his promise that he would never again appear in or for Australia as an Australian meant that the ECB, under the cloud of European law, exercised their discretion to relax a previous regulation that players who had done this were not eligible to play in the following season.

I must stress that this is no personal vendetta against Harrity – he is a more-than-swift bowler whom I may have to face. And he has a notoriously short fuse, exemplified by the time when at Neath in 1995 on the Young Australia tour he 'beamed' Tony Cottey in his frustration at a combination of a turgid pitch and the eccentric brilliance of the diminutive batsman now at Sussex. Nor do I have anything against any of the other EU players, who are just earning a living. Nor, indeed, against the agents, who are doing likewise. One of them – David Ligertwood, of Athletes1 – has been instrumental in many of these players gaining contracts and as a result has achieved a fair degree of notoriety, especially amongst the cricketing hierarchy.

I admit to having some sort of vested interest here, being a client of Ligertwood's, and I know that I could be accused of hypocrisy. But I do believe that this almost farcical situation is not necessarily the fault of Ligertwood and co. It is true that he is particularly forthright in his desire to fight tooth and nail for his clients and is using his legal background and knowledge to his considerable benefit, but for me the real culprits are the counties.

After all, they are the ones who are prepared to employ these players, the ones whose short-term and blinkered planning will eventually, I believe, drag the county game to its knees.

I do not wish to preach a 'holier than thou' attitude but at Glamorgan we do not employ any EU players. We did have one in recent years in Dutchman Roland Lefebvre, and we might have had one last season in Ali Bukhari – well, that was what we thought he was called until the extremely quick left-armer turned up in Derby as Mohammad Ali – before it was decided not to offer him a contract. For this coming season we will have just one overseas player in Mike Kasprowicz, with financial constraints precluding a second. But we are, and always have been, fully committed to producing our own players, and utilising our new academy under the estimable Steve Watkin.

Personally, I am in favour of the 'authentic' overseas players because I believe that, as long as they are of sufficient quality, they bring much to our game. But the current combination of these and the EU players is untenable.

Legally the ECB have their hands tied in attempting to impose restrictions on the EU players – although they could introduce incentives into the counties' hand-outs to encourage the nurture of home-grown talent – so the responsibility falls squarely upon the shoulders of the counties to self-regulate.

At recent county captains' meetings, when the eloquent Matthew Fleming has raised this issue, there has been minimal support for EU players. And I have it on good authority that it is a similar story at the First Class Forum meetings. Yet these players are still being recruited.

Upon signing, they are required by the ECB to sign a declaration that it is not their intention to represent any other country than England for whom they can, of course, play once they have served a four-year qualification period. But who is to say that they may not turn their back on county cricket and return to their native land at any time?

The madness must end.

For me, at the time, this was a strong piece but it was heartfelt and I felt that it needed to be said. Not that it has had much effect, though. The influx of these mercenaries continues, and the fact that Andy Flower, a veteran of 63 tests for Zimbabwe, is playing for Essex in 2004 as a domestic player underlines the desperately short-term reasoning being undertaken by the majority of counties. By signing these players the counties are signing their own death warrants. Things could worsen still further with the recent European Court ruling on Maros Kolpak, a Slovakian handball player, who was not permitted to play for his German team because of a law allowing only two non-EU players per team. The judgement was that any citizen of a country that has an associate agreement with the EU should have the same rights as a European worker. The West Indies and South Africa fall into that category, so this could mean that many of their cricketers could play in county cricket as domestic players, without even requiring an EU passport. That is scary. And, despite an agreement between the chief executives of all the counties not to sign any of these players, Leicestershire went against this in March 2004 by signing South African left-arm spinner Claude Henderson.

I do happen to think that there are too many counties, or rather too many players. In January 2002, I penned an introduction to the *Cricketers' Who's Who*:

The county system has glaring deficiencies. Nobody can dispute that. Anyone setting up such a system today would surely never set about it using the geographical spread of counties which has evolved down the ages. The Midlands is heavily over-populated, for instance.

In my opinion, there are too many professional cricketers in this country earning a decent living; and too many of those are in a comfort zone with no real ambition to represent their country, which should always be the ultimate aim. Too many are interested in the pampered lifestyle, fretting about such peripherals as securing a sponsored car rather than putting in extra work in the nets or in the gym. For some, things come too easy.

But signing these EU players is not solving the problem, rather exacerbating it. I must again stress that I am not against overseas players *per se*. In fact, I think they are good for the county game, as illustrated by the constructive contributions made by most of Glamorgan's foreign imports during my career.

Viv Richards was the man who changed Glamorgan cricket. He arrived in 1990 to play for a team, which, despite possessing talent, was unused to success, with losing a permissible inculcation. Richards changed all that. He was a winner, who did not tolerate sloth or indifference amongst his colleagues, and his arrival gave Glamorgan credence and kudos, as well as inspiring the club's most successful season for 20 years. He was 38 when he signed and may have been past his peak, but in his three years between 1990 and 1993 (in 1992 he was on tour with the West Indies), he revealed himself as the 'great' batsman we all knew him to be, despite a suspicion towards the end that his eyes were not quite what they had been, substantiated by some close shaves with fast bouncers. But his pride precluded the wearing of a helmet, though he did have one in his bag.

But what struck me most about him was that he was such an incredible natural athlete. His reactions in the field, even at such an advanced age for a professional sportsman, were stunning. I have memories of him fielding at square leg in one-day games for the off spin of Robert Croft and the off cutters of Steve Barwick, tempting the batsmen to risk a single to him, then pouncing panther-like with frightening speed to scupper such fanciful notions.

Richards made the whole of the Glamorgan side stand taller. His mere presence emboldened even the most timid, especially when he swaggered out to bat, chewing gum and exuding an aura which intimidated even the most experienced and most skilful of bowlers. I did not bat with him often, but there were a couple of occasions when I looked around as he strutted out and wanted to say to the cowering opposition, "He's on my side."

What a joy it must have been for Adrian Dale to have shared that club record partnership for any wicket (425) with the great man against Middlesex in 1993, both recording double centuries. Dale tells a humorous tale of how Richards berated him for running after he had struck a sweet shot through the covers which was always destined for the boundary. "Don't spoil the shot," cautioned King Viv.

Richards did not offer much in the way of technical advice, but used to enjoy giving tub-thumping dressing room speeches, which always involved liberal use of his favourite word – 'Karaktar'. I can recall him once telling me that it took 'a big man' to respond with a century after I had suffered the ignominy of a pair in a day at Luton in 1992; that hundred coming in a game at Neath during which Richards had to be hurriedly awoken from a nap (not an uncommon occurrence) when it was his turn to bat.

But there was a darker side to him, not least the occasional sighting of a violent temper. Once, during warm-up before a game at Chelmsford, Dale and Croft were desperate to bowl. But as all the Glamorgan batsmen had had their fill, the two youngsters decided to have a bowl at John Stephenson, the Essex batsman practising in the next net. Richards immediately spotted this and flew into the most uncontrollable rage – "I cannot play with guys who do this," he fumed, before attempting to convene a special committee meeting to discuss the matter.

On another occasion, at Llanelli, he very nearly refused to play in a Sunday League match, when it became apparent that the pair of batting gloves and Glamorgan baseball cap he had left in the drying cupboard at Cardiff had been stolen. Quite what the theft had to do with the rest of the team was unfathomable, but as Hugh Morris went out to toss up, Richards was still adamant that he was not going to perform. But Morris bravely included his name on the team sheet and as we batted first, Richards' hotheadedness was given time to cool a little. Not enough, though, to prevent him ranting at the rest of us, "Haven't you seen runs scored before?" when a silence descended upon the field as he was plundered for 35 in three overs of his usually useful mixture of canny spin and seam.

That match came in the middle of a curious six-week period for me when Richards declined to speak to me. I am still not sure why. I had been getting on quite well with him, even taking him to a gym in Worcester to show him how to use the various weights machines, which, given his impressively chiselled physique, I thought he must have been using all his life. He teasingly called me 'Big tits' after some winter bench pressing had enlarged my pectoral muscles.

But on that day in deepest west Wales I was sporting six stitches in a swollen eyelid ("You think you're f**king 'ard, do you?" asked a moronic, drunken local on the boundary edge) courtesy of a dodgy pitch in Newtown, mid-Wales, for an ill-conceived unofficial Wales v. England benefit fixture. So when Morris (before the kit storm fully broke) playfully asked Richards if he had seen the team's new boxer, the West Indian fixed me with a look of brooding derision.

We were back on speaking terms when Richards delivered his *coup de grace* for Glamorgan – a first piece of silverware for the county since 1969 with the Axa Equity & Law Trophy being won amid chaotic and emotional scenes at Canterbury. Fate had decreed that the final match of that Sunday League season (which was a 50-over competition for the only time ever) should be between the top two teams, Glamorgan and Kent, who were equal on points. It was a winner-take-all showdown in front of a crowd of 12,000.

Big crowds fazed me then, and, when we fielded, I was a bag of nerves, more often than not praying for the ball not to come my way. I had fielded well that season, making the backward point position my own in one-day cricket, always in the inner circle saving ones and diving around. But for some reason that day, I ended up spending most of my time on the boundary. Maybe captain Hugh Morris sensed my unease, but my lack of confidence was betrayed by my insouciance towards being a peripheral figure.

I cannot even now bring myself to re-watch the excellently put together video, complete with the moving music of *Perfect Day*, of that momentous day. Once was enough. My batting technique was in tatters; my stance an ugly self-invention with my front foot pointing down the wicket and my head bobbing around. "You look like a crab," a friend told me, and I batted like one too, scoring 3 before being caught at backward point, having already been dropped there as the ball skewed inelegantly off an open face.

The match fell between the third and fourth days of the final Championship match of the season. On the third, Kent dismissed us for 144 in reply to their mammoth 542. But curiously they declined to enforce the follow on, with their minds on resting their bowlers for the following day rather than the immediate matter of a facile victory.

This move enraged Richards, who, at the end of the day's play, walked out on to the balcony at Canterbury, then without a partition and serving both changing rooms, and boomed: "If you guys f**k with the game, the game will f**k with you." From that moment I knew that the match the next day was ours. There were some cowering faces in that Kent dressing room as I peered in.

Fittingly, Richards was with Tony Cottey as the winning runs were hit, and – this is most telling given that pronouncement – he was caught off a no-ball. Cricket proved to be a harsh mistress to the flirting, pesky men of Kent and it favoured our fearless Antiguan. Richards' tearful embrace with Morris may have been a little fulsome with our changing room suddenly full of all manner of people, but the victory clearly meant much to him. It sparked the best night of celebrations I had in my time at Glamorgan. "You were pissed before Viv and Cotts got off the field," Morris later told me, as I greedily guzzled the ubiquitously-available champagne. "There didn't seem to be a lot being sprayed or spilt," said a friend watching on TV. After such a long wait, there seemed no point wasting it.

The Bat and Ball pub outside the ground was overwhelmed with the sound of Welsh singing, and I was determined to revel in it despite Colin Metson's congratulation, typically veiled in deprecation even at this most exhilarating of moments: "Well done. For the first half of the season anyway."

Metson was a funny chap, probably still is. He was my room mate at the time – mainly, I think, because I was the only one who would put up with him. In the end a combination of unpopularity, ineptitude with the bat, and *ennui* curtailed his career. But he was a magnificent wicketkeeper, who, at that time, was keeping better than anyone I have ever seen, Jack Russell included. But the England selectors did not come calling, and, after 1993, Metson, with that ambition seemingly blocked, was not the same force behind the stumps. He practised less and his standards began to slip. It was such a shame that his batting was so insipid and ineffective, because it promised more. Its lack of fulfilment was epitomised by Metson's constant contention that his highest first- class score of 96 contained a four adjudged to be leg byes but which in fact came off the bat.

He had no time for team bonding and would spend most of his time in his room, number crunching on his calculator in readiness for his winter job with a local shipping and haulage firm. I got on reasonably well with him, but it was his pursuit of perfection that led him to the unfortunate habit of making the most inappropriately caustic remarks, thus often (probably inadvert-ently) conveying the impression that he was a cut above the rest of us. The equalling-biting dressing room returned the favour by dubbing him and his then wife 'The Duke and Duchess of Cowbridge' in recognition of their perceived aloofness.

Aloof was how I perceived the three other sub-continent players who preceded the gregarious Waqar during my career at Glamorgan, despite them all being exceptional players. I have to say in their defence that I played very little with all of them. First, there was Javed Miandad, a magician of a batsman who once did not turn up at the start of the season when contracted to play for Glamorgan; and then there was Younis Ahmed, another Pakistani, whose reputation for not being, let us say, the most trustworthy person in the world was borne out by frequent visits to a flat I once occupied in Zimbabwe by all manner of spivs looking for a Mr. Ahmed, the cricketer. He played county cricket for Surrey and Worcestershire, and my abiding memory of him is his oft-repeated complaint, in an accent that was a mellifluous mix of aristocratic English and Pakistani: "20,000 runs and no f**king benefit." I think he was missing the point that loyalty is at the heart of the awarding of benefits.

And then there was Ravi Shastri, the tall, elegant Indian, who was generally popular, not least with the ladies. But I have probably never really forgiven him for his "run out by a f**king kid", which I overheard after a mix up between us at Swansea.

Another overseas star with whom I also had a few run out mis-understandings was Australian Matthew Elliott. I should have realised that we might have a few problems when I saw him shuffling sideways, crab-like, down the stairs at Sophia Gardens, courtesy of his dicky knee, first injured in a mid-wicket collision with Mark Waugh in a Test match against the West Indies. But the left-hander from Victoria was far from aloof. He was a wonderful team man, a typical Australian in that respect. He came to us with a question mark hanging over his attitude to that team ethic, which was perceived as being the reason for his puzzling exclusion from the Australian side. But he soon endeared himself to us by suggesting the introduction of a team song to be given airing every time we won. Owen Parkin duly provided the excellent lyrics and Elliott led the song on the table:

Over the Severn and down to the Taff
Like lambs to the slaughter they take on the daff
Only now do they know how hard the Welsh will fight
As they trudge back to England beaten out of sight
We are Glamorgan, dragons you and me
Together we stand as the pride of Cymru.
We play to conquer, we play to thrill
We play for the glory of the mighty daffodil.

There is no feeling like it, singing that song; the whole team, sometimes the whole squad, linked in arms bellowing it out. I felt very Welsh, very proud when I sang that.

Elliott did on occasion, though, reveal an odd, peppery side to his character. A fiery incident at Colwyn Bay is recounted elsewhere but the most glaring example came at Northampton where a seemingly innocuous incident irked him so much that his temper got the better of him. During the tea interval Keith Newell accidentally knocked over some orange juice on the table that runs down the length of the dressing room. Unfortunately, some of this found its way into Elliott's bag. Upon seeing this, Elliott lost it, as they say, before going back out to bat with me. He then proceeded to play the most ugly heave imaginable to the medium pace of Tony Penberthy before stomping off. For the next hour he sat on the floor of the toilet with his feet on the seat, brooding and sulking. But aside from some momentary fits of pique when I had run him out, this was a rare show of moping. After Elliott came other two Australians, Jimmy Maher and Mike Kasprowicz, a couple of Queenslanders who may be differing characters but who are generally also cheerful souls. Maher was the first to arrive in 2001 when Elliott was unable to return. He came with a better one-day record than four-day, and soon revealed a liking for the on- side in his forthright strokeplay.

And he soon became popular through his gregariousness and accessibility to supporters, especially at the bar. He revealed himself as a wonderful mimic, especially of colleagues' gaits and laughs, as well as a vividly imaginative story teller; none more so than in the tale of his live TV faux pas in 1995. Queensland had just won the Sheffield Shield for the first time in their history and by all accounts the players were still celebrating days later, when Maher and Stuart Law were invited on to a live show to discuss their success. When asked how he was feeling, an emotional (and no doubt still intoxicated) Maher replied, "I'm as full as a coon's Valiant" – an offensive piece of Australian slang referring to the alleged overcrowding of some of the Aboriginals' vehicles. The comment became a major racial issue, with Maher clearly unaware of the vastness of his audience when he said to Law in the taxi on the way home, "Stuey, don't tell anyone I said that." Maher, in no way a racist, was most contrite, but dropped another accidental clanger in 2003 when he was asked about fellow Australian squad member, Darren Lehmann, who had been banned for racist remarks made against the Sri Lankans. "The trouble with Darren is that he calls a spade a spade."

At times I found Maher a difficult player to captain. He yearned to be in charge – eventually being rewarded with the Queensland captaincy – and was never backward in voicing his opinions. However, I do have to say that he always voiced any concerns to my face. There was never any suggestion of him talking behind my back, or stirring. For, in 2001, during dinner at Le Monde in Cardiff, Maher had told me that he thought that he should be captain instead of me. I told him I was thinking of resigning. "Yeh, I think that would be the right decision," he said in that matter-of-fact Australian way.

Maher did irk me a little with what I saw as a publicity campaign for his return in the 2002 season. I thought that we needed a bowler as our one overseas player because of Steve Watkin's retirement and the inability of the other seamers to lead the attack, but Maher had other, no doubt self-interested, ideas. And he wasted no time in ingratiating himself with the Welsh media in his attempt to secure another contract. Ironically, it was one of his state team mates to whom we turned, as well as re-signing David Hemp from Warwickshire in the hope of making up any shortfall in the number of runs without Maher. Hemp had been unhappy that he was not being considered for both forms of the game at Edgbaston, so I told him that he could open for Glamorgan in both forms if he signed. It was a gamble because he is much better suited to the middle order, but he had scored over a 1,000 runs at number three the previous year and I had always considered him a good player of quick bowling. But this plan of mine did not work. Hemp's return has not been the success I, or he for that matter, imagined.

Kasprowicz's arrival was, though. He is a gem, one of the nicest people I have met in cricket. I made a number of mistakes in my time at the helm at Glamorgan but signing Kasprowicz was not one of them. I had been tempted to sign Wasim Akram instead, but I eventually became frustrated by his reluctance to give assurances about his availability. So I went for the 6ft 4inch Queenslander, who won an Australian Schools rugby union cap as a lock. His presence at the touch rugby warm-ups certainly added a physicality as well as a know-how, no doubt kept up-to-date by his brother Simon, who is a member of the New South Wales Waratahs Super 12 squad.

And, although he made a quiet and relatively ineffective start to his Glamorgan career – just like Watkin he needs to bowl a lot of overs to establish rhythm – his whole-hearted and thoroughly professional approach was rewarded in 2003 with two separate nine-wicket innings hauls against Durham. His second innings figures of 9-36 at Cardiff were the second best in the club's history. I will freely confess that constant up-close viewing of his bowling has revealed that he is a much more potent threat than I had imagined him to be. Certainly not a 'pie-thrower', as Martin Searby of *The Daily Telegraph* described him when he played for Leicestershire against us. And his affability and unstinting devotion to the team ethic was recognised by his fellow players when they voted him as the winner of the inaugural Byron Denning award in 2002, given in memory of the much-liked former Glamorgan scorer to the person deemed to have contributed the most as a 'team man'.

But his courteous credulity could leave him prey to the pranksters of the Glamorgan dressing room. At Durham in

2002 he came off the field to find a note asking him to call a reporter. Dutifully he dialled the number and asked for the reporter. "I can be anyone you want me to be," came the seductive voice of a woman on a sex chat line.

I have already mentioned my misgivings about Ottis Gibson, but the South African Corrie Van Zyl and West Indian Hamish Anthony were also poor choices as overseas players during my career. In mitigation, Anthony did come under strong recommendation from Richards, but it probably says much about both his and Van Zyl's cricket that the most salient story in my mind about each of them concerns an off-field incident.

The first concerns Van Zyl and I must take more than my fair share of the blame. Glamorgan were playing a Sunday League match against Derbyshire and that evening were travelling up to Scotland to play a benefit match for Gilbert Parkhouse, the only Glamorgan batsman ever to have scored a first-class century against every other county. The match was at a place called Cheadle, which we faithfully looked up on the map and found directions for. Only trouble was, we arrived at Cheadle in Cheshire, instead of Cheadle in Staffordshire. Another 'shirt' offence, thankfully before its introduction.

Mind you, it seems that such place confusion is fairly common amongst cricketers. Chris Lewis turned up in Newport, Gwent, when he should have been in Newport, Shropshire for an England get-together at Lilleshall. And Simon Base, a mad but likeable fast bowler who used to vent his frustration by biting the bails, once arrived in Croesyceiliog, Carmarthenshire, when he should have been in Croesyceiliog, near Cwmbran, some 130 miles away, for a Glamorgan second eleven match.

Geography was not Anthony's forte either. Hugh Morris gave him a lift to London one day so that the Antiguan could meet up with some friends and was rather flabbergasted when he asked Anthony where he wanted to be dropped. "Anywhere in the main street," was the reply. For all my concerns about the excess of foreigners earning a living over here, I too very nearly flew the flag of convenience. For, in the early 1990s, I gave serious consideration to qualifying to play Test cricket for Zimbabwe. I spent five winters in that once wonderful country, beginning in 1990 when myself and Adrian Dale went there to play for an all-black side called Bionics.

Barry Dudleston, the first-class umpire and one-time Zimbabwe coach, organised for a group of us English (or Welsh!) professionals to play club cricket and help the rapidly expanding coaching programme, which was designed to reach as much of the indigenous population as possible.

I was met at the airport by team manager Mac Dudhia, who, while extremely friendly and cordial, told me that I was to be captain of the side and that Richard Blakey of Yorkshire had scored 1,000 runs in ten innings the season before. I was expected to do something similar. No pressure then, especially when one considers my calamitous end to the 1990 English season. Living in Zimbabwe was an eye-opening experience. Despite my association with the blacks and Indians (I later played for Universals, a Muslim team) most of my social communication came with the white community. They were wonderfully hospitable and fun company, but colonialism had left its indelible mark on them.

At first, I found it difficult to come to terms with the curious arrangement of being waited on hand and foot by a domestic housekeeper. It may sound like heaven, and indeed for someone as undomesticated as me, it was, but still it did not seem right, especially when I witnessed the belittling and demeaning tone employed by some of the whites to these 'servants'. The worst of this was commonly reserved for the waiters in the various sports clubs around the city where some whites regularly met to imbibe their favoured Castle lager or their 'soapies' – a local concoction of cane, lemon barley and soda water.

But that is not to say that many of the white Zimbabweans are not more liberal minded and fair. Andy Flower's black armband stand, along with the black Henry Olonga, against the death of democracy in his country in 2003, earned him hero status throughout the world. And rightly so, for he is a man of integrity and intelligence, and one I am proud to call a friend. He and his family were especially kind to me in Zimbabwe; his brother, Grant, a willing drinking partner as well as a sufficiently obsessed fitness training partner, his father, Bill, always a sage advisor, and his mother, Jean, a friendly face and cook for this lost Brit abroad. The whole family has done so much for racially integrated cricket in Zimbabwe, in terms of coaching and encouragement, that it is a crying shame that, at the time of writing, only Grant remained there. And I wonder for how long that will be.

Alistair Campbell's family were also overwhelmingly welcoming, as were many others. The left-handed Campbell is one of the finest talents I have seen in the game, but a sadly unfulfilled one, retired from professional cricket by the age of 30 through a combination of his own mediocre performances and the mess in which Zimbabwean cricket has now landed itself. And I found frequent lodgings at the home of Matthew Streeton, son of Sir Terence Streeton, and a former British diplomat who had fallen in love with the country. Remarkably, given the ongoing troubles, he still remains in Harare to this day; confirmation that he has become a 'local' coming in a humorous incident during England's tour there in 1995 when Streeton was appointed liaison officer for the tourists, only to be sacked within the first week for being too friendly with the Zimbabwean team. England were worried that their secrets were being passed on!

I thought that Zimbabwe were fortunate to be granted Test status in 1992. They have produced many fine players, notably Graeme Hick whom I reckon would have become one of the all-time great Test players if he had played for Zimbabwe, away from the menacing glower and unrealistic expectation of the British press and public. And David Houghton was the most destructive player of spin bowling I have seen. Andy Flower, with his reverse sweeping as strong as his conventional sweeping, was not far behind in that department, and his exceptional mental strength (up there with Mike Atherton's) propelled him deservedly into the upper echelons of the international rankings for most of his career.

Add in a chap called Kevin Arnott whom I reckon was as good a fielder as another brilliant Zimbabwean, Trevor Penney, and maybe as good as another, the legendary Colin Bland, and it is clear that the former Rhodesia is a fertile breeding ground. What was, and still is lacking, was the infrastructure.

The financial poverty of the game was illustrated by the fact that I had to give Andy Flower a pair of my boots for him to use at the 1992 World Cup in Australia and New Zealand, and poverty in terms of know-how by the ridiculous decision to appoint the Essex journeyman, Don Topley, as their national coach. Topley is a friendly enough chap, if a little self-absorbed and most definitely bitter after Essex released him just before his benefit was due. But his elevation after being employed as the club coach at Harare Sports Club invited ridicule. Of course, Zimbabwe did manage to win one game in that tournament, against England, captained by Topley's county captain Graham Gooch. It was said that the night before the game at Albury, Topley had been criticising some of his charges in front of England players, only to revel in the glory of his team's surprise win the following day.

However, Gooch still had the last word with one of the best put-downs I've heard. "I won't let you forget this all next season," Topley had boasted to his skipper.

"Not sure I'll be at many second team games actually, Toppers," came Gooch's classic response.

During 1993 I had some communication with Peter Chingoka, the chairman of the Zimbabwe Cricket Union, about the possibility of my qualifying for Zimbabwe. Test cricket was a lure, as at that stage England recognition was a distant prospect, but sanity, thankfully, prevailed. "You'll miss county cricket too much," was my father's advice, and Mike Atherton's "You can't play for another country" was at the heart of my eventual dismissal of the notion. It would not have seemed right, and I am most thankful that the urgings passed without too much progression. Having said that, they probably did contribute to my playing too many seasons in Zimbabwe. That first season had gone remarkably well and I had gained a good reputation. The standard was competitive then, with most of the future Test players performing weekly in the domestic league, but the elevation to Test status brought a dramatic drop in standards. "It's no good for you playing here now," Bill Flower had cautioned. But despite a couple of months playing for the Primrose club in Cape Town, I returned for the easy life.

Alan Butcher had once advised me to go to Australia. "I saw what it did to Alec Stewart," he said. "It changed him mentally, made him tougher." I wish that at some stage I had followed his counsel. All that sledging might have steeled me a bit younger. There was some of it in Zimbabwe, especially whenever we played Old Georgians, with the Flower brothers and other talkers like Craig Evans, Gavin Briant, Mark Burmester and John Rennie in their side. Then I struggled. "They've got a psychological hold over you," a team mate remarked. I think he was right. Their banter, which sometimes descended into normally taboo comments about family sexual relations, distracted me.

Eddo Brandes, the burly chicken farmer, famous for bowling out England at Albury and for later capturing a hat-trick against England in Zimbabwe, is just as well known for his classical riposte to Glenn McGrath's sledging. "Why are you so fat?"

asked McGrath. "Because every time I f**k your wife she gives me a cookie," was Brandes' unforgettable reply.

That is quite mild compared to some of the things I heard out there. Andy Flower once almost reduced a previously mouthy young Australian bowler to tears – he even complained to the umpire – with his observations on what the bowler's mother did in her spare time.

Myself and Adrian Dale had gone there with the intention of portraying ourselves as aggressive English professionals, and if that meant saying a few choice words then so be it. But those good intentions lasted just one match. Our debut came against Old Hararians, whose opening bat happened to be Russell Tiffin, now an international umpire, albeit a moderate one (but as you will see, that is not for me to say). We thought that he had edged a ball behind early on, but the umpire had not concurred. So we let Tiffin have a few volleys of good, old-fashioned abuse. He said nothing, but once fixed me with an aggressive glare.

The mid-morning tea break (these were 60 over games starting at 9.30am) soon arrived, and, as we sipped our tea, two of the opposition players sidled over. "If we were you two, we would not be chirping Russell. He's a hard man, you know. Fought in the war. Probably killed people." Two Glamorgan cricketers' already pallid faces suddenly turned even whiter. It reminded me of the comment of South African Brian McMillan to Shane Warne during an ill-tempered Australian tour to the Republic: "Warnie, hundreds of people get killed in this country every day. No one will notice one more."

The dangers of a foreign land soon became ever more apparent. One afternoon, Dale and I returned to our house, which we shared with Paul Weekes (the Middlesex all-rounder) to hear an almighty commotion going on at the back. There, we discovered Ed, our domestic housekeeper, with a machete in his hand, wildly trying to slice through the railings of an outside store room. Inside this was a petrified painter, whom it was thought was stealing the odd pot of paint for himself. We got there just in time to save him.

And a couple of weeks later, Dale also had a close escape. We were practising in the nets at Harare Sports Club, which are only separated from the back of Robert Mugabe's palatial residence by a narrow road. One of Dale's deliveries was struck into that road and he dutifully scurried after it. Unfortunately he was unaware that the road was zealously guarded by a bevy of soldiers armed with AK47s. As Dale searched amidst the undergrowth for his errant ball he suddenly felt one of the aforementioned rifles being thrust forcibly into his chest, with an accompanying volley of unintelligible Shona invective.

He was frog-marched up the road, and Lord knows what might have happened had it not been for the intervention of Malcolm Jarvis, the Zimbabwean left-arm seamer and himself a war veteran, whose smooth talking defused a potentially ugly situation. It is a shame someone has not done the same for the country as a whole.

CHAPTER SEVEN

FLETCH

"Let's get this road on the show then." It was with this accidental, but rather humorous, transposition of words that Duncan Fletcher concluded his first chat with his new Glamorgan charges in 1997. Fletcher had succinctly outlined his coaching methods and, more specifically, his management structure. By applying the principles of his former career in computers he likened the squad to a business, with the captain, Matthew Maynard, as the managing director and he, the coach, as a consultant. As well as these two, lines of communication would come through three other members of the management team, in this case, Hugh Morris, Steve Watkin and Tony Cottey. These were senior players to whom others could talk if they felt they were unable to speak to Maynard or Fletcher.

It was a totally new concept for us and, despite the incongruous ending to his opening salvo, Fletcher had immediately revealed himself as a clear, incisive thinker on the game. But, more importantly, he had not portrayed himself as some dictatorial newcomer, who wanted to change everything. This was in direct contrast to the Australian Jeff Hammond, who arrived in 2000 and rushed headlong into the job, instantly reinforcing his reputation as a typically brash Australian. Hammond announced that he was not going to get too involved initially because he wanted to have a good look at everyone before passing judgement. But, within a couple of hours, he had informed left-arm spinner Dean Cosker that he would never regularly take wickets in first-class cricket unless he radically altered his action, and had told batsman Alun Evans: "Stop standing like you've got a carrot up your arse."

Fletcher (we were not sure what to call him initially and I eventually settled for a semi-respectful 'coach') stressed that Maynard was still the man in charge and would make the final decisions. It is a system he has utilised with every side he has coached and is now particularly effective with the England squad, where, at various times, youngsters like Marcus Trescothick and previous renegades like Phil Tufnell have been afforded extra responsibility, usually with pleasing results. I had heard rave reviews of the Zimbabwean during my winter stints in his native land (but did not first suggest his name to Glamorgan, as Maynard intimates in his book, *On the Attack*) where there was nothing but respect, in some cases reverence, for his leadership. He never played Test cricket, but famously led Zimbabwe to victory over Australia in the 1983 World Cup, and his emigration to Cape Town, where he became coach of Western Province, had been met with dismay north of the Limpopo.

I had been introduced to him very briefly by Mac Dudhia, manager of my first club side in Zimbabwe and an unreserved fan, when I represented Mashonaland against Fletcher's touring Western Province in 1994. Even so, like everyone else at Glamorgan, I did not know what to expect prior to his arrival in 1997. All the club had to go on was an awful photograph in which he bore a remarkable resemblance to Benny Hill. Fletcher parked himself down in the spot next to me in the Sophia Gardens dressing room, and, for a couple of weeks, we hardly said a word to each other. I was intrigued by the man, as were the rest of the team. There was no pre-season overseas tour that year and, fortunately, we were blessed with good weather. In fact, two weeks of unbroken sunshine produced the best build-up to a campaign I can recall. There was a mixture of outdoor nets, fielding and fitness every day with Fletcher meticulously organising everything. But otherwise he said very little, standing at the back of the net, observing and storing every minute detail in his memory bank. It was during a three-day bonding break at Christ College, Brecon, that he really came into his own, introducing us to his full repertoire of fielding exercises. At first they seemed impossibly intricate but, once learnt, they were invigorating and fulfilling. He placed great emphasis on fielding – it has always been a facet of the game at which Zimbabweans have excelled – as well as physical fitness.

There was the Roundabout, which involved the whole team in three groups, moving round to incorporate the under-arm pick up and throw, an over-arm shy at a single stump, then backing that up and throwing back to the wicketkeeper. This had become a fairly common exercise at the time, but Fletcher added his own variation, whereby the backer-up had to throw the ball back to the thrower as if throwing the ball to the bowler in a match (something that Fletcher felt was not practised enough), and he wanted the throws-in hard – no half-hearted efforts.

In all his exercises, he insisted on throws being over the top of the stumps, standing crouched with his baseball mitt fixed in the position where he wanted the throw. "That's three frames out," he would shout in reference to the waywardness that would buy the batsman valuable time in a referral to a third umpire using the TV. And there was the Crossover, which was an individual fielding/fitness exercise involving four cones, with Fletcher making you retrieve balls along the floor, running in a figure of eight. It was all fed with pin-point precision by the man himself, and made you stretch, pick up and throw.

Then there were the dreaded ten catches. I never saw a coach so adept at introducing and maintaining an intensity to a fielding practice as Fletcher. His hitting and catching skills are supreme. He affords no easy options to the fielder, and this is no better illustrated than in this catching routine, which, like the Crossover, is both a fitness and a skills exercise. Fletcher will hit steepling catches, which require you to run, dive and stretch until you have caught ten. To say it is lung-bursting is an understatement. It can reduce grown men to quivering wrecks. The biggest mistake you can make is not to catch the first one, because Fletcher will have made you run a long way and stretch for it, so the prospect of still having to catch ten with your lungs and legs already crying out for mercy is not a pleasant one. Some of the less aerobically-gifted cricketers have attempted to lessen the physical burden by deliberately throwing the returns over Fletcher's head (apparently Tufnell tried it in South Africa) so that he runs out of balls to hit, but, more often than not, this results in further punishment and a steely glare from the Zimbabwean. And he usually conducts this exercise with a masochistic grin on his face, dancing with delight if you drop one because it means that there is more chance of your fitness yielding before you reach ten. "I love it when the guys are working hard," he used to say.

He has a unique method of hitting slip catches, which involves having his left hand (without batting gloves) on the splice rather than the handle of his treasured Gunn & Moore bat. Early on in 1997 he split one of his fingers quite badly doing this but declined to make a fuss and initially refused treatment on it. And he abhors the way most English professionals let the ball go when it bounces in front of them during this close-catching practice. Most contend that they could break a finger, but this cuts no ice with Fletcher, who often sarcastically remarks, "Well done, you saved a certain wicket", when someone drops a catch.

I have it on good authority that Fletcher was not afraid of

strenuous physical activity himself when he was a player. As captain of Zimbabwe he had no coach to assist him, so he disciplined the side himself, often making the team embark on the picturesque three-mile run around the Harare Sports Club and golf course after net practice. When a couple of likely lads tried to take a short-cut, Fletcher stayed behind with them to do more training, doing everything that he asked them to do. He surprised and delighted us by encouraging us to play soccer and touch rugby, both before and after play. This drew howls of dissatisfaction from supporters, especially the older brigade, but Fletcher maintained that it brought the competitive spirit out in us, as well as improving agility, conditioning and awareness. He would hand-pick the sides – often youngsters against oldies (or *Piccaninns* versus *Medullas*, in African dialect) and referee strictly and enthusiastically. I was intrigued by the strength and trust of the instant relationship struck between Fletcher and Maynard, two of the more contrasting personalities you could ever imagine. On the one hand, the quiet, conservative, reflective, sober (mostly!) and calculating coach; on the other, the extrovert, impulsive, hard-drinking and slightly crazy captain. But the common thread was that both had the most fertile of cricketing brains, forever espousing theories and the wildest of plans.

Fletcher and I gradually got to know each other – two rather shy personalities whose initial conversations centred mainly on another shared passion, rugby union. But I would like to think that we developed a mutual respect and that we got on. We had to, really, because we often travelled together on away trips. He called me Sport Billy because of my fondness for all things sporting, when really he could have been talking about himself. His passion for sport, especially cricket and rugby union, takes some beating. His admiration for the oval ball game began in his schooldays at the famous Prince Edward School in Harare, which also produced the likes of golfer Nick Price, and cricketers Graeme Hick, David Houghton and Trevor Penney, where he would surreptitiously listen on his transistor radio to the Springboks in action.

When at Glamorgan he would watch or, if involved with cricket at the time, videotape any rugby match on TV. Once in 1999 I took him and his wife, Marina, to the Cardiff versus Llanelli Swalec Cup semi-final and he knew as many of the players in action as I did. He immediately spotted the Llanelli open-side flanker, Ian Boobyer, as being a class player and asked why he was not in the Wales squad. A few weeks later, Wales coach Graham Henry called up Boobyer for the summer tour to Argentina.

His attention to detail came home to me the day before the first game of that 1997 season. We were playing Warwickshire at home, and my opening partner, Hugh Morris, and I were busy in the nets, readying ourselves for the fearsome challenge of Allan Donald. We had the bowling machine cranked up to 90 mph in a last-minute bid to replicate the speed we could expect to face, and to try to condition our reflexes accordingly. Fletcher strolled from the furthest part of the ground, picked up the machine and lifted it two yards to the left. "That's where Donald bowls from – he bowls wide of the crease." So he does, we thought, as the perspicacious coach walked away. A slight adjustment, but a most important one.

When he came to Glamorgan he brought with him some completely new notions on field placings, challenging traditional theories with hard evidence. For instance, he believes third man and fine leg should be much finer than is usual in this country to prevent those infuriating snicks that beat them on the inside. "Never get beaten on the inside" can still be heard today in the Glamorgan dressing room when such an incidence occurs.

Fletcher likes his sides to play hard and be competitive. Contemporaries from his Zimbabwe days talk of a no-nonsense character who occasionally had run-ins with the authorities because of his unquenchable desire to win. The South African A side, which toured England in 1996 under him, was an aggressive unit that upset a few, but at all times he backed his players. Fletcher's greatest strength is his ability to stay on an even keel, whatever has happened during the day's play. This was clearly demonstrated after our ignominious 31 all out against Middlesex in 1997. This was our first really bad day under his guidance and, in truth, we were shocking. There were even mischievous mutterings that some players were more interested in watching the British Lions play that afternoon than seeing off Angus Fraser and co. As we gathered in the dressing room afterwards and Maynard called on Fletcher to speak, I was expecting the worst. Surely we were about to feel the full wrath of our new coach. But he just calmly stated that we had had a bad day and that it did not make us a bad side – we had a Sunday League game the next day and we had to pick ourselves up for that and show some character.

We did, winning that game. Fletcher's man management was to the fore again. However, he did confess to me once that it is generally the long-suffering Marina who bears the brunt of his frustrations after a day's play. Apparently she can interpret the signals. If Fletcher is very quiet, he is best left alone to stew. Only twice did I see him lose his temper. The first time was when Maynard badly dislocated and broke his little finger while doing the Crossover after play in the first Championship match of 1999. Fletcher hurled a ball into the advertising hoardings and swore loudly before abandoning the practice. I do not think that it was because he felt responsible for such a nasty injury (it required an operation) but his anger was borne of the frustration that he would be without his skipper for the next six weeks. The other, more serious fit of pique occurred at that most beautifully picturesque of grounds, Abergavenny.

Dressing room practical jokes are commonplace in county

cricket – the school dormitory atmosphere and the long periods of time spent together lend themselves to it. Here, Robert Croft decided to snip Fletcher's socks so that when he went to put them on they would fly up past his knees. It is quite a common trick, played for years in dressing rooms up and down the country. Croft, in an idle moment, had acted on his own and waited expectantly as the coach came out of the showers, dried himself and began to get dressed. The reaction was not what anyone expected. There were twitters of laughter as it happened, but Fletcher was fuming. He barked at Mike Powell, who had only recently broken into the team and was playing on his home ground, "What are you laughing at youngster?" and stormed out of the room. Maynard went after him to try to calm him down, but it was to no avail. He was seething. And I had to drive him home! He did not say a word all the way home. Nor for the remainder of the game. I honestly thought that he was going to pack his bags and go back to South Africa. He thought the prank had been planned by the whole of the team and that his authority had been undermined. He was wrong on both counts, but it took many meetings full of apologies before he relented and we could get on with the business of attempting to win the Championship. Maybe Fletcher had over-reacted, but he had also made an important point: the coach has to stand apart from the team. He cannot be one of the lads.

He emphasised this point by rarely socialising to a late hour with the team. He would have a quiet pint after the day's play, but then he would be away. He did, however, enjoy the team meals on away trips, which formed such an important part of the team-building process. His central philosophy to success on the field was a happy dressing room.

There was one particular meal at Leicester, which began with physiotherapist Dean Conway initially refusing to wear the green shirt awarded for 'dick of the week', which was both nerdy and suffocatingly tight – unsurprising, given that it had been an unwanted present from a grandparent to the 5ft 5in Tony Cottey. It developed into a lively evening, highlighted when Robert Croft stood on his chair to sing, and went straight through it. Fletcher was not one of those leading the inevitable shouts of "You fat bastard", which were led by Croft's 'Toilet Twin' (in reference to their lavatorial humour) Cottey, but he was loving every second of it.

He is not a big drinker but for some unknown reason he seemed to quite enjoy attempting to get me, another lightweight, drunk. This culminated in a particularly unlikely episode when Fletcher returned for his second stint with us in 1999. The Australians were based in Cardiff for the World Cup and a special lunch was held at Sophia Gardens for them. Fletcher was seated next to me and every time I turned away, my glass of red wine was filled to the brim by the giggling Zimbabwean. I began to return the favour and by tea time we were both substantially inebriated. It was not one of those drunken episodes where we became so serious as to discuss the meaning of life – I am not a great believer of *in vino veritas* – but he did speak in hushed tones of the Australians, whom we had formally met the day before, and their self-imposed alcoholic abstention for the two weeks prior to their opening match.

We moved on to the nearby Beverley Hotel, where matters deteriorated until I staggered into a taxi. Once outside my house I could not hold back the overwhelming desire to relieve myself and did so in the street, much to the astonishment of my next-door neighbour. Apparently Fletcher stayed the course a bit longer than I did and was spotted attempting to eat petunia flowers outside the hotel when he obviously became a bit peckish later on. It was a rare moment of public revelry from an essentially private man. Croft probably should have known better than to attempt his jape, because discipline was high on Fletcher's agenda. He introduced a new dress code and fines system, which may sound petty but, in reality, worked a treat. Lateness was not tolerated (although Waqar was granted some latitude as the hard season wore on) and Fletcher's mischievous sense of humour surfaced in his delight at catching anyone canoodling with their partners at the ground. "PDA, £5" he would write on the fines sheet on the dressing room wall when he spied what he deemed a 'public display of affection'. There were some murmurings of discontent amongst the team at Waqar's increasingly tardy behaviour, but, as long as he was winning us matches, I did not care a jot and thought it was clever handling by the management team. Sadly, Fletcher felt that he could not commit himself to Glamorgan for the 1998 season. He was still coaching during the winter at Western Province, and felt he needed a rest.

When he returned in 1999 we immediately noticed a change in attitude. Fletcher was much more aggressive in his coaching methods, much more eager to radically alter players' techniques. We went to Cape Town on a pre-season trip and Fletcher was there. But he wasn't there, if you know what I mean. He still wanted to rest, so left the majority of the coaching up to John Derrick, for whom I felt sorry. The affable and extremely capable man from Aberdare was again caught in a locum role, as he had been in 1996 and 1998. Derrick had left the playing staff in 1991 and immediately found employment as a coach at the Ebbw Vale indoor school. He did some marvellous work there, and it is no coincidence that the majority of the young players coming through into the Glamorgan ranks now are from the eastern side of Wales, most of them tutored by Derrick at the centre perched on a hill next to Ebbw Vale's Eugene Cross Park rugby ground.

Fletcher immediately spotted Derrick's potential and was eager to introduce a reciprocal agreement for him with Western Province, which sadly never materialised. But when Fletcher did pop into the nets at Newlands, he was soon on to me. He said he could not believe that I was still not technically proficient at playing the slog/sweep. Playing spin is a facet of the game where Fletcher has particular theories, advocating the now much-used 'press' forward before the ball is bowled, as well as the use of the sweep and slog/sweep. And the latter is something I have always found difficult to grasp, despite some time spent in the nets on it. I actually think that Fletcher has a tendency to over-exaggerate its importance. For me, it should be the last option on a turning wicket. One should always look to play down the ground first – an altogether less risky option. Matthew Maynard plays the shot very well, but he can also hit the ball straight with incredible power. I would much rather see him doing that than employing the sweep/slog. As England coach, Fletcher has dramatically improved the team's ability to play spin abroad, especially in the sub-continent where notable triumphs over Sri Lanka and Pakistan have been achieved. But at home the preoccupation with the sweep has often made them look foolish against even the most moderate of spinners, something on which the Sky TV commentators have not been slow to pick up.

In Cape Town I sensed Fletcher was already a little agitated with our ability as a side to move forward technically. He was especially critical of a number of the younger players. But one thing was for sure – when Fletcher turned up to take a fielding practice before a one-day game at Constantia, there was an intensity and urgency about it that had not been seen for a while. Sadly, this was not to last. While the England team were giving a shambolic performance at the World Cup in 1999, Glamorgan were faring little better. And things were to take a turn for the worse when it soon became clear that Fletcher was one of the favourites to take over from David Lloyd as England coach. At first, he attempted to keep it a secret, but then began to canvass opinion amongst the senior players about his suitability for the job. He spoke to me about it on a number of occasions. He seemed to have the impression that the England players at the time were an awkward bunch, and was questioning whether he wanted to work with them. I just said that I knew a couple of them personally and thought they were okay, but did not feel well placed enough to comment on the current team spirit. My Test experiences had been too brief to make a balanced judgement.

We were playing Kent at Canterbury, and, during the match, Fletcher slipped away for his interview with the EWCB. He landed the job, as I thought he would, despite Simon Pack, the then international teams director of the EWCB, greeting him with "Hello, Dav" when he arrived; confusing him with future Sri Lankan coach Dav Whatmore, another interviewee. He decided that he wanted to stay with Glamorgan for the remainder of the season; a decision which, with the benefit of hindsight, was probably wrong. His mind was understandably elsewhere. What is more, England were being humbled by New Zealand at the time, and questions were being asked as to why the future England coach was still at Glamorgan. Nonetheless, that time with us was not entirely futile. For, during it, Fletcher spotted two players who were to go on to achieve big things with England. In fact, in two consecutive Championship matches in September, he discovered two batsmen who were to go on to become a productive opening partnership for him during his tenure as England coach.

Firstly at Taunton, Marcus Trescothick made a magnificent century, which caught Fletcher's eye. On a bouncy, lively pitch, Jacques Kallis attempted to rough up the youngster with some hostile, quick bowling, but Trescothick was more than a match, hooking and pulling powerfully, as well as picking Steve Watkin's slower ball and sending it soaring towards the first of the three churches behind the old pavilion. We could sense that Fletcher was excited about him. He talked of little else during the game, asking us about him and then summoning the

Somerset coach, Dermot Reeve, for a chat. I sensed then that, one day, Trescothick would be given the chance to play for England. He did not make the tour to South Africa that winter but made his debut in a one-day international against Zimbabwe the following summer.

The following week at Headingley, in totally different circumstances, Fletcher spotted Michael Vaughan. The Yorkshire batsman only managed two runs in two innings, but our prescient coach observed him closely in the nets and saw something special. Vaughan was not enjoying the best of seasons overall and, when Fletcher mentioned to me that Vaughan would more than likely go to South Africa, my response was, "It will be a disgrace if you pick him." This was obviously borne out of rivalry at the time, but it does prove that national selector is unlikely to be one of my employment possibilities later in life!

All of a sudden, everyone in the country seemed to want to know what Fletcher was like. Because of my journalistic connections, I seemed to be asked more than most. I had been doing some writing on the Zimbabwean players for *The Sunday Telegraph's* World Cup supplements that summer of 1999, so when they held an after-event get together with all their contributors, I found myself being grilled by the likes of Barry Richards, Colin Croft and Ian Chappell about him. Legends all, and they were hanging on my every word! "Good bloke, excellent coach, will not relish the excessive media scrutiny," is an abbreviated précis of my reply. They all seemed more interested in the last part of that than the rest. "He might struggle then," was their assessment in that department. But Fletcher has never seen it as the coach's role to be a glib media spokesman. He will speak to the press, but he will be guarded, concise and always, always, supportive of his team.

This was in direct contrast to his Glamorgan successor, Hammond, who quite often had to be prised out from in front of the camera. One of his first priorities after arriving was to secure an individual contract with BBC Wales for his thoughts and views. When anything to be autographed arrived in the team room Hammond would be the first to scrawl across it. Fletcher would never sign anything like that. "That is for the players," he would say. It was not that he was being lazy. He just recognised that the limelight belonged to the players. He was just the consultant, remember.

I have to say that not all the Glamorgan players were totally enamoured with Fletcher, because some felt that he had his favourites with whom he worked closely while, unwittingly or otherwise, discarding others. And sometimes his initial impressions were difficult to alter. Mike Powell has discovered that; in that game at Taunton when Trescothick was so convincing Fletcher, Powell endured a rough time against Andy Caddick, struggling especially against the short ball. Fletcher has never forgotten that and it will always hinder Powell's England aspirations, which are realistic in my view. He now plays the short ball well, and has moved on mentally since the days when he used to join me at the crease with such diffident offerings as: "They've got men around the bat and it is turning. What am I going to do here?" He is certainly no less a player than Ed Smith, who was capped in 2003.

I suppose I was one of Fletcher's favourites. I would receive my daily fix of strenuous exercise by asking him to preside over a fielding blow-out after the end of play, usually involving numerous Crossovers and a round of ten catches. He would taunt me with "Herschelle would have got that" when I missed a ball, in reference to one of his Cape Town protégés, the outrageously-gifted Herschelle Gibbs. That summer, Gibbs dropped Australia's Steve Waugh in a vital moment in a World Cup match, Waugh apparently teasing him with, "You've just dropped the World Cup." In fact, Gibbs had held the simple catch at mid-wicket, but had then attempted to celebrate a little too early. "I knew something like that would happen somewhere along the line with him. I always told him to beware of being too cocky," lamented Fletcher.

But Fletcher would have been cursing Gibbs in a very different manner in the summer of 2003 when the opener, who had been first advised by Fletcher to try his hand at the top of the order, scored 179 against England at Edgbaston. And more irony would have come in the presence of Eric Simons as South African coach in that series. Fletcher used to continually refer to Simons, his former Western Province all-rounder, as a 'legend', an unusually gushing epithet, and would often talk of a letter, which Simons, upon his retirement from first-class cricket, had penned to him. "He will make an excellent coach," Fletcher used to contend, again revealing a clairvoyant quality.

Even though 1997 was my most productive season, it would be wrong of me to attribute all of my success to Fletcher's arrival and his technical work with me. Indeed, after two weeks he had said nothing to me so I plucked up the courage to approach him. "Have you spotted any problems with my technique?"

"No, I think that your bat is coming down nice and straight. You and Matthew (Maynard) look in fine form."

As the season progressed he would stress the need to be patient while opening the batting and not go chasing wide balls too early in my innings (something I was prone to do).

"Let them come to you," he would say. Often he did not need to say anything, just a look was enough. I got 69 in the first innings against Worcestershire but it was a frantic, slapdash innings. Some time after I was out, I saw Fletcher looking at me.

"Was I too loose today?"

"What do you think?" was all he said. I knew.

His crusade to convert me to the slog/sweep began after I had scored 153 against Durham at Cardiff. I scored a hundred before lunch on the first day – "I never thought I'd see the day," said a disbelieving Tony Cottey, who still remembered me well as a blocker – and I thought it was one of my better innings, fluent but controlled. In an interview afterwards I said that the Durham bowlers had bowled 'in nice places'. In fact, they had fed me with a liberal supply of off-stump half volleys, but I couldn't say that. I was just delighted to have scored my first century against Durham. But what had irked Fletcher – and indeed a supporter who wrote to me afterwards "Did you not want to get 200?" – was the manner of my dismissal. James Boiling, a good friend and team mate for the Combined Universities and the Bionics club in Zimbabwe, had snared me caught and bowled with his off spin, bowling around the wicket with a man carefully positioned very straight on the drive. I had been hitting a lot through there and Fletcher felt that my inability to slog/sweep had precluded a most viable option. I resolved to work on it, but never succeeded.

Fletcher was a breath of fresh air in his insistence that the modern game is far superior to all that has gone before. His views were in contrast to those of Don Shepherd, on which we had been reared at Glamorgan. Shepherd is a lovely man for whom I hold the utmost respect, and, as I have said, his remarkable achievements quite rightly announce him as a legend of Glamorgan cricket. He also possesses a rich knowledge of the game, but sometimes he can be overly fond of the old-fashioned way.

Fletcher would have no truck with this. Once I heard him talking of Colin Bland, his compatriot, still regarded by many as the finest fielder ever. "I've got ten boys at Western Province who are better than he ever was," was Fletcher's reaction. Even Shepherd will admit that the standard of fielding has soared with the increased attention to physical well-being, but I have also seen Fletcher smirking when watching tapes of the 'old days' when batsmen plundered runs off seemingly innocuous bowlers with three slips and a gully. He is well aware that all other sports have made dramatic strides over the years, so why not cricket?

Fletcher will always be remembered in Glamorgan history as the coach who arrived and immediately led us to the County Championship. It is some legacy, and, while I would guard against saying that it was all down to him, because we were a fine side at our peak then, he certainly did bring something new 'to the party' (a favourite phrase of his, as the national press has discovered).

I think that his biggest influence was on the youngsters Darren Thomas and Dean Cosker, but he also seemed to revitalise Hugh Morris, stimulating him with increased fitness through ball games rather than mundane training sessions, and with feverish cricket technical talk. Morris, no doubt, soaked up as much information as possible in the event of being appointed to the post at the EWCB, for which he had confidentially applied.

Fletcher saved Thomas' career. He had burst on to the county scene as a 17-year-old with five wickets on his debut in 1992, but had unfortunately become Steve Barwick's drinking partner – a most arduous and wearing task. Barwick (known universally as Baz) had left the staff at the end of 1996 amid some acrimony when he, Neil Kendrick, Alistair Dalton and James Williams were all informed of their release on the second evening of a three-day second-team game in Worcestershire. The first three had all declined to take any further part in the match. It created a furore, but it was ridiculous for the cricket committee meeting (where contracts were then resolved) to have been arranged when it was.

It was a disharmonious way to end a fine career, which had seen Barwick revert very successfully from brisk away swingers to off-cutters, very much as Don Shepherd had done. He became famed for his one-day economy, opposition teams holding meetings solely about him and how best to counter his miserly stuff. Barwick was not shy of explaining the rudiments of his success to opponents in the bar afterwards, once famously spending what seemed like an age at Colwyn Bay, detailing to Lancashire's John Crawley how he should not even entertain the thought of advancing down the pitch at him until his bowling arm was well past the vertical.

Barwick's predilection for lager and tobacco was, and still is, legendary around the county circuit. His attitude flies in the face of all the modern thinking of sports physiologists, but, despite imbibing at least six pints of the amber nectar every night, he never carried any excess weight and would turn up every pre-season and land the ball on a sixpence. Mind you, he would not want to do a lot more. By some quirk of fate he was always injured on pre-season tours but always available for the first game of the season.

It was a shame that Barwick and Fletcher did not cross paths. Just as Australian David Boon said that he would have paid good money to have watched England's fidgety number 11, Peter Such, face the fabled West Indian attack of the 1980s, then so I would have shelled out huge chunks of my salary to have witnessed Barwick perform Fletcher's ten catches. Barwick's biggest problem was that he needed a regular partner to indulge in this colourful lifestyle. It had been Ian Smith, the talented but undisciplined all-rounder from Durham, but his metabolism was not quite as forgiving as Barwick's, and the extra pounds emasculated his once swift bowling.

Thomas, too, was piling on the pounds – strange to relate given that he is now the fittest man on the Glamorgan staff, regularly reaching level 15 on the dreaded bleep test – and his bowling was suffering. But Fletcher recognised his potential, and worked tirelessly with him. Fletcher's interest alone was a boost to Thomas' confidence. And to Cosker too, who was at his most effective in Fletcher's first season. Both of them gained future England A call-ups because of Fletcher's influence. I think Fletcher has done a good job with England, bringing much of the common sense and sound man management that he offered to Glamorgan, as well as a pragmatism that does not exclude flair and free thinking; and, just as at Glamorgan, he forged a strong relationship with a skipper he had never previously met. Nasser Hussain and Matthew Maynard are two very different characters. Hussain drinks little, for a start, but there are common threads that would have endeared both of them to Fletcher and his coaching philosophies. Firstly, both are very passionate and thoughtful about their cricket. Indeed, they are among the deeper thinkers in the game, and both will have found a willing listener and suggester in Fletcher.

Secondly, both are naturally dominant personalities within any dressing room; characters who enjoy the kudos and responsibility of being in charge. And, while Hussain is much more demonstrative, passionate and emotive, neither takes the inclusive route of constantly seeking others' advice – something I was inclined to do as captain. During 1999 I briefly took the reins when Maynard was injured and I found the personal onus and accountability wearing. The team endured a sticky period and Fletcher did admit to me: "I'm sorry. I should have got more involved." I was not his omnipotent managing director, like Maynard or Hussain. And even though I do not know Michael Vaughan, England's newest leader, well enough to make a totally cogent argument, I doubt if he is either. He will be more democratic, and Fletcher will have to modify his role accordingly.

High on Fletcher's agenda with England has been the need for consistency in selection, something conspicuously lacking in the times before his tenure. A good example to me is Chris Adams, the Sussex and former Derbyshire batsman. His muscular and forthright batting (as well as some well-placed self publicity) ensured his selection for the 1999/2000 tour to

South Africa. He played in all five Tests and, even though he failed to come to terms with the leap in standard, at least he can rest in the knowledge that he has had a fair crack of the whip. A whole series in the side is sufficient for an individual to know whether or not he is good enough to cut it at Test level. Adams knows. I am not sure. Never will be.

Who knows what might have happened if Fletcher had become England coach in 1998 rather than 1999? I misfired in 1999, only finding real form late on, once the winter selections had been made, but Fletcher, who has always been at pains not to be seen to be favouring anyone from Glamorgan, did confide to me recently that he had proposed to the selectors that I go on the A tour that winter to the West Indies, as much as a role model as anything else. "A top professional" was how Fletcher once described me to a reporter. Now that means something to me. And even though he has become a full member of staff at the EWCB I still would not bet against Fletcher having some future involvement at Glamorgan. He likes Cardiff, renting a flat there even when England coach, and I think that there are a number of well-positioned people still keen to utilise his talents again.

CHAPTER EIGHT

ROUNDED WITH CONSUMMATE EASE

"**A**nd Hackney rounded James with consummate ease," reported *The Guardian* newspaper after the UAU rugby final at Twickenham in 1988 between Swansea and Loughborough Universities. And indeed he did. The match was a tight, closely-fought encounter, the outcome of which hinged on one try. This was naturally scored by Steve Hackney, a winger who went on to represent Leicester and England B with some distinction. He took a quick drop out on the opposite side of the field from where all the forwards were waiting, and beat one man, leaving him with some 30m of open space before the last line of defence. Unfortunately for Swansea University, that last line was me.

It was with some trepidation that I loped across from right to left on that famous, beautifully-manicured turf – the only time I played there, later turning down a Under-21 final with Gloucestershire in favour of a Glamorgan Colts cricket match ("Why?" I ask now). Hackney stepped off his right foot, veering back infield. "I've got him," I thought, stopping and stretching my right arm out to embrace his solid frame.

But then, in a millisecond, disaster. For the second time in this book I have used that word when it is not wholly applicable, but again it was a life-turning moment for me and one that still embarrasses me to this day. Just as quickly as he had stepped on to his right foot, he now stepped off his left foot. And how. Off he went like the wind. I did not lay a finger on him as he scooted outside me and sped the remaining 50m unhindered. I probably should at least have dived to try to unsettle his thoroughbred stride pattern. But it all happened too quickly. "We thought that he must have been in touch, because you didn't try and tackle him," a friend later told me. If only he had been. He had some five metres to spare. No one has ever said it to me. But I know. I cost Swansea University the UAU title that day.

It could have been a glorious week for me. That was on the Wednesday. On the Saturday I played for a strong Gloucestershire side including internationals Mike Teague, John Orwin and Gordon Sargent in a County Championship semi-final against the old enemy, Lancashire, who included a current international in Wade Dooley, at the Vale of Lune. I did not make any glaring errors there, but produced a generally anonymous performance in another close match. Indeed, I might have been the hero, had not my chip ahead (a favourite contact-avoiding tactic of mine) in the dying minutes bounced into touch. The line was at my mercy, untenanted. But it was not to be. The near miss encapsulated my rugby career: nearly, but not quite, good enough.

I have little doubt that Hackney will not recall me. Asking him to do so would be like asking me to name the bowler whom I hit for 20 in an over (he was unlucky, whoever he was) when Lydney played Optimists in 1984. But I most certainly remember him, because he taught me a salutary lesson. I was too slow for top-flight rugby. I had suspected as much. I had been a scrum half at school, "deceptively casual" apparently, and had made my debut there for Lydney at the age of 18. I think I was about fourth choice. Probably the only choice left. I was just back from my first term at Swansea University. "Are you fit?" the coach asked on the phone. My affirmative reply was a

197

blatant lie. It was against Bridgwater and I recall my mother coming to my bedroom on the morning of the game. "Your father is worried. He thinks you are so nervous that you are going to make a fool of yourself." He was right on the nerves front. This was my pinnacle.

I think that I learnt something about concentration that day. I don't think I have ever concentrated so hard. All the line-out calls. All the chivvying of the forwards and shouting of moves. I made sure I did it all. I felt good that evening. But despite my encouraging start I was soon forced to switch to full back at Lydney because of the robust effectiveness of Julian Davis, a fine player who later jousted for a place at Bristol with a youthful Kyran Bracken. "His greatest strength is his strength," he used to say, somewhat amusingly, of the future England scrum half. Davis was not exactly weak either. And a bit fiery too, especially with his beloved cider – 'the mad apples' – inside him, as Adrian Dale once discovered in a misunderstanding in a Chepstow bar.

I had a decent service as a scrum half – "the most natural passer in England" in 1989 according to Ian Peck, the Cambridge double Blue – but was very much a "non contact" provider, as succinctly observed by my pal, Simon Bryant. I was certainly not in the mould of Davis, who was the latest in a long line of tough-as-teak scrum halves from Lydney.

I was not the most forthcoming of tacklers, let us say; not relishing the more physical encounters partly because of a poor technique, which rarely involved the use of my shoulders, and partly through a mistrust of my physique, which was generally pencil-thin, except for the stomach region, by now regularly supplemented by the weekly drinking binges after rugby. My tall frame can easily disguise the fat, as Alec Stewart found on my Test debut, punching me playfully in the stomach to announce in surprise, "I thought that would be rock hard". Sadly not.

Mind you, my tackle count was astronomical compared to my mate Paul Morris, who operated the most welcoming of escort agencies from outside half. "This way, please. Through you come," might as well have been his advice to any opponent wishing to run towards him. His forte was goal kicking, but he suffered some pitiless slagging from certain sections of the Lydney crowd, mainly because of comparisons with his father, John, a stalwart of the club (captain for 11 successive seasons) and a good enough scrum half to have played in an England trial.

I suppose the fact that my cricketing career was prematurely curtailed by injury could have easily been foreseen by those close enough to witness my many rugby mishaps. A twisted ankle virtually every game, despite heavy strapping, was the least of my worries. I suffered terribly from 'dead legs' – or haematomas to be more medically correct – resulting in a lump like a golf ball appearing in each of my thighs, scar tissue that has reduced my flexibility and may well have hastened my knee problems.

I talked earlier of my striving to be accepted amongst my home town peers. I think by playing regularly for Lydney at rugby I achieved that. But even then I think I was different. Ask any rugby follower about Lydney and his reply is almost certain to contain words such as 'hard', 'tough' and most likely 'dirty'. And I cannot deny that any of those is inapplicable. But palpably none of them apply to me. Never have done. Never will. I was different.

I think the rest of the team considered me the 'flair' player, who could win them games and therefore had to be protected. As I have said, I did not have pace but what I did have at full back and in the level just below first class, was the know-how to join the three-quarter line at the right time; the ability to time my run so that I could split the opposition defence. Mind you, I have to say that opposition defences were in no way as drilled and organised as they are today. Creating the extra man in those days caused havoc. Nowadays I think I would get clobbered a lot more frequently than I did then.

I marvelled at the unity which that Lydney dressing room instantly created. I am sure that is the same in many rugby changing rooms but I was amazed how men from such differing backgrounds and livelihoods suddenly bonded together; willing to literally fight and spill blood for each other. And there were some hard men in that dressing room at Regentsholme. The hardest I played with was a chap called Stevie Collins, not the Irish boxer, Steve Collins, but a man with an equally destructive mean streak. Just ask Steve Smith, the former Sale and England scrum half, about Collins. He will know all about him. Sale visited Lydney in 1983 in a John Player Cup match, televised on Rugby Special. At the time it was the most exciting day of my life. The day the TV cameras came to my tiny, little rugby club where I had been playing mini-rugby since I was eight. Lydney had a decent side then too. I can still name it: Butler, Richards, Vine, Saville, Hardacre, Price (C), Howell, Sargent, Price (P), Brooks, Lindley, Curtis, Jones, Davis (K), Collins. There may be two internationals in Peter Butler (a full back recruited from Gloucester for that one season specifically to be the goal kicker – it was a failure) and Sargent, but they are clearly not household names. But I make no apologies for naming them. They were my heroes. Sale had the England captain in Smith. But Lydney could, and maybe should, have won.

However, for years after, all the talk centred around Collins and how he had stalked Smith; scared him to death they said, once sending him flying with an illegal, late elbow. And many years after that match, Collins did something else I would never forget. We were playing Berry Hill, the local rivals with a comparable reputation for rough-hewn rugby. Their pack, and one of them in particular, kindly decided to treat my legs and

HAPPY COUPLES: Jane and me after our wedding, and guests Michael Atherton and Robert Croft, who clearly found the event hilarious.

FAVOURITE
PEOPLE:
My mother
Margaret and
father Peter,
and, below, Jane
and Bethan
(then aged 2).

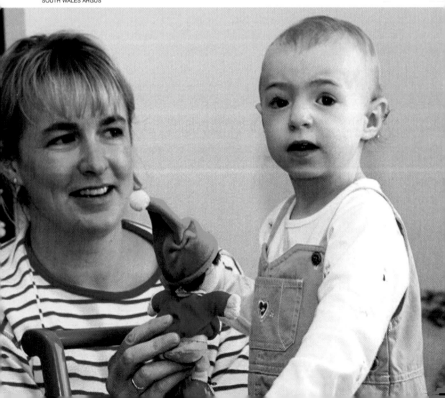

HUW EVANS

A BIG HAND FOR THE COACH: Duncan
Fletcher inspired us during our Championship-
winning campaign.

RUGBY MOMENTS: Lydney under-13s *circa* 1980 (above). I'm holding the ball, as usual!

In the press box at Kingsholm, Gloucester (left) and, below, on my way to a try for Lydney.

Bruce Seabrook/GPA IMAGES

GLOUCESTER CITIZEN

DARK DAY: Jane is first on the scene to treat the stricken Gwyn Jones after his terrible accident at Cardiff Arms Park in December, 1997.

DOCTOR IN THE HOUSE: Gwyn's graduation in 2003.

GLAM ROCKERS: Team-bonding stuff in the Brecon Beacons (above) with Steve Watkin (left) and Alex Wharf.

Congratulating 'Racehorse' Simon Jones (right) after his England call-up in 2002.

Strong-arm stuff from Matthew Maynard (below) in the dressing-room at Sophia Gardens

TOMORROW'S MAN: Mike Powell, pictured celebrating a catch with Matthew Maynard and keeper Mark Wallace, has the talent to play for England.

CAPTEN CYMRU: Skippering Wales to victory (left) against England in a one-day international at Cardiff in 2001.

NATIONAL TREASURE: The Division One League trophy, which Glamorgan won in 2002.

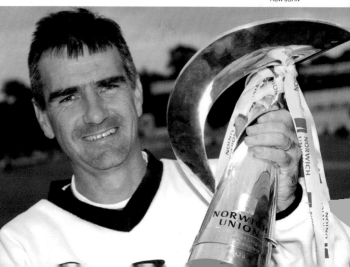

BAY OF PLENTY: Leaving the field (right) at Colwyn Bay after my record 309 not out against Sussex in 2000.

Left: With Matthew Elliott after our opening partnership.

back like a door mat. I was in some pain and as we gathered around for a breather, Collins asked, "Who woz it Jamerr?"

"Lester, I think," I said, referring to Roger 'Lester' Pickett, a man-mountain of a prop in their massive pack.

I did not see what or when it happened, but when I bumped into Collins the next day, his hand was in plaster. He just winked at me and said, "I'll look after yer, Jamerr." I never discovered what happened to Pickett, but Collins had broken his hand. For me. Even the hardest men can break bones. I don't think he was out of action for long.

My shunning of any potential fisticuffs once produced a moment of rare hilarity on the rugby field. Lydney were playing Matson, a Gloucester Combination side renowned for their thuggery. They play their home games in the middle of a run-down council estate, and among many such stories, it is fabled that a rabid woman spectator once prevented the opposing winger from scoring by throwing her bicycle into his path. But, thankfully, this County Cup match was at Lydney. It was much anticipated, and its mid-week evening kick-off ensured a healthy crowd. Everyone knew that the match was going to erupt into an unsavoury free-for-all. It was just a question of when.

It took less than a minute. From the kick-off, in fact. Both sets of forwards met and fists began to fly. The backs began to enter the fray too. All except me, of course. And surprisingly, in my view, their full back too, a chap called Les Jones who also played for Gloucester and Pontypool. As the brawl continued unabated, much to the delight of both sets of supporters, who had clearly been awaiting such violence, I spied Jones coming towards me. I was nowhere near the melee. In fact, I was as far as I could be away from it. But he was definitely coming towards me. "Oh, shit," I thought, "my proud boast of never having had a fight is about to end. He's coming to get me." As he advanced, I braced myself for the inevitable haymaker. But all that came forth was the sweetest sounding Glawster drawl.

"Hey, Jamerr, fancy an arm wrestle?"

It was widely perceived in the Glamorgan dressing room that I might have preferred to have been a professional rugby player than a cricketer. Mind you, that was probably because very few of them actually saw me play a proper game. But they did see me play 'touch' in the mornings and observed my passion for that and all other things rugby. I even became a little worried at times that I was over-obsessed with it, talking whenever possible about it, whether it was lamenting the parlous state of Welsh rugby or picking my best ever British Lions fifteen with Robert Croft, who seems unable to comprehend that there are some decent rugby players outside of Llanelli.

As you can imagine, there was never a shortage of willing listeners or protagonists in such a rugby-mad nation. Hugh Morris, who played fly half for Cardiff Institute (now UWIC), Aberavon and Newport, was one. Wicketkeeper Adrian Shaw was another, until I played a part in finishing his first-team career for him. I say that with a heavy heart because Shaw was a most likeable, humorous colleague, but on the morning of a game at Maidstone in 2001, he fell ill with food poisoning. Mark Wallace was called up to replace him, promptly scored 80 not out and took eight catches. As captain, what could I do? Shaw has not played a Championship match since, although he has slotted in nicely to his new role as second team captain/coach. He has long avowed his intention to coach, spending many winter hours teaching cricket in primary schools in the Vale of Glamorgan, so I hope this avenue bears fruit for him. He has an attitude to sport and life with which I can readily identify. He trains exceptionally hard and is always realistic about his or the team's chances in any situation.

So I was amazed that some team members began to interpret his pragmatism as negativity when advising me on this selection dilemma. After all, one of the reasons he had been brought into the first eleven by Matthew Maynard had been his lively humour and devotion to the team ethic. Like me, I think he lacked a sturdy inner belief, but he became more confident, especially with his batting, where he overcame the perils of being an early leg before candidate on account of his nerves. And, unlike quite a few county cricketers, he has an earthly awareness of the relatively low status we register in the fame stakes. All the trappings of occasionally being on TV, always being in the newspapers, staying in five-star hotels, having a sponsored car and all the other pampering can lead some individuals into believing that they have a higher profile than they really have. "Who's going to recognise us in the street?" is his constant refrain to any upstart.

Even I, once, strayed beyond my station, complaining to Glamorgan about my sponsored vehicle, a bright red Mercedes A Class, which I reckoned to have more than a passing resemblance to Noddy's toy car. "You're only a county cricketer," chided Adrian Dale, another realist then working in the club's marketing department. Indeed. Shaw had a kindred spirit at Glamorgan in Stuart Phelps, a left-arm spinner from Briton Ferry, who once was preferred in the first team to Croft, and has since seen action in the Gulf, but who was known for his laconic one-liners, with his croaky west Wales intonation. "You live your life like a rock star," he once told one of the players whom he deemed to be more concerned with the partying, designer gear and the flash car than the cricket.

Shaw was a more than decent centre for Neath. He did play a little on the wing but is easily irked by the winger tag. "49 games, 49 tries" is often heard at Sophia Gardens, when assessing Shaw's first-class career. Now, Shaw is no braggart, but he does have a habit of making the most outrageously hyperbolical statements, especially when recounting how many bottles of Budweiser beer he has imbibed the night before. More famously in the annals of Glamorgan dressing room history, he once proclaimed: "Any man, over any distance" in

211

reference to his speed compared to the rest of us. Shaw is indeed quick, but unfortunately possesses the most inelastic pair of hamstrings known to man. As a result, he takes a while to warm up in the mornings, and, within a couple of days of his brave declaration, he had been skinned on the outside in a game of 'touch'. I think it may have been by Simon Jones. That is no disgrace, because Jones is a formidably athletic specimen, whom Andy Harrison, our former fitness adviser, reckoned could easily have been an elite 400m runner. It may have been by Mike Powell, even Jacques Kallis, but no matter. If you are going to make such statements, you must expect the ribbing too. And Shaw has never had any problems with that, an ability to laugh at himself being another endearing personal trait.

So Shaw always had some forthright opinions on the oval ball game, as well as the latest gossip on the Neath squad, garnered from his likeable father, Dai, the Welsh All Blacks' seemingly eternal team manager. Shaw junior used to swear a lot, and once Alan Jones, then in charge of the Glamorgan Colts, was becoming concerned about this. He called Shaw senior into the changing room at the end of a game at BP Llandarcy. "What's the little **** been up to now?" said the father before Jones could speak.

And in the Sophia Gardens dressing room there was another man of rugby who was to have an exceptional bearing on my life, both sporting and otherwise. I once described him thus: "He's a mixture of physiotherapist, psychoanalyst and agony aunt – and he's not a bad drinking partner either". Dean Conway, who began as Glamorgan's physiotherapist in 1989 and went on to do the job for England. To call him rotund is being kind to the former prop, who achieved Wales Youth honours and had brief sorties with Cardiff and Bridgend at the higher level. But he is better known as a product of Mountain Ash and the most gregarious of companions – oh, and also as the matchmaker who introduced me to my future wife.

It was a balmy summer evening in 1996 when Conway for once stayed true to his assertion that he would meet me for a drink. He is notoriously unreliable, not from any hint of deceit but from an affable inability to say no. But thankfully he pitched up that night at Brannigans in Cardiff, a popular nightspot once frequented by cricketers aplenty, none more so than Waqar Younis during his stay in Wales – a tendency unfortunately not unknown to the local constabulary, who one night picked him up outside in his sponsored Jaguar on a drink-driving charge.

Married couples are usually uncomfortably reluctant to admit that their eyes first met in a nightclub. But Jane and I have little choice. We were introduced by Conway, which, on account of his arch gossip-mongering, is akin to meeting on live TV. It was clearly love at first sight, with Jane thankfully not recognising me as a Glamorgan cricketer. Suspecting that I was some sort of a hanger-on, this most attractive lady proclaimed: "You're too much of a wimp to play cricket." And there was me thinking it was a prerequisite.

When Jane announced that she was once the physiotherapist for London Welsh RFC, much banter ensued; a mortal enmity between London Welsh and Lydney stemming from their respective efforts in 1995 to achieve promotion from National League Division Five South, including a dramatic 17-17 draw at Lydney, with Rob Mills kicking a last-minute penalty to tie the scores. "I can still see that kick going over," says Jane to this day. "Our coaches, Bill Calcraft, (the former Australian flanker) and John Dawes (former British Lion) were inconsolable." No sympathy, I'm afraid.

"You can't marry someone from Lydney," Jane's co-physio-therapist for the Exiles at the time, Virginia Marcell, later told her. Jane thankfully ignored that tongue-in-cheek advice and we were wed little more than a year later. And without wishing to descend into soppy sentimentalism – even if I did propose outside St. Mark's Cathedral in Venice – it is no coincidence that, in that time, my cricket demonstrated a confidence stemming from a renewed *joie de vivre*. As my best man, Adrian Knox – prompted by my father – commented when speaking at my wedding: "A happy man is a successful man." He knew. Jane had changed me, made me more confident, more able to banish those nasty negative thoughts, often giving me pep talks the night before a game and telling me how many runs I should score. I couldn't always oblige, but I tried mighty hard.

Being the husband of the physiotherapist of Cardiff RFC (or the Cardiff Blues as they are now known in the brave new world of Welsh regional rugby) does have its perks, especially when it comes to free tickets and the friendship with some wonderful rugby people. But it also has its downsides. Becoming a die hard Blue and Black supporter has not been difficult because I have always had something of an affinity with the self-styled 'Greatest club in the world', but it is an inevitable upshot of the bigoted parochialism that has so blighted Welsh rugby that the capital city club are roundly despised. And so I have had to endure my fill of rancour and ridicule, not just from my west Wales team mates at Glamorgan, but also one Newport fan at Rodney Parade who quickly put me straight – "Stick to cricket, James" – when I protested loudly to the referee about a decision.

Indeed, it must be said that Cardiff have not always helped themselves since the advent of professionalism, at times signing top players randomly, with more deference to their performances in a recent Six Nations tournament than any thought of how they might slot into the team at the Arms Park. That inevitably brought accusations of being the big spenders of Welsh rugby, prepared to go to any lengths to buy a team. There is a fair degree of truth in this, but it is also true that many other clubs in Wales have frittered away thousands of pounds on the equally over-inflated wages of averagely-talented rugby players. Cardiff have not been the only miscreant in a system that has rewarded mediocrity and at one time brought this once-proud rugby nation to its knees.

Thankfully, Cardiff Blues are now seen to be actively encouraging the advancement of their home-grown talent, as seen in the emergence of the likes of Rhys Williams and the Robinson brothers, Jamie and Nicky, and will be all the better for it.

13 December 1997, 3.13pm
Cardiff v. Swansea at the Arms Park

Cardiff win a scrappy line out, which scrum half Robert Howley has to retreat to secure. They win the ball, and play proceeds up field towards the River Taff end of the ground. As everyone watches play progress, something catches my eye back downfield whence it had come. There is a player lying motionless. Sickeningly motionless. Face down, arms by his side and legs splayed out. He is wearing the blue and black colours of Cardiff. I did not need to look any closer. I knew it was Gwyn Jones. Don't ask me why. Two weeks earlier Gwyn had led Wales out at Wembley (their temporary home while the new Millennium Stadium was being built) against the mighty All Blacks. He was 25 years of age, with – would you believe it – 13 caps, a superb open side flanker with the rugby world at his feet. The fact that I might be witnessing the end of his career was now immaterial. Everything happening now was transcending rugby, placing sport in its rightful position some way down the list of life's priorities.

I did not know him personally at that stage but had met him briefly when I interviewed him for *The Western Mail* at Merthyr RFC where he had been due to make his long-awaited debut for Cardiff. The pitch was frost bound and the game called off ("Thank God," Gwyn later revealed to me, "because I had been roped into celebrating a friend's graduation the previous evening"). Jane was the first upon the scene. "I can't feel my arms or legs," said Gwyn. Apparently, he had looked down to see a thumb, which he only realised was his when he recognised the unique strapping that he used on it. Play stopped and a deathly hush enveloped the ground.

Jane had signalled immediately for the doctor. Luckily, consultant surgeon Professor John Fairclough, who later became far too acquainted with my left knee, was at the match. Amidst a flurry of other medics he ensured that the proper procedure was followed, with Gwyn being meticulously moved on to a stretcher. For what seemed like an age the game was stopped.

The gravity of the situation touched everyone present. Commentator Jonathan Davies had to leave his position for a few minutes to collect himself; Leigh Davies ("the hardest player I ever played with or against," according to Gwyn) stood by the waiting ambulance in tears. The game really should not have continued. How could the players concentrate?

Gwyn had been the first one to Howley when he fell on the ball. In true open side flanker fashion, he had remained on his feet in the 'bridge' position to win the ball for his team. However, as he did so, he was hit from front and back. His head was pummelled into his chest, causing spinal damage. My initial thought, and I'm sure that of many others present, was that he had broken his neck. No break was revealed, but he had suffered severe spinal compression.

As Gwyn was taken away in the ambulance with his distraught parents, Alun and Esyllt, no one could have imagined that there was more tragedy to come that fateful afternoon.

Early in the second half as Swansea hooker Garin Jenkins prepared to throw in at a line out, he was tapped on the shoulder by a policeman. Jenkins' father had suffered a heart attack on the terrace behind, and the Wales international was over the barrier and into the crowd like a shot. Another ambulance appeared and Jenkins accompanied his father, still clad in his white Swansea kit.

That evening I went with Jane to the University of Wales Hospital in Heath, Cardiff, to see Gwyn. Seeing him totally paralysed was a distressing experience, but it also became the start of an enduring friendship. He underwent an operation to relieve the pressure on his spine, and his recovery was painfully slow; first at the University Hospital, then at Rookwood Hospital in Cardiff. I went with Jane to visit him regularly; a routine interrupted by my England A tour to Kenya and Sri Lanka, from where I sent a message of encouragement signed by all the players for him. Robert Croft also arranged one from the England players in Sharjah for a one-day tournament. "Be strong," Alec Stewart said on it.

When Gwyn told Jane: "Tell Steve to score some runs," I felt bad for not doing so on that trip. The accident had affected me deeply, as is illustrated by the piece I wrote in my weekly *South Wales Argus* column.

Last Saturday was one of the saddest days of my life. To be at the Arms Park to witness such tragic events was to realise that sport, after all, means very little. It put everything in my life into perspective. At times I have considered cricket to be the be all and end all, getting horribly depressed when things have gone wrong – being inconsolable after scoring nought – but what does all that matter now?

I am actually angry with myself for getting so wound up about those minor, trivial things when I consider what Gwyn Jones and his family are going through at the present time. To see Gwyn lying there motionless was a sickening experience. My wife, Jane, was the first to get to him and described it as her worst experience as a physiotherapist. She is understandably deeply distressed by the whole situation and is struggling to come to terms with it. I myself feel as if there is a black cloud hanging over my life, so I cannot even imagine to understand what Jane and everyone at Cardiff Rugby Club is going through. I went with Jane and Jonathan Humphreys to the Heath Hospital on Saturday night where we spoke to Gwyn's parents, who are doctors themselves and two of the nicest people you could ever wish to meet. They were immensely brave, considering the circumstances, and we chatted for nearly an hour, even joking about Robert Croft's recent appearance on A Question of Sport.

I still cannot believe it has happened, but all I know is that Gwyn is a fighter and if anyone is going to battle through this, it is him. There should be no thought of him playing rugby again, but just to recover fully and be able to lead a normal life again. My hopes and prayers are with him as are, I'm sure, those of the whole of Wales.

Gwyn had visitors and messages of support from all over the world, and he was particularly proud of the fact that Ian Botham called by, his son, Liam, having just joined Cardiff as a powerful, hard-working winger, desperately keen to make his own way in sport, having spurned cricket despite bagging five wickets on his first-class debut.

Once back home in the trendy Pontcanna area of Cardiff, Gwyn's rehabilitation continued with Jane and I still visiting regularly. At first, lots of his rugby playing colleagues called by, but their presence noticeably dwindled as the days and months wore on, Leigh Davies and Robert Howley being his staunchest allies. Whenever I called by, Gwyn never wanted to talk about his injury or his progress, just sport in general. His knowledge of all sports is almost encyclopaedic, and he was ever eager to discover what was happening in the cricket world, especially at his beloved 'Glammy'.

It was only in 2003 when I was laid up at home for six weeks after my knee operation that Gwyn began to open up to me about his accident. He was magnificently supportive in that time and told me that, for the first nine weeks at home, he was unable to even use the remote control for his TV. "Once I could do that, I felt I was on my way," he joked. Certainly any notions of self pity I might have had were instantly banished.

During my convalescence, Gwyn qualified as a doctor, a magnificent achievement given that he has not made anything like a full recovery. He decided to celebrate at the Le Monde restaurant (a favourite of those excellent trenchermen, Mike Gatting and Graham Gooch, whenever they are in the Principality) in St. Mary's Street, Cardiff, and invite all those people he felt had helped him in his recovery.

I was on crutches and in considerable pain but there was no way I could have missed it, given what he had been through. At one stage Gwyn caught me looking quizzically towards the toilet, with all the tables and chairs en route to it. "You're trying to work out the easiest route there, aren't you? Welcome to my little world." I smiled almost apologetically, but my mind was saying, "Yes, but I'm only in it for six weeks. You're in it for ever. You're a brave bastard."

Initially, Gwyn was most reluctant to go out in public, and understandably so. But Jane was insistent that he had to start somewhere, so she organised a night out at a local curry house, with some of the rugby players. Gwyn has never forgotten that because it did indeed set him on his way. And in November 2002 I was invited to a Rugby Legends dinner in Cardiff at which Gwyn was presented with a bravery award. He mentioned me and Jane in his acceptance speech and I freely admit that I was scarcely able to keep my emotions in check. I am not the most emotional of people, and it would be an exaggeration to say that tears were flowing down my cheeks, but my eyes were not entirely dry either.

Gwyn still cannot walk with complete sureness and confidence, but he has made remarkable progress. Before returning to his medical studies he began forging a formidable reputation as a rugby commentator with both the Welsh language channel S4C and the BBC, as well as becoming a controversial columnist with *The Western Mail* newspaper.

He certainly speaks his mind and has upset a few people along the way, notably two recent Wales coaches, Steve Hansen and Graham Henry, both New Zealanders. But he has become well-respected because he is brave enough to voice his opinions, which are always well thought through and based on a perceptive rugby knowledge. His work commitments mean that he will not be seen in print from now on, which will be a loss, but his commentary will continue. So, I hope, will our friendship.

CHAPTER NINE

KING OF
COLWYN BAY

A drian Dale had just scored his first double hundred for Glamorgan, sharing a 425 partnership – a record for any wicket – with the incomparable Viv Richards against Middlesex at Cardiff in 1993, when I remarked to him: "I could never imagine scoring 200. Not in any sort of game." It was a curious comment. In fact, eleven years on it looks downright ridiculous, because I am now the proud holder of the record for the most double centuries by a Glamorgan batsman. I finished my career with six, with Javed Miandad next on the list with four. But it was born of my fabled lack of confidence, and was how I felt at the time.

I had acquired the habit of scoring centuries. "Hundreds are what people notice," was a repeated mantra of both my father and Alan Jones, but to double them up was a hinterland I had barely even considered. So it was very much to my surprise that during the subsequent winter in Zimbabwe I managed an unbeaten double century for my club side, Universals, in the delightfully sylvan surroundings of the Queens Club, Bulawayo. It was even more amazing considering that my form had been so dire that I had pleaded with my Muslim employers to allow me to return home to Britain for Christmas. I played a couple of games of rugby for Lydney and even considered not returning to Africa, but when I did go back I felt refreshed. I was dropped on nought and then made hay. But what about a triple century? I'm not even sure the childhood reveries on my lawn stretched that far. No Glamorgan batsman had ever scored one before the 22nd and 23rd of August 2000. Over those two never-to-be-forgotten days I scored 309 not out. Maiden centuries may be a little tedious but I make no apologies for going into some detail about my triple hundred – not that many players have that luxury. And I also make no apologies for quoting liberally from a piece that Scyld Berry wrote for my benefit brochure, where he attempted to get inside my mind before, throughout and after my marathon innings. I spoke to him and thought that I had given an honest psychological appraisal of my state of mind then. But looking back, I realise that I was holding back a little.

The 2000 season had not been a particularly memorable one. I had begun well with two centuries in the opening two games – both, unusually, accompanied by ducks in the other innings – but then my form had fallen away markedly. The fixture list for that season contained a new twist for Glamorgan. We played a four-day game against Nottinghamshire at Cardiff, finishing on the Saturday before making the long trek north to Colwyn Bay that evening in readiness for a Sunday League match against the same opponents the following day. I made a palliative 77 at Cardiff but then my uneasy mind was further weakened with a second ball duck on the Sunday, a delivery from the Australian Paul Reiffel rearing unexpectedly from a length. The quirky fixture list then afforded us a day off before beginning the four-day match against Sussex.

A night away with no cricket the next day usually only means one thing for county cricketers – a night on the tiles followed by a day of desperately trying to dry out before going back into action. But I resolved to have a reasonably early night, as I had noticed that such 'bonding sessions' had left me still feeling lethargic two days later. I decided to run back from the ground on the Sunday evening to our hotel in Llandudno. I reasoned it to be some three miles, a gentle jog back. It turned out to be nearer five and by the end I was shattered and light-headed. I did go for a couple of quiet beers but was in bed by midnight and determined to rise early and go to the hotel swimming pool for a recovery session. By the morning the smells wafting from the breakfast room were too much. I decided rest was the answer to my batting problems and a day spent strengthening my resolve, attempting to exorcise the demons that were bringing negative thoughts at an alarming rate of knots.

Succour came in the fact that I had scored a career best 259 not out at the ground the previous season in remarkably similar circumstances, while in the middle of a debilitating run drought. It had taken me a shade under 12 hours (719 minutes) and, by the end, I was praying for captain Matthew Maynard to declare, despite my proximity to Emrys Davies' record score for Glamorgan. I was on my last legs – physically, rather than mentally, shattered. This may sound a little strange, but I do not think that it was a good innings. I never felt good. Maybe it was because I batted for a long time with Jacques Kallis, who made a stellar hundred, and his classical deployment of his broad-looking blade contrasted with my more strained, earthly offerings.

That was certainly the view of Nottinghamshire's Barbadian Vasbert Drakes and of their South African coach Clive Rice. Myself (43) and Kallis (24) were not out at the end of a remarkable first day in which Steve Watkin had reduced the opposition to 9-6 in the opening hour with a spell of 5-0 in 16 balls. Yet again, eavesdropping in the bar of the hotel, which the teams were sharing, I heard the genial and fun-loving West Indian declare: "I might have to have a few drinks tonight; Kallis' bat looked wide this evening." He clearly was not too worried about my nudging open face. And then, in the winter, Duncan Fletcher told me that while he was back in South Africa he heard Rice on TV being less than complimentary about Glamorgan, and about me in particular.

Kallis confused me at lunch on the third day. I had completed my double century but was still short of my career best 235 – also against Nottinghamshire, at Worksop in 1996. But Kallis kept saying, "Well played, Jugs." I thought he was referring to the tradition of a batsman having to buy a jug of beer if he achieved a career best. My "I haven't got it yet" was greeted with a quizzical look from Kallis, who soon informed me that he was referring to the hours I had been spending on the bowling machine (of which one type is named Jugs) with Duncan Fletcher and, at times, Kallis himself. It was ironic that the opponents this time were to be Sussex. My first-class debut had been against them in 1985. Well, that is what the record books say. In fact, I did not make it on to the field at all. It was the last game of the season and I was a late call-up (I was to have a few more of those) for Alan Lewis Jones, who dislocated his shoulder in practice. I had not even passed my driving test then, so I had to hurriedly organise a lift with a family friend who happened to be working in Cardiff at the time.

I was not ready for first-class cricket then, and was fortunate to be selected ahead of the likes of Tony Cottey and Michael Cann, and the weather gods concurred, only allowing just over 60 minutes' play in the whole three days. Hugh Morris and John Hopkins were the Glamorgan openers and they survived the short period without too many alarms, although I do recall Morris being struck a fearful blow in the groin area by Imran Khan (how would I have coped with him?) and all the players on the balcony giggling furiously at all the usual "one ball left" type jokes, as Morris' girlfriend of the time sat below us, her face reddening by the second.

Fast forward to 1987. I had missed my second year examinations at Swansea through a virus and had only played a handful of competitive club matches when I received a call from coach Alan Jones. "You're in the first team for the Tilcon Trophy (a one-day tournament then played annually at Harrogate) and then for the Sussex championship match. They will give you a run in the team."

I don't know which was the stronger feeling, elation or embarrassment. It was brilliant news that at last I was to be given an extended opportunity in first-class cricket but how was this going to look to my tutors at Swansea, in front of whom I had appeared a few weeks earlier, seemingly at death's door? I had been ill. But it had also been an opportune illness. I had been partying hard, and my studying was in no sort of order to be examined. It all looked a little suspicious, but what the hell. *Carpe diem*. There was no play for three days at Harrogate, resulting in three bowl-outs.

Now, you may have noticed that I have not mentioned my bowling thus far in this book. There is good reason for that. It is hopeless. No, in fact it is worse than that. I quote Don Shepherd, who knows a thing or two about the art, who described me as "the worst bowler I have ever seen." And he has not even included the word professional in there, so I presume that I have pipped even the most inept park bowlers to his carefully appointed title. It is difficult to know where it all went wrong. I was a leg-spinner as a youth, once even capturing two wickets for the Welsh Schools U15 eleven (I was bowling because I was captain) and I recall the team manager whispering to me before the international against England, who included two leg spinners called Nasser Hussain and Michael Atherton, "You're our secret weapon."

I wish I had kept myself a secret. I got smashed everywhere. I think at that stage I had a reasonable action. Nothing special, but passable, and certainly not the sort that had people rolling around with laughter. But within a couple of years that was not the case. I had reverted to off-spin in a vain attempt to avoid embarrassment, but failed horribly. My head jerked involuntarily away at the point of delivery, resulting in a low, slingy and probably crooked bowling arm. This inability to bowl actually dented my general confidence. Every young professional is expected to bowl in the nets, and rightly so, but I just made a fool of myself. I used to plead with Alan Jones to send me out and make me run as many laps of the field as he wanted. Anything not to bowl. As I became a more senior player I was able to avoid this humiliation more readily, busying myself with extra fielding, fitness or simply throwing balls to a colleague for extra batting practice.

So it will be of some surprise to read this. I quote *Wisden* for fear of being branded a bare-faced liar:

> *Rain ruined the Harrogate Festival, where all three matches were decided by the system of each player bowling two balls at a single stump, the side scoring the most hits being declared the winners. June 12. Gloucestershire beat Glamorgan 4-3. In the first round, S.P. James of Glamorgan and K.P. Tomlins of Gloucestershire were successful...*

What it does not say is that the ball that did hit only just made the base of the stump before its second bounce, which would have rendered it a no ball. It also turned quite prodigiously, not from any spinning skill on my part but more likely from striking a crease in the coconut matting on to which we were bowling. So on to Hove we went. It rained for the whole of the first day. "This is your fault. Your career is doomed," said Greg Thomas. The rain was certainly following me around. Maybe this pluvial beginning to my first-class career goes some way to explaining my later yearnings for interruptions and an adjournment of the time to bat. Rainy days in county dressing rooms are often the most buoyant and boisterous, the release of any pressure prompting pesky schoolboy behaviour. Some play cards, some go training, and some just talk gibberish, filling their time by selecting upcoming England teams. Mike Powell and Mark Wallace are more likely to be animatedly discussing some notional eleven, such as their Hard (or Tasty as they like to call it) Eleven. In 2002 it might have looked something like this:

Adam Hollioake (Capt) (Surrey)
Matthew Hayden (Australia)
Peter Bowler (Somerset)
Adrian Rollins (Northamptonshire)
David Byas (Yorkshire, but by then spending a curious final year over the Pennines at Lancashire)
Iain Sutcliffe (a boxing Blue, then of Leicestershire now of Lancashire)
Andrew Flintoff (Lancashire)
Ridley Jacobs (West Indies)
Andy Bichel (Australia)
Chris Silverwood (Yorkshire)
Alex Wharf (Glamorgan)

Peter Willey (England) umpire

Brian Close (Yorkshire) coach.

Each selection is greeted with a playful "I reckon I could have him" from somewhere within the room, or a "Now he is tasty. Have you seen the size of him?"

It should be noted that I would include Powell himself in that side, having spent many winters pushing weights with him and having seen him lift 130kg on the bench press. And, of course, he has been involved in the odd scuffle, too. There was the much-publicised one with his close pal, Ian Thomas, at Colwyn Bay in 2002, when he completely lost his rag during a touch rugby warm-up, forcing myself and coach John Derrick to ban him for two games – a most difficult punishment to mete out to a close friend. And there was a less known contretemps with Matthew Elliott, two nights before my 309. I did not actually witness it close hand because I was some 150 yards up the street in Llandudno, but it seems some alcohol-induced, humorous face- slapping turned a little nasty. But, like the earlier incident, it was stopped before it got out of hand. With all due respect to Elliott, I know who my money would have been on!

Or Powell and Wallace might have been choosing their Cool Eleven, which could have read:

Carl Hooper (Capt) (West Indies)

Kim Barnett (Gloucestershire – a surprising choice maybe, but they thought he was endearingly carefree)

Mark Waugh (Australia)

Graham Thorpe (Surrey)

Mark Alleyne (Gloucestershire)

Craig White (Yorkshire)

Keith Piper (Warwickshire)

Neil Smith (Warwickshire, another surprise, but they liked his imperturbability when hit for boundaries)

Carl Greenidge (Northamptonshire)

Devon Malcolm (Leicestershire)

James Anderson (Lancashire)

Mark Benson (England) umpire

Jimmy Adams (West Indies) coach.

I have also heard them selecting a team of 'More Heads', who are reckoned to have more head than hair (in other words, baldies); or a 'Bogwash' eleven, which consists of those county players whom they reckon were bullied at school, and had their heads washed down the toilet. There have been two Derbyshire opening bowlers, a recently-capped England batsman, an Essex captain, a former Cambridge university colleague of mine, and a Glamorgan lyricist among those 'selected'. I think that they were considering including me until I told them that I once (erroneously) acquired the nickname of 'Gripper' at school, after Gripper Stebson, the bully from the popular 1980s BBC TV series, *Grange Hill*.

Powell and Wallace, along with others, also talk in their own language, a patois formed from their own cricketing rhyming slang, which delights and boggles in equal measure. This is how an early morning dressing room conversation might have gone after the previous night's floodlit victory.

MW: That was a Murray last night.

MP: Yep, we were up the guts. Lucky the ump didn't drop his shopping with that Lb at the end.

MW: Hell of a bead on though. Fatty's by the end.

MP: Slinging 'em last night, boy.

MW: Didn't get home till late. Couldn't have a gypsy's for that jobsworth.

I arrive.

MW: How's your Brett, Sid?

SJ: Just had it drained.

MP (giggling): Oww, Sid's knee is tired, boys. Get it? Drained?

Wallace, have you got that Angus for me?

MW: Yes, it's under the Mike Powell over there. I'm off for a David.

MP (noticing my grumpiness): I think Sid's tits are out. He hurt his Mal last night as well. And I think Maynard's gone in the Gregory.

Some explanation may be required! A 'Murray' is a good win, after the Sussex and former Zimbabwe batsman, Murray

Goodwin. 'Up the guts' is a favoured expression in the Glamorgan dressing room to denote a no-nonsense, determined approach. 'To drop one's shopping' is an expression much used by Adrian Shaw as an alternative to the colloquial 'shit oneself'. Lb – short for Lbw. 'I've got a bead on' is Alun Evans' way of saying that he is sweating. 'Fatty's' has already been explained, meaning knackered. 'To sling 'em' is short for 'slinging z's', i.e. sleeping. 'Gypsy's kiss' is traditional rhyming slang for piss. The 'jobsworth' is the drug tester. 'Brett' Lee = knee. 'Sid' is my awfully corny nickname (I've never complained about it though, because that is never a good plan) after the late actor Sid James. It was first coined, I think, by Matthew Maynard when he was helping Geoff Holmes with some pen portraits for his benefit brochure.

Generally the nicknames in the Glamorgan squad, just like any other sporting team I suspect, are facile but seemingly indispensable, derived by the simple process of adding a 'y' to the surname, or some part of it. Thus Powelly, Crofty, Newelly, Wharfy, Wally, Watty, Shawsy, Hughesy, Parky, Hempy and Daley – which inevitably leads to 'Arthur', that famous second-hand car salesman, and some better sobriquets.

Ian Thomas is known as 'Bolts' because he has some in his back after an operation. Likewise Owen Parkin has been known as 'Calamari' (a spineless mollusc), partly because of a similar operation, but I suspect there is a hint of a lack of courage, too. Dean Cosker is known as 'Lurker' for his tendency to surreptitiously loiter around. Simon Jones is called 'Horse', short for racehorse, there being no doubt that he is a thoroughbred physical specimen, and this often leads to him being called 'Ray', short for the delightfully-rhyming 'Ray Sauce'. Alun Evans is rather cruelly known as 'Troll' for his unique looks, grimaces and accent. And, just as most cricketers called Smith are known as 'Smudger', so Darren Thomas joins the list of Thomases known as 'Teddy'.

The origins of Steve Watkin's 'Banger' (it is certainly not Marcus Trescothick's love of sausages) and Andrew Davies' 'Diver' are less clear, certainly not as self-explanatory as Tony Cottey's 'Cotts', David Harrison's 'Hazza' or John Derrick's 'JD' – although he was known as 'Bo' once, and more recently as 'Axeman' for the very rare occasions when his generally smiling, happy-go-lucky personality turns a little darker.

Back to the translation. 'Angus' Fraser = razor. 'Mike Powell' = towel. 'David' Gower = shower. 'Tits out' means angry. 'Mal' Meninga (Australian rugby league player) = finger, but not thumb as the sometimes dopey but extremely likeable Alun Evans found to the great amusement of everyone else when he asked broken thumb victim Powell, "How's the Mal?" 'Gregory' Peck = neck.

As illustrated by the Croft/Fletcher story earlier, practical jokers are in their element. In fact, by the most uncanny of coincidences as I was writing this chapter, laid up at home with my injured knee, I received a phone call from John Derrick. It was raining at Worcester and in the background I could hear laughs and giggles as if some party was going on. It was 10am, but rain was falling. And in progress was an uproarious meeting to ascertain the identity of the most recent person who had been meddling with other players' socks. Derrick's attitude to this type of behaviour was clearly a little more *laissez-faire* than Duncan Fletcher's. Derrick said: "I've got someone who wants to speak to you." It was Wallace. "It was me and Powelly. We didn't mean any offence."

They were owning up to a 'crime' committed more than a year before, when one of my socks mysteriously disappeared from the dressing room during play. I then received a letter in the post warning me to obey instructions and not to mention it to anyone else in the team. "Make sure that in the morning during touch rugby you wear your sweatshirt around your waist. If you do not, your sock will have it. Be afraid, be very afraid," it read. A week later I received my sock in the post – in five pieces. "You will know better next time."

Ah, the pranks of youth. At least I took it in good part; one senior player reckoned that if it had been him as skipper, he would have dropped the miscreants if he had found them. But I was not getting myself involved in any such tomfoolery as I contemplated my first championship innings for Glamorgan at Hove. I was more worried about how quickly Garth Le Roux was going to bowl. I soon found out. He might have been ageing a little, but he decided that I should receive the traditional, time-honoured greeting to first-class cricket – three bouncers from the first three balls. Welcome, youngster.

Fast-forward to Colwyn Bay. I had no idea that Sussex would become an integral part of my cricketing history as I settled down to read Simon Hughes' second book *Yakking Around The World* (nowhere near as good as his first, *A Lot of Hard Yakka*; the superbly honest and illuminating account of life on the county circuit) in contemplative solitude. A willing Dougie No Mates now. My room mate, Adrian Dale, was out playing golf with his father, so I was alone and thinking about how I would combat Jason Lewry, their left-arm swing bowler, who had dismissed me earlier in the season at Hove. I was never particularly comfortable against left-arm swing bowlers, especially the ones who swung the ball back into me late. Umpires seem to adore it when a left-armer does bring the ball back sharply, and often seem to have a finger up before the ball has even struck the pads. "Hit it back where it comes from" (in other words through mid on) was always Graham Burgess' advice on playing them, but my natural inclination was to aim towards extra cover. Thus the problem. So in between Hughes' chapters I kept repeating the mantra, "Hit it back where it comes from."

An additional concern was that I had been struggling for most of the season with my leg side play, but I probably did not need new coach Jeff Hammond to gleefully pronounce to the press after I'd scored a hundred at Edgbaston: "He played okay but his leg side play needs a lot of work." The only occasion I left my room during the day was to buy some food, and on the way back to the hotel I was tempted by the 'Closing Down Sale' signs of a clothes shop opposite. My questionable taste in clothing led me to purchase an awful stripey top, which was neither a long-sleeved T-shirt nor sweatshirt. I wore it once, I think. I kept it as a lucky memento for a while, though.

There was a team meeting that evening, not to smooth things over between Powell and Elliott – that had already been done – but for the coach to emphasise the need for patience at the crease. We were looking to score too quickly, he told us. We all nodded our heads and went our separate ways. I am not a big fan of meetings. I know it is clichéd, but I would much rather people 'walk the walk' than 'talk the talk'. I recognise that there is a place for team discussions but what happened the following day emphasises their frequent futility. On the morning of August 22, I went out to the middle to inspect the wicket, just as I would do on the first day of any four-day match. It looked damp and green, very much like the Sunday wicket on which I had been dismissed so early. Mindful of what had happened to Nottinghamshire at the hands of Watkin a year before, I immediately told skipper Maynard that we should bowl.

I passed Glamorgan fan Mike Morgan, known to all as 'Mad Mike from Newport', and not without good reason, though he showed that he has a heart of gold by cycling all the way up to Colwyn Bay for my benefit year. He said: "Same as last year now, Steve."

"Not on there," I replied in a typically negative reaction to the pitch. I also mentioned to Edward Bevan, BBC Wales' cricket correspondent: "It would be nice to have a bowl on there. It's sure to dart around." I have never been allowed to forget those comments. Mind you, that must be nothing compared to the ribbing that Sussex captain Chris Adams must still receive, because his opinion on the wicket concurred with mine (indeed, Maynard's did, too, until he went out to toss and realised that it had dried). Adams won the toss and inserted us.

"So it was that one of the most costly insertions of all time was made. If you send a team in, you want four wickets by lunch, not by tea the following day," wrote Berry. I had not told him what I had said to Morgan or Bevan.

Any early inning nerves were soon assuaged by some friendly leg stump half volleys from Lewry. The ball was not swinging. *"Records are not compiled in adverse circumstances: Jim Laker didn't take 19 wickets on a belter at the WACA in Perth against batsmen with fantastic bat-pad techniques. In Steve's case one advantage was that Glamorgan chose a Reader ball for this match, not a Duke, which would have swung more and helped Sussex's swing bowlers. As the opening stand between Steve and Matthew Elliott grew to lunch and beyond, this piece of planning handsomely paid off. Elliott started to trade in boundaries, more so after he inside-edged a ball on to his troublesome knee, causing an inflammation that was to end his season,"* wrote Berry.

Indeed, it was Elliott's last day at the crease for Glamorgan until his return in 2004. His 'jelly knee', as he likes to call it, had given up on him. There were some dissenting voices at the club suggesting that it was perfect timing for Elliott because he fancied returning home anyway. But I thought them harsh. And it was certainly not because of his spat with Powell. But he was finding the rigours of a full county season demanding and, when my wife looked at his knee, she reasoned that there was something seriously wrong with it. He returned home and immediately went under the knife, not appearing for his state side, Victoria, until after Christmas.

As with many records, mine required an outrageous slice of fortune in order to be attained. Please do not think for one minute that I am striving to compare the two of us as batsmen, but Brian Lara, on his way to the highest first class ever of 501 not out for Warwickshire against Durham in 1994, was dropped on 18 by opposition wicketkeeper Chris Scott. Apparently it was a sitter, and Scott turned to his slips and remarked: "I bet he goes on to get a hundred now." And so I will be eternally grateful to Richard Montgomerie, who dropped me on 15.

It is strange how batsmen sometimes are reluctant to admit that they have had some luck. And I was the same here, because there was some uncertainty as to whether it was a drop at all. I sliced a full ball from Lewry with an open face (surprise, surprise!) and the ball went fairly gently towards Montgomerie at gully. He spilt it, and myself and Elliott crossed for a single. I asked umpire Jeremy Lloyds what he thought. He seemed unsure, but I think he may have been being kind to me.

Elliott had no doubt, and neither did most of my colleagues. It had been a catch. I maintained that it might have been a 'bump' ball, but deep down I knew it was a catch, too. After that, I played well. I usually did at Colwyn Bay. The pitch is invariably flat, and its slowness meant that I could play my idiosyncratic hook and pull shot (both feet off the floor, arms flailing) with impunity while the boundaries are short and inviting. After I had scored 184 there in 2002, much was made of my record; apparently, in 12 innings I scored 1,221 runs at an average of 135.66. Sorry to bore you with such bald statistics but even I cannot be self-deprecating about them. If only there had such rich pickings at other grounds.

I knew that I must have done reasonably well there when I once heard the ever-lugubrious Bob Willis refer to me on Sky Sports, with a rare hint of levity, as "The King of Colwyn Bay". I scored my maiden Championship century there in 1992 against a Lancashire side captained on a rare occasion by Mike Atherton. He did much of the bowling, too, in tandem with left-arm spinner Alex Barnett. It was not a particularly satisfying century for me because it came in the second innings and I felt that Lancashire were precipitating a declaration rather than going all out to bowl us out. But it was not the filthy declaration bowling often seen in three-day cricket. Atherton was a steady county bowler in those days before his back problems. And he tempted me on 98 by bringing the field up to Barnett. I took up the challenge and was fortunate that my lofted drive just about cleared mid-off.

Against Sussex I was indebted to Elliott's positive lead. He was in imperious form on the way to the two of us breaking Glamorgan's first wicket record partnership, previously held by Alan Jones and Roy Fredericks, our 374 eclipsing the 330 made by those two superb left-handers in 1972. Elliott was particularly severe on Mark Robinson, a Yorkshireman on his third county, whose honest trundlers, which often bounced more than you expected, were causing county batsmen problems that year. Robinson possessed the most outrageous and exaggerated follow through, which once nearly led him to a premature end when a Matthew Maynard exocet straight drive hit him flush on the forehead before he could move. But here he was in no such danger. Rather it was the spectators on the bank opposite the pavilion at the delightful Rhos-on-Sea ground who were fearing for their safety as Elliott continually deposited Robinson's decently-directed length balls over mid-wicket with a customary swivel pull off the front foot. It was a class Test batsman treating a hard-working but ultimately ordinary county seamer with contempt. I was the commoner tucking in to the left overs at a banquet graced by royal presence. Elliott played that well. He left, sated, for 177 but I ended that first day, still greedy, on 193 not out. Glamorgan were 547-1. So much for the team talk about not trying to score too quickly. I think that generally I could be classified as an above-average county batsman, but what at times elevated me above even that was my ability to compile big scores. My conversion rate from fifties to hundreds was high, a point Matthew Maynard was always quick to pick up on. And my late-found talent for double hundreds embellished that. I am not sure what to put it down to. But what I do know is that I hated getting out, for whatever score. I was enraged to be wrongly given out caught for 235 at Worksop in 1996. And in whatever match, even a benefit, I might smile and act as if it did not matter, but every time I went to the wicket I put my reputation on the line. I remember my benefit match at Cowbridge in 2001 when I strolled in at number four to face Peter Hardwick, a canny middle-aged left-arm spinner. He immediately brought in a silly point, which riled me. "How dare he?" Second ball I charged down the wicket and missed. Stumped for nought. I laughed, but inside I was seething. I had been outfoxed.

Back at Colwyn Bay in the bar after play, Dr Andrew Hignell, Glamorgan's honorary statistician, informed me that I needed seven more runs to pass Miandad's record of four double hundreds. In fact, there was much talk in the bar that night; a lot of it about records. Emrys Davies' 287 was mentioned but I tried to play down such fanciful talk with lines like, "It only takes one ball and it's all over." Indeed, that is one of cricket's greatest truisms, but deep down I realised that I might never again have such a good chance of breaking that record. The previous year I had ended the second day on 172 not out, but I was shattered. There was little left in the fuel tank. But now I felt okay. I was tired, naturally, and had experienced some cramps in my hands and forearms while batting. I usually did during longer knocks; I had to grip the bat uncommonly tightly in order to achieve any semblance of normal control over it, so it is not surprising that I suffered so. I learnt much over the years about hydration, most notably from our first proper fitness adviser at Glamorgan – a former St. Helens rugby league player, Andy Harrison, whose early morning urine tests provided some stark evidence. One player was so dehydrated that were he in hospital, he would have immediately been placed on a drip.

His tests revealed that the cricketers' staple fluid intake of a few pints of beer after play, then tea or coffee for breakfast spelt dehydration of the highest order. Yellow urine became the enemy. So I knew that I had to rehydrate quickly and plentifully. A mineral replacement drink helped, too. And off I went for an Italian meal with Adrian Dale, with all sorts of thoughts buzzing around inside my head. It is difficult to switch off when you have been batting all day. Indeed, sleep can be very elusive in such circumstances. Berry captured this cleverly at the beginning of his article.

It is one of the misapprehensions of cricket. Umpires are assumed to be merry innkeeper types, Falstaffian figures, whereas they have as many anxieties as the rest of us. In the same way, after a batsman has played a very long innings, the consensus is: 'he'll sleep like a baby tonight!' The reality is different, less cosy. We underestimate the effort involved if we assume that batsmen enjoy a good night's rest while they bat. Long innings are played partly in the mind, and there they stay during the early hours, animating the author of them, making him toss and turn, while his supporters sleep.

I did drift off to sleep, almost immediately, though not as quickly as Dale, who is often snoring within seconds of his head touching the pillow. But I soon awoke with violent cramps, not just in my arms but in my calves and hamstrings too. I thought of what I had done that day and of what might be in store the next. What the papers might think of my innings. Surely they would make much of the fact that I had not been dismissed at

Colwyn Bay for nearing 18 hours. What adjectives would they use to describe me? That always fascinated me, sometimes even enticing me to attempt to play as described – say phlegmatically, or studiously, or even fluently. *The Daily Telegraph* Fantasy Cricket once described me as cherubic. That made me laugh. I'm not sure I could play like that!

This cocktail of physical pain and mental oscillation continued for much of the night, with the result that I awoke the following morning tired. Not grumpily tired though, but pleasurably and contently tired. I sat near Steve Watkin and his wife Caryl at breakfast. "Make sure you have the same thing as yesterday," said Mrs. Watkin. Muesli with yoghurt on top then. And then, in a surprising flouting of superstition, some of my beloved poached eggs on toast as well. Either I was subconsciously preparing for extra work or was conceding that it did not matter if I was dismissed early. After all, 193 is not bad, is it? On the way to the ground I picked up a message on my mobile phone from Alan Jones, congratulating me on breaking his record, but also ending with the words "300 is not far away." I began to feel nervous. There was a burden of expectation, which seemed to border on presumption, hanging over my head. I needed a good start to the day to ease my nerves. James Kirtley provided it with a juicy leg stump half volley which I clipped for four.

Now he felt better able to support the weight of expectation from crowd, team-mates and watching parents, and to go on to something special. When non-striker he allowed himself to think about the milestones. When taking strike he continued to bat in normal Jamesian mode, battering the blockhole, fidgeting that front foot forwards, hustling that first run until it was wiser to conserve his resources. He even brought out his slog-sweep for a rare change when Umer Rashid left deep mid-wicket open, wrote the ever-perceptive Berry. I wonder if one day he will describe a young batsman as "angular to the point of Jamesian."

I do like his description of my style though, hammering my bat into the crease (there used to be huge craters on the Lydney outfield where we used to play as kids when the men had finished, as well as on my home lawn from this) and pressing forward. I can hear David Lloyd on *Sky Sports* saying: "There's a lot of movement." Indeed there was. And there continued to be on that August 23rd. It is funny how one's attitude can change during a career. When I was young, records and milestones meant nothing. To Hugh Morris they meant everything, a justification of his very existence as a cricketer. His obsession with pounding a remorseless path into the Glamorgan record books used to puzzle me. But here I was, blissfully alert to every passing milestone; Miandad's number of double centuries, my own personal best, then the clip to fine leg off Will House (the part-timers were on by then) to pass Davies' 61-year-old record and finally the nudge to short third man (it had to be, didn't it?) off left-arm spinner Rashid for the 300.

There was a moment of humour on 296 when I glanced towards the scoreboard to see one of the operators climbing a ladder with a number three at the ready to indicate 300. Talk about tempting fate. I cursed him inwardly and the Sussex fielders picked up on his presumption, chirping me for the first time in the whole innings. I hit a full-blooded drive, which was brilliantly stopped, and, for a moment, I thought maybe I was not fated to reach the magical figure. I actually laughed. A nervous laugh, though. Ever heard of the nervous 290s?

The milestone was greeted by my usual understated, courteous celebration; off with the helmet, a wave of the bat to the dressing room and then to the four corners of the ground. Nothing too ostentatious; no kissing of the daffodil on the helmet; no leaping around. That was never my style. It is not in my character. Only once did I receive the crowd's applause for a hundred with an exaggerated reaction. It was at Hartlepool in

1994. I had been left out of the side for a couple of weeks by captain Hugh Morris and had received a late call-up for the Sunday League clash to cover for Matthew Maynard, who had a neck injury. I made the long journey to the north-east only to find that Maynard was okay. Morris sportingly left himself out of the side in order to let me play, but still, when I passed the 100 mark, I indulged in a puerile display of air-punching and arm-waving. It was a petty demonstration of my indignation at being dropped.

I reflected on this as I travelled all the way to Sittingbourne in Kent that night to play in a second eleven match, and I felt embarrassed. Morris is essentially a good man and did not deserve such petulance. I was not in the side, because I was not scoring enough runs; as simple as that. I had never stooped to such publicly childish behaviour again. Call me over-sensitive, but it was this boorishness that first came to mind when, in early 2003, I discovered that Morris, at the age of 39, was suffering from throat cancer. Any guilt was soon overtaken by shock though, and, as captain, I made a point of keeping in regular contact with him and reminding him that the thoughts of everyone at Glamorgan were with him. For they were. Thankfully, an early diagnosis and a course of radiotherapy seem to have zapped the disease and Morris has returned to work. Equally as shocking was the tragic news in 2002 that Rashid had drowned in an accident in Grenada during Sussex's pre-season tour there. I might have been overjoyed to reach 300 but the man whom I reached it off is no longer with us. That's perspective for you.

But there was none on the evening of August 23rd. Inevitably there was much media interest in my achievement; the BBC even dispatched a satellite van to the ground to do a live interview, and the freelance journalists on the ground had a field day as the many newspapers who did not have reporters covering the game frantically sought them. Again I was awake for most of the night. Indeed I did not sleep properly for a week afterwards. But it was an odd experience, different from the previous night even, in between the inevitable cramps, reliving the day and its vast glories. I still do not know why Matthew Maynard did not declare once I had reached 300. Glamorgan had already passed 700, so I could see no reason to continue. But he did briefly.

I finished on 309, which immediately brought jokes from my team mates that Peugeot would soon be on the phone to offer me one of their cars bearing that number. Unsurprisingly, they did not ring. But at least I had something a little different to add to the much-deliberated design of my benefit tie: 309 emblazoned above a heraldic crest containing the three lions and crown of England; the daffodil of Glamorgan; the blue lion of Cambridge; and a simple SPJ.

The Colwyn Bay game, which we won after two-and-a-half days of hard labour in the field, was to be followed by a day spent travelling to Derby for a Sunday League match. The week before, I had asked captain Maynard if I might dash off on the Friday in order to accept the *Sunday Telegraph's* offer of a place on their table at the Cricket Writers' annual bash in London, and then a spot of reporting at the Benson & Hedges Cup Final between Glouc-estershire and Warwickshire the following day. He seemed a little reluctant to consent, and only did so with a corollary warning "Make sure you get a hundred first". I think I earned my supper that Friday evening.

There was one message of congratulation that stood out among many which arrived. It came from Peter Davies, son of Emrys.

Guildford, Surrey.

Dear Steve,

I have just seen on Ceefax that you have passed the 287 scored by my father, Emrys, against Gloucestershire in 1939. I was then 8 years old and, frankly, I don't remember it at all. But I have spent the following 61 years rather proud of that record of his.

He would have approved warmly that, if it was to be beaten, it should be by a home-grown (sic) opening bat. I am sure it is on his behalf as well as mine that I say "Very well done" to you.

He was at his playing peak in 1939. He was chosen to tour India with MCC that year, but the outbreak of war prevented them from going. Unlike him, you have had the distinction of wearing the England cap, and many of us Glamorgan exiles hope there are more to come.

One other record of his may give you a further ambition. I was at the Arms Park, when the tannoy system played "Happy Birthday" as he walked out to bat on his 50th birthday – and duly scored another half century!

Yours sincerely,
Peter Davies.

Unfortunately I was unable to even make my 36th birthday as a player, but I hope one day to be able to send such a message myself. It may be a little late in his career now for Matthew Maynard, and only Mike Powell of the current crop of young Glamorgan batsmen has so far shown anywhere near the necessary penchant for big scores, but he and the others can be heartened by my late development in that department. My record will be broken one day, but if it is not in my lifetime then I am sure that Bethan will gladly oblige with the felicitations.

CHAPTER TEN

CAPTEN MORGANNWG

C apten Morgannwg. Who would have thought it? I certainly didn't. Indeed, I reckon that if Tony Cottey had not left the club in 1998 to join Sussex, I would never have led Glamorgan. Cottey had been Matthew Maynard's vice-captain – and a very good one, too – but was tempted by the seductive praise of Chris Adams and the promise of a five-year contract down at Hove. The threat of his departure caused ructions at Glamorgan, but as a mere foot soldier, not privy to the high-level discussions and negotiations at the time, I am not able to pass detailed judgement on what I consider to have been a most regrettable episode.

What I do know is that late in the season of 1992, myself, Cottey and Adrian Dale were all capped together; not at tea during a county game, as is customary, but at the St. Helens Balconiers end-of-season do at the Dolphin Hotel in Swansea. This was a slightly unsatisfactory arrangement, foisted upon us by rain that day. The receiving of a county cap is a momentous occasion for any professional cricketer. It means that you belong. It also means the following, in differing order of importance for differently motivated people:

1. That you have produced enough suitably noteworthy performances to be considered a first-team regular and that you

might even be given the option of opting out of a game against one of the universities.

2. A noticeable hike in salary.

3. A guaranteed sponsored car. Well, it is supposed to, but at the beginning of the 1993 season the upshot of not having won a trophy for 24 years was that the marketing department was struggling to find suitable deals for vehicles, so Adrian Dale and I had the use of a Vauxhall Astra and the team kit van between us. The van was so large that the neighbours were seriously considering reporting me to the council environmental department for obstruction and light deprivation. Finally, Paul Russell, now Glamorgan's chairman, came to the rescue with a sleek Audi number.

4. The start of an illustrious career, which you hope might lead to (a) an England cap (and another hike in salary) and/or (b) a lucrative benefit in ten years' time.

I can only presume that the powers that be at the time did not think that all of us would reach 4b). If you consider that Robert Croft had also been capped earlier that season then you can imagine the problems that were engendered later on when all four of us became integral members of the successful Glamorgan side of the nineties.

This was the crux of Cottey's argument in 1998. He wanted to know some sort of pecking order for the awarding of benefits. It is a ticklish issue, because benefits can never be guaranteed, certainly never mentioned in a contract, due to the ever-inquisitive eye of the taxman, who decrees that they can remain tax-free. Clearly, Croft would come first, but Cottey was told that nothing further was cast in stone. He asked for a three-year contract, rather than the two-year deal he and Dale had been offered, and which Dale had signed. Glamorgan would not budge, although it was rumoured that there was a last-minute verbal promise that, whatever happened, there would be some place at Glamorgan for Cottey in that third year. Cottey had a well-earned reputation amongst the players for swift, abrupt changes of mind, but now, when we most wanted him to think again, he did not. My sadness at his departure, deepened by the news that a close colleague had advised him to leave, was captured in my *South Wales Argus* column.

Tony Cottey is a Glamorgan man through and through. Nobody can ever have worn the daffodil on his chest more proudly than 'the little man with the big heart' – a sporting cliché if ever there was one, but so fitting for this man. Guts and determination oozed from every pore every time he walked out to bat for Glamorgan, often in a crisis after more celebrated figures at the top of the order had failed.

It was apt that he should be the man to hit the winning runs in 1993 to clinch the Sunday League and end Glamorgan's barren spell stretching back to 1969. With his usual wit, he described that hit as 'a straight drive over the keeper's head'. He even forgot to grab a stump as a memento but the sight of him charging off the field, fists clenched, with the great man, Viv Richards, will remain with us all forever. Representative honours have somehow passed him by, except for selection for a TCCB XI against Young Australia in 1996. Surely he deserved an A tour at least, and I know he was quite close that year – Mike Atherton said he had been extensively mentioned at selection.

Most of all, though, he was THE MAN in the dressing room. When people talk about the great team spirit we have at Glamorgan they should remember it mostly stems from Tony Cottey – he is the life and soul of the party whether things are going well or not.

I consider him a good friend. I have known him since 1985 when we got off on slightly the wrong footing because I took his place for my second eleven debut at Usk. Since then, though, he has forgiven the snooty schoolboy from Monmouth and we have got on famously.

Life will not be the same next year.

He should not have left. Both he and Glamorgan were equally

culpable. And he has mostly regretted his decision, spending four fruitless seasons on the south coast until an incredible spurt of form in 2003 and a second Championship winning medal brought belated fulfilment. And there can be little doubt that he got his sums wrong. Despite the guarantee of a basic salary well above that which Glamorgan were willing to pay, he would have been much better off staying at home. He would have got a benefit. Probably before mine. And he would have been captain. As it was, Matthew Maynard telephoned me and asked me to be vice-captain. Naturally, I accepted, but just as I had been to Nick Knight in Sri Lanka, I was a poor deputy. Good deputies are always full of ideas, ever eager to be involved, ever speaking at team meetings. I was not. I was too concerned with my own game. Not that I think it would have made any great difference to Maynard's captaincy. Whilst it would be harsh to say that his successful brand of leadership was based on autocracy, especially given my earlier observations on his being easily led (off the field, that is), his strong, dominant personality meant he usually wanted to do things on his own as captain. Even Cottey became frustrated at times because of Maynard's unwillingness to act on his multitude of suggestions.

Only once can I recall changing Maynard's mind for him – at Canterbury, in 2000, for a NatWest Trophy match. The pitch was damp and green, and the weather overcast, but the skipper had this wacky idea of batting first. Everyone else in the side disagreed, so I put this to him. I found it humorous that he should declare, like some American President "We live in a democratic society" when quite often we did not. Not that we necessarily should have done. "Captaincy by committee on or off the field is lamentable," are words I recall once reading somewhere (in fact, they were written by A.E. Knight in a treatise called 'The Complete Cricketer' in 1906) and have been oft-repeated since. But Maynard did not captain by committee.

He stepped down at the end of the 2000 season. He had been

tempted to do so a year earlier, but a boozy trip to Ireland had revealed that all the players wanted him to continue. I certainly did. But he was becoming increasingly weary with the off-field commitments of the job, especially his dealings with the cricket committee, which never seemed to be particularly cordial or concordant. He was instrumental in bringing in the Australian coach Jeff 'call me Bomber' Hammond to toughen up attitudes, especially those of the younger players. "We've tried the other way with them, let's see how this goes," were Maynard's words to me as regards the young, maverick talents, such as Alun Evans and Wayne Law.

Unfortunately, I do not think that enough research was done on Hammond. A BBC Wales reporter asked the chairman of Eastern Province, his previous employer, about him. "Do you want me to say what the Welsh public will want to hear, or the truth?" he cautioned. So alarm bells should have been ringing. In fairness, the impressive presentation he made upon his arrival, outlining his methods, to which he invited not only players but the whole staff (administration, marketing and ground) and even the media, demonstrated his persuasiveness. And he announced his 'tough' tactics by taking us into the Brecon Beacons for a couple of army training days, spending the night on a concrete floor in a hut without lights or heating, arising at 6am to perform aerobics in the snow. I am not generally a fan of these 'team building' exercises, especially at Glamorgan where there is a natural togetherness anyway, but I became even less so when I only narrowly avoided death on the car journey home.

Keith Newell may be known for his rather laid-back nature but the rigours of an assault course on top of a sleepless night had left even the most resilient of us drained. So, as I rather selfishly dozed off in the back seat, I was suddenly awoken by Mike Powell in the front passenger seat, screaming "Newelly!" There was a thud as we hit the central reservation of the A470 near Pontypridd. Newell had fallen asleep at the wheel but, thankfully, Powell had been resisting his slumber sufficiently to have noticed. It was not soon enough to avoid considerable damage to the wing of the car but soon enough to allow Newell to regain some semblance of control, and, miraculously, we bounced back into the outside lane, all of us uninjured.

I have already mentioned Hammond's early, undiplomatic coaching tips but he also introduced some bizarre warm-up drills, which soon raised eyebrows. He was fond of us hitting golf balls up and down on the edge of our cricket bats. Apparently the Australian Test team does this but he never explained why we were doing it. There was also a fielding exercise called the 'triangle', which involved running at balls hurled at you as hard as possible. This was anathema to any ball player reared on the importance of the 'sympathy' of a pass. A startled Steve Watkin dislocated a finger for the first time ever in its first outing. The sheer length of his sessions – warm-ups were taking over an hour – was wearing, as were his idiosyncratic sayings. "More heat, more heat," he would exclaim as we did the 'triangle'. And he was forever exhorting me to "tuck your wings in", which I found to mean that I should not release my hands too far away from my body in my pick up. He also bemoaned what he described as 'the Glamorgan way' of batsmen tapping the bat between their feet in their stance. One innovation of his that I did like was the increase in intensity he brought to indoor net sessions by making two batsmen (as opposed to the usual one, who normally bats on his own) run as if they were in the middle of a one-day innings. It is a simple idea, but one rarely used.

Sadly, it took just one Championship match for Hammond to irretrievably lose the respect of the team. The match in question was at Worcester – a rain-affected affair in which we did not bat – and Hammond, who had already displayed his unquenchable thirst for the amber nectar at Watkin's stag night, apparently over-indulged a little during one of the long evenings. While we were bowling the next day, one of the players had to nip off the field to relieve himself, only to find Hammond fast asleep on one of the wooden benches in the lovely old pavilion. Astonishment and disbelief might well have turned mutinous if Maynard had not shown strong leadership by speaking starkly to Hammond and then addressing the players in his absence.

So when, half-way through that season, Maynard called me aside to inform me that he was giving up the captaincy, I understood what he meant when he said "and he hasn't helped" gesturing at Hammond, while explaining his disillusion with the job he had done so well for five years. I wasn't sure if I wanted to do it. "You'll be captain of this club one day," Duncan Fletcher had once told me, "but make sure that you have done everything you want to in the game before you do." I wonder whether he said the same thing to Michael Vaughan?

Croft was making no secret of his desire to take over. He had once told me how much he wanted it when he generously invited me and Maynard, complete with families, to stay at his house on the hill overlooking Hendy, near Pontardulais. "I want to do it to see if my ideas and methods can work," he told me as I declared limited interest in a job that I considered to be a burden. The coveting of it flummoxed me, because of its hassles and unusually high level of responsibility. "I can't believe how much responsibility you've got," Wales' rugby captain Rob Howley later remarked to me.

It is no state secret that Croft and I did not always have the smoothest of relationships in my time at Glamorgan, punctuated by a small number of disagreements. Mind you, minor disputes are inevitable within a county dressing room. For six months of the year, players from differing backgrounds and differing outlooks on life are thrown together, living in each others' pockets and seeing much more of each other than their families. And in between times myself and Croft have been friendly, but any dispute between us has usually centred around the fact that we are very different characters. Croft is extroverted, a naturally loud and attention-seeking comic. I am introverted, quiet, shy, and generally lacking the confidence to be the showman.

He is an excellent cricketer, who has achieved much more in the international game than me, but I reckon that even he might agree with my contention that he is not now the attacking off-spinner he was in his early days. Years of one-day cricket and unresponsive county pitches, which have often seen him used as a stock bowler, have rendered him flatter and quicker than he would like. Not that he has been idle in attempting to rectify that, nor in attempting a number of variations (including the so-called 'statue' ball where he pauses in his action) in a bid to pacify the constant clamour that finger spinners need something different, something mysterious in their armoury. The 2003 season was one of his most successful for some time in first-class cricket and it amazed me that Gareth Batty of Worcestershire – so palpably an inferior cricketer – can have initially been chosen ahead of him for England, especially given Croft's exceptional record overseas. But of greater wonderment to me is how he has not figured more in England's recent one-day plans, as he has comfortably been the best one-day spinning all-rounder during my career.

Immobile fielding has been cited as one reason why he has been overlooked. Indeed, Alec Stewart's comment to fitness trainer Dean Riddle during my Test debut was telling. "You've got to sharpen up the Daffodil," I overheard him say, after Croft had been slow to react at mid-on. But Croft has recognised the importance of physical fitness, training manically during the winters, rediscovering the motivation to stick rigidly to a lung-bursting treadmill programme, alternating minute intervals between 17 and 14 kilometres per hour, which, for those uninitiated in the rigours of a gym running machine, is swift going. As a youngster he was slim and fit but not quite so svelte during his middle cricketing years, despite always showing a dedicated work ethic to his bowling.

Unfortunately, his batting has not always received the same sort of attention, which is a shame because he has enormous talent. He should have been batting at number six for Glamorgan in first-class cricket throughout his career. But, for a number of reasons, he has not. His first-class output has improved dramatically in recent years and he has at last made a consistent success of the pinch-hitter's role at the top of the order in one-day cricket, but the suspicion still exists amongst opponents that he does not 'fancy' it, substantiated by a liberal peppering with the short ball whenever he arrives at the crease. Some have said that he lacks courage when batting, but in my view that is always a dangerous criticism to level at anyone. Ask Mike Atherton about his comments on Steve Waugh in 1994.

"The one who really got up my nose was Steve Waugh, who spent the entire series giving out verbals – a bit of a joke when he was the one bloke wetting himself against the quick bowlers." So the man who is second in the all-time list of Test match run scorers can't play the short stuff? Whoops, Athers.

More often than not, poor technique is construed as cowardice. Mike Kasprowicz does not play the short ball terribly well, turning his head away and punching a glove hopefully at it, very much as Steve Watkin used to, but I would wager much that neither of those two beanpoles is scared. Neither is Croft, and his sometime inadequacies have thus been misconstrued. He was determined to remedy them, and spent many hours on the motorway travelling to see Graham Gooch to work on his technique. And when we shared a room together on an England fitness week in Lanzarote he alone took his bat with him in order to arise before the rest of us to do his work with Gooch. There is no doubt that his technique has improved, despite an exaggerated initial backward movement which still remains, and has certainly moved on from 1997 when Glenn McGrath, having fed Croft a leg stump half volley, loudly berated himself. "What am I doing? All I've got to do is hit him on the head." That might not prove so easy nowadays.

When Maynard pushed Croft up the order to pinch-hit in one-day cricket in 2000, I was unhappy. I wanted to open and felt that I was the right man to do so. I telephoned Maynard to tell him that I thought that Croft was incapable of making a one-day hundred – not necessarily a prerequisite for the role, but something Maynard said he was hoping for. So now that Croft has achieved that milestone (four times) I am happy to hold my hand up and admit my error of judgement. But I can still remember the pain I felt when Croft and Matthew Elliott walked out to tumultuous applause at Lord's in the Benson & Hedges Cup Final that year. I thought I should have been doing that and, for all the magnificent atmosphere of that day and Maynard's subliminal hundred, it is not an occasion I will ever recall with any great fondness. I felt, at that stage, I should have been higher up the order, something Maynard validated later in the season by promoting me to number three.

It took me a while, but eventually I came to recognise that, later in my career, I was best suited to a middle order slot in one-day cricket as the game changed and maximum use of the first fifteen overs became crucial. I realised that I was useful in the less entertaining middle overs between 15 and 40, when running between the wickets and strike rotation are key. And, in due course, I came to learn how to finish games, how to absorb pressure and see the team home in tight situations. It took a while, mind, and I can only truly say that I first felt totally confident doing it in 2002 when Glamorgan won the National League Division One title.

The days of an opener dropping anchor and trying to bat through the innings in one-day cricket are gone – unless, of course, the pitch is offering lavish assistance to the bowlers. I know that the old-fashioned critics will say that the best players can still score quickly, with the fielding restrictions as they are, by playing 'proper' cricket shots, but I still think risks need to be taken – calculated ones, but risks nonetheless, like hitting over the top and running down the wicket. For that reason, I do not think that someone like me, or, for that matter, Mike Atherton (despite his protestations to the contrary) would fit this bill. In fact, I can recall a one-day game as long ago as 1993 when one of the Glamorgan players remarked that it was a shame that we had not kept Atherton in longer after a stodgy half century. Mind you, I should take much of the responsibility for his turgidity that day, having persuaded him to take more than the odd glass of wine with me the previous evening. I had injured my thumb very early in the construction of an equally turgid and fortunate century (at least it was a four-day game) the previous day and had no chance of playing in the Sunday match. "You brave bastard," was Atherton's response when I revealed the thumb was broken. But even 'Iron Mike' was looking a little jaded that grey Manchester day.

Croft and I have never fallen out about pinch-hitting but we have over other issues. The first came very early in our careers, in 1992, at Chelmsford, when I, somewhat childishly on reflection, became incensed with some of his unrelenting teasing. At the time, it was being stressed that the whole team make sufficient effort to encourage the bowlers in the field; no problem for the garrulous Croft but awkward for me, as it was throughout my career, resulting in my uttering asinine stuff like, "Let's get one." Croft picked up on my unease, as well as my unoriginality, to remorselessly mimic this until I snapped, "I'll see you after". Still he continued. "I'm going to f**king have you after," I barked. I didn't, of course. I've never 'had' anyone – just witness my shunning of the physical stuff at rugby. But in later years cries of "Let's get one" in the field, often from a mischievously giggling Croft, always produced a wry smile from the both of us. There is something about Croft and Chelmsford. There was a famous spat between him and Mark Illott during the NatWest Trophy semi-final of 1997. Then, in 1998, skipper Maynard felt the need to take him aside there at the end of the four-day game to speak to him about his attitude. Even his great mate Cottey had become concerned about his surly introspection, which sometimes led to an indifference to his team mates. Maynard spoke to a couple of senior players, including myself, and it was agreed that Croft should be spoken to. He was enduring a difficult period with England, which had begun with the Australians handing him that very public dissection of his batting technique against the short ball, and was being heavily criticised in the media; but that was no reason to be taking it out on his team mates.

But I know, even from my brief flirtation with international cricket, how difficult it might be to deal with the baleful intrusions of the press and public, even if I never suffered the same level of scrutiny as Croft. And anyway, I had been united in discontent with Croft in 1994 when we found ourselves sharing a room in London for a second team game after being dropped from the first team by Hugh Morris – me for Alistair Dalton, and Croft for Stuart Phelps. Neither exactly became a household name. This was a low point for both of us, and lamentation and incredulity raged within our room. In retrospect it did us both good, with second team coach John Derrick offering the sagest of advice to us two moaners. "Just get out there and prove yourself on the field." We did.

Cottey was good for Croft. They were the closest of room mates, sharing the same sense of humour. As I mentioned, they were dubbed the Toilet Twins, and, for a time, were a good stand-up double act. Crucially, Croft would listen to Cottey, and if Croft was out of order, Cottey would tell him so.

Often, being the sole Welsh representative in the England

team (or British Lions, as Croft puts it) brings with it a peculiar and at times heavy burden, but Croft has used his outgoing persona to good effect. There is little doubt that his face is the most recognisable in Welsh cricketing circles, at least before Simon Jones' emergence at Test level. He does not need Cottey nowadays because he has mellowed and matured as a person.

But I did disagree with Croft over his decision not to tour India in the winter of 2001. He and Andrew Caddick declined to travel in the wake of security fears after the events of September 11th. I thought Croft should have gone and told him so. I realise that his mother was not well at the time, but I just felt that once the EWCB had decreed that the tour was on, then Croft should have gone. I made some hasty comments (for which I apologised to Croft) to Delme Parfitt of *Wales On Sunday,* which were sensationalised a little, suggesting that if Croft did get another chance, team spirit might be affected. Whatever, it cost him dear for he was not selected for England again until the Sri Lankan leg of the 2003 winter tour. And I suspect that, while they have vehemently denied it, the selectors had held that refusal against him. Not that Croft should have retired from international cricket, as he did in early 2004. That was also an incorrect decision in my view; no doubt fuelled by indignation at the injustice meted out in Sri Lanka, when he did not feature in any of the internationals. But I had it on pretty good authority that he had a more than even chance of making the subsequent West Indies tour. It was a curious decision of his and I told him so.

I suspect Croft might have been holding something against me in 2000. I may be wrong. It was his benefit year and on his committee was a fellow called Ian Williams. Williams is a life-long Glamorgan supporter whose prematurely greying hair and distinctive gravelly voice had long been a feature of Glamorgan games home and away before I really got to know him at Easter, 1995. We became friends while I was at one of my lowest ebbs – with my leg in plaster after an accident with a glass door in Zimbabwe, having been unthoughtfully informed by captain Hugh Morris that I was not to feature in his plans for the start of the season. Williams proved a patient listener as well as a quenchless imbiber of ale, and his sage counsel found fruition in a career-defining season for me. I scored a Glamorgan Sunday League record number of runs in a season (815) and an eye-opening 230 not out in a day at Leicester, all fuelled by a brooding sense of injustice and a burning desire to prove my worth. My impending benefit year in 2001 was another not inconsiderable factor in my deliberations over whether I wanted to take on the captaincy. Maynard had coped admirably with this twin encumbrance in his first year in charge in 1996 and offered this advice: "I think you can do it, especially with 'Wales' to help you."

'Wales' is the nickname acquired by the aforementioned Williams, a solicitor based in Cardiff but originally from Griffithstown near Pontypool. It originates from an alcohol-fuelled trip to America and Williams' inability to fill in his immigration form, confusing 'Name' with 'Country of birth'. And Maynard was right, because I could not have chosen anyone better equipped to fulfil the onerous, and let it be said, thankless task of benefit chairman. But I never properly asked Croft if it was okay to 'steal' Williams from his committee, causing a good deal of unnecessary friction.

A benefit is a curious year (well, almost two years when one considers all the planning and mopping up afterwards) when cricketer becomes businessman. It was a year that proved extremely profitable – just over £160,000 tax-free – and engendered a strong relationship between myself and Williams, but my reserved persona dictated that I was never entirely comfortable with the modus operandi of the year. I was most appreciative of the exceptional groundswell of support I received, in recognition of my service to Glamorgan, but at times I was embarrassed at what I sometimes perceived as the 'legalised begging' involved.

Public speaking has always scared me rigid, but here I found myself having to do it at every function. I made sure I kept it short and sweet, just a list of thank-yous, really. I could not help but improve after my first embarrassing effort at my launch dinner in the Coal Exchange in Cardiff Bay. I had scribbled down a lengthy list of people to thank but had not thought for one minute that there might be some applause after each of these, the result being me warbling embarrassingly on when no one could hear. And at a lunch at the Reform Club in London, where I hinted, with a glance at the table kindly taken by *The Sunday Telegraph*, that the media might be a preferred future occupation, some inebriated wag shouted, "You'll have to be a bit more eloquent than this." Thankfully, some subsequent expert tuition from Edward Bevan has ensured that, these days, I can make a half-decent fist of being at least a comprehensible summariser on BBC Radio Wales.

I felt awkward at attending some functions where I knew that the people contributing barely had two ha'pennies to rub together, but felt compelled to announce my final figure – as is the norm – as a gesture of thanks to all those generous souls who did support, whether rich or poor. I was humbled by the uncomplaining help given to me by people of differing standings. At one end of the celebrity scale, the legendary Gareth Edwards spoke, gratis, for me at a memorable dinner at Monmouth School; spellbinding an awestruck audience and delighting them with his opening line, "I think I've got an old one of mine in the attic somewhere", after Paul Russell had just donated a remarkable £6,000 for a signed and mounted 2001 British Lions jersey, equally generously supplied by Cardiff's David Young. And Max Boyce, also without asking for a fee, spoke at Cheltenham Racecourse in a joint dinner with Gloucestershire's beneficiary Mike Smith. At the other extreme,

Lloyd Davies, an omnipresent Glamorgan fan who delights in shouting "Let 'im 'ave it" every time an opposition batsman nears the crease, arranged a thoroughly enjoyable race night in the Bridgend Railway Club. All the events were successful and the attendees pleasant, save one chap who told me: "You probably won't do too well today. You're injured, the team's doing poorly, and, of course, you're English."

Croft's influence and help should not be overlooked. His curiosity and persistence had kindled the interest of cricket nut Andrew Jones, of Stephens & George magazines in Merthyr Tydfil, whose offer to print a benefit brochure free of charge extended to me and Adrian Dale the year after. For me the most enjoyable event came at Lydney where I took a star-studded rugby side, including seven internationals in Wales' Mike Rayer, Derwyn Jones, Jonathan Humphreys, Mark Ring, Hemi Taylor and Mark Bennett as well as England's Malcolm Preedy, to take on my former team. Current Cardiff backs coach Geraint John marshalled the backs and a mellowed Andy Booth atoned for his effrontery at Neath with a tackling display bordering on the heroic, aided by the former flanker, Bennett, his fellow brief detainee at Her Majesty's Pleasure after an ugly skirmish with some farmers from Kidwelly during our time at Swansea University. After much pre-match bravado many Glamorgan cricketers showed their true mettle through non-attendance, but of those who did play, Mike Powell displayed an unsurprising physicality, Darren Thomas a clever sleight of hand and foot, David Harrison a know-how one would expect from the son of a former Pontypool back row forward, and Adrian Dale, despite his jocular protestations to the contrary, irrefutable evidence that he is not the Jonah Lomu presence on the left wing he imagines himself to be. Even Williams was offered the opportunity to prove that he was once a decent flanker for Panteg RFC. As for me, I did score the first try of the evening – not the gimme some thought it to be, but rather the product of some electric running from Simon Morris, an old team mate at Lydney; and I did fervently ensure that a one-on-one with my old mucker Adrian Knox did not result in a try.

After due deliberation I had decided to announce to the club that I wanted to be considered for the post of captain, not from any fervent desire to lead but because I thought that I was the best man at the time. I had thought that it boiled down to a straight choice between myself and Croft, but, surprisingly in my view, Dale became a late contender, mainly, it would seem, at the behest of coach Hammond. He was wary of both Croft and me, having especially noted my aversion to many of his methods. That left Dale, who had had an exceptional summer and who got on with Hammond better than most. But, clearly Hammond did not get his way, and in October I received a phone call, while on holiday, to say that I was to be captain of Glamorgan. 'Capten Morgannwg', as my wife, Jane, kept telling me. Not quite the 'Capten Cymru' to which every Welsh rugby player aspires, but nonetheless a most weighty honour. There was no communication from Hammond. And the messages I left for Croft remained unanswered.

I immediately informed Mike Fatkin, the club's chief executive and Ricky Needham, the chairman of the cricket committee, that I did not want Hammond as coach. I did not feel that I could work with him, and there was little doubt that he had 'lost' the team. I was told I had no choice. He was on a two-year contract and they could not afford to pay him off. Next was my choice of vice- captain. It was a delicate decision. I sought the advice of former Wales rugby captains, Gwyn Jones and Mike Hall. Hall cautioned: "You've got to make sure someone like Crofty is involved."

But I interpreted Croft's silence as reluctance and, despite Maynard's assertion that I should not have a vice-captain, and instead just appoint a 'senior pro', I went for Dale. I felt I needed a close ally in what was already shaping up to be a difficult period. He was then my closest friend in the game, someone upon whom I knew I could rely, and someone who had similar views on cricket. If Croft had been more forthcoming, I might well have appointed him vice-captain. That would have been the correct decision for the team, as was later proved by the events of 2002. Maybe I should have been more decisive in my attempts to contact him. But when I eventually did so, he sullenly refused my invitation for him to join the Duncan Fletcher-style management team I was planning, saying that he just wanted to do his own thing. I was a little miffed that Dale found out from the chairman of the club before I told him of his elevation personally, but that was just an early indication of the frequent leaks in communication that are bound to affect the archaic machinations of a committee-based system (thankfully now streamlined at Glamorgan). At least I never experienced the same committee intransigence of which some of my predecessors complained – in fact, most of my dealings were remarkably straightforward and amicable – but there were numerous examples of supposedly confidential information being leaked. Often, I worried that I was a prime suspect given my media interests, but soon came to discover that one local paper had access to an obliging mole.

It would not be an exaggeration to say that my captaincy tenure was jinxed. Prior to 2001, I had had no knee problems – aside from the accident in Zimbabwe, which affected my right knee and was merely a deep cut that partially severed the patella tendon. But suddenly, early in the New Year, I felt a twinge while doing some routine shuttle runs. I soon ran it off and thought nothing more of it – until a month later, while performing a weekly SAQ (speed, agility, quickness) session with Andy Harrison, I felt a much sharper sensation in the same area. Within an hour, I could not walk. I had torn my medial meniscus and was operated upon the next day. At that stage, there was no threat of my missing the start of the season. But not long after we had reported back for pre-season training, my rehabilitation ground to a halt when I felt the same sensation again. Another arthroscopy meant that I was to miss the two opening Championship matches. Dale was in charge.

Hammond had been amazed when I told him how the players felt about him. Bravely he stood up in front of them and admitted his folly of the previous year. But I think I tried a little too hard to stamp my authority and introduce some new ideas, drawing on some quotes from England rugby flanker Neil Back to attempt to motivate the troops, and asking club president Tony Lewis to speak to them before presenting them with their new 'baggy blue' caps. Apparently my comments about alcohol intake caused consternation. I had merely said that I would not stand for any repeat of an incident the previous year at Bristol, where a ferocious thunderstorm, which flooded the ground, had triggered excessive drinking on a grand scale by some players. It's called taking the 'gamble' in cricket, whereby one is hoping that bad weather will ensure no play the next day. The Bristol ground was bone dry the next morning. Defeat, naturally, ensued. A heavy one.

Bristol again proved to be eventful in 2001. I had returned to the side for the Benson & Hedges Cup campaign, mindful of there being a less-than-harmonious atmosphere. Maynard was struggling to come to terms with being in the ranks, especially if he disagreed with any plan or philosophy. I found his contradictions to myself, Dale or Hammond during team meetings difficult to handle, so I went to his room and assured him that, while I valued his opinions highly, I would much rather that he voiced any problems to me in private.

The next day was to change my career. I was batting well in partnership with a rampant Jimmy Maher when I attempted to pull a shortish ball from Gloucestershire's swing bowler, Jonathan Lewis. I only succeeded in inside-edging it on to the inside of my left knee. For a moment, there was nothing more than mild discomfort. Then, suddenly, agony. And I mean agony. I was writhing on the floor, hyperventilating, close to fainting through pain. I was led off, limping. A bruised knee was diagnosed, but the reality was much more damaging. From then on, my knee swelled up every time I exercised vigorously. It was initially thought that it was a result of my two cartilage operations, but subsequent specialist advice disagreed and suggested that I might have momentarily dislocated my knee cap that day.

Word came back to me that a number of players were not happy with my choice of vice-captain. It was a divided camp, with a group wanting Croft as the deputy and I felt threatened, insecure in my position. I felt that every decision I made was being questioned. I enforced the follow-on at Essex and felt let down by the reaction, despite Dale's faithful "Let's back up the captain's decision" as we walked out. I always believed in enforcing the follow-on, mainly because I hated it as a batsman. There seems little to play for when you walk out having followed-on. As it was, Essex did pass our score, but I hit a hundred to win the match for us. My over-sensitive nature was tested by my almost voyeuristic addiction to read what supporters were writing on those wonderful new creations – internet message boards. My wife kept telling me that I should not 'beat myself up' by constantly reading what was said, much of which was uncomplimentary. But I did, and there is a particular person named 'Izzie' whom I would like to meet one day, preferably in a dark alley with my 'minder', Mike Powell, alongside me!

As early as the end of July, I was minded to resign the captaincy. I told Williams and he told me not to be hasty, but it was almost a blessed relief when Andy Caddick broke my hand badly at Taunton. It gave me time to consider my position. I went away to the Cotswolds for the weekend with Jane and

Bethan, and had almost resolved to pack it in. While it was an honour, it was surely not worth all the hassle. I have never been a natural leader of men and I was being shown up. In that game at Taunton a young, inexperienced Simon Jones had asked me how I wanted him to bowl at Mark Lathwell; in the team meeting, Maynard had said full and straight, I had favoured the bouncer theory, so my vague "just bowl aggressively" betrayed both my naivety and lack of confidence as a skipper.

So it was with opportune timing that I happened upon a chance conversation (it may well have been initiated by the club's hierarchy, whom, it has to be said, were unstintingly supportive throughout my tenure) with Tony Lewis, during the annual match at Colwyn Bay. He reassured me that I was the man to be captain and drew some surprising parallels with the early years of his tenure, citing characters who were similarly helpful or disruptive. And during that game Hammond announced that he was not returning. His contract would not have been renewed anyway. But I have to say that my relationship with him definitely improved through the year. I certainly respected him a lot more by the end. We spent considerable time together in some fruitful one-on-one batting practices where he continually emphasised the need for patience at the start of my innings and not to 'go too hard at the ball'. And he gave some well-thought-out and timely team speeches. But, sadly, too many were not listening. There were some, notably Adrian Shaw, Alex Wharf and, of course, Dale, who thrived under Hammond, but they were in the minority. It was a shame because he is not a bad man. His heart was in the right place. He just got off to an inauspicious start and never recovered.

My hand mended sufficiently for me to return for the last couple of games of the season. In my absence the side had played some excellent cricket in Division Two of the National League, and my return to fitness coincided with a day/night match at Hove, which would see us lift the trophy if we won. I don't think Hammond was keen for me to play, because Ian Thomas, the chunky left hander from Newport, had done well in my absence, but I asked Dale his thoughts. "If you're fit, you play," he said.

I did, but I didn't score many runs and we lost. I felt like a gatecrasher, and indeed word reached me that some players thought that I should not have played. Because of other results we had won the title before our last match against Middlesex at Cardiff, but I was determined to make a point in that match. I saw my parents before the match and told them to enjoy it because it was going to be my last game as Glamorgan captain. We won, I scored some runs, and I rather sheepishly lifted the trophy – just as I did a year later at Cardiff on the last day of the season when the National League One title had already been won. On that occasion a spectator told me I looked as if I was waiting for a bus as I awaited the presentation. He was right. It applied to both presentations, which I found strange because the moment had passed. As I lifted that first trophy, I was not elated; it was only the Second Division, and there were other divisions occupying my mind. I did though, in a moment of clairvoyance, tell the crowd that I would see them back again the next year when we were Division One champions.

Vacillation ruled my life. To be or not to be captain. That was the question. Reassuring support came from Dale, the club's hierarchy and from most of the more junior players. It would have been easy to have resigned, but in the end I resolved to battle it out. However, I knew some things had to change. First, there was the position of coach. Contact had been made with Jack Birkenshaw of Leicestershire, who might have been a little old but was universally respected, but that soon fell through. My only reservation with John Derrick was his closeness to some of the players, especially the older ones with whom he had played a lot of cricket, and its subsequent effect upon discipline.

But when the club informed me that, for financial reasons, it was felt prudent to look within the club's existing coaching staff, I was not unhappy. In fact, I knew that I could develop a strong working relationship with him. I knew that Derrick had felt a little hamstrung by Maynard's yearning to run his own show during his two previous locum stints in charge, so I was happy to allow him carte blanche in his organisation and running of the team's affairs.

Next came the issue of the vice-captaincy. I had known in my own mind for some time that it had to change if we were to achieve a more cohesive team unity. I also knew that I risked losing the close friendship of Dale. He had done nothing wrong in my eyes. He had been loyally supportive and had led the side well in my protracted absence but, in the end, the well-being of the side had to hold sway. I handled it badly, though. Dale was on a six-week holiday in New Zealand and I could have got hold of a phone number; but I panicked a little when I saw an article in the *Western Mail*, which was about the appointment of Adrian Shaw as second team captain/coach. A statement from the club said that they were sure that John, Steve and Adrian would work well together. This, of course, was referring to the coaching team of John Derrick, Steve Watkin and Adrian Shaw but the reporter, Andrea Morgan, took it to mean John Derrick, Steve James and Adrian Dale. So I fired off this e-mail to Dale.

Arth,

This is probably one of the hardest things I've had to do and I am conscious that I probably shouldn't be doing it via e-mail. I was hoping to wait until you got back, but things are happening apace and I fear that you may hear some other way anyway.

Basically I decided about a week ago that I'm going to ask Crofty to be vice-captain next season.

I know this will be a massive disappointment to you and rightly so. Even though it may seem so, it is no reflection whatsoever on what you did last year. I thought you did a superb job when you filled in and I could have asked for nothing more in terms of support or loyalty.

However, I think you realise how divided the side was and how this very nearly led me to resigning the captaincy.

I do feel that in some quarters it was perceived that you and me are too close and too similar in our cricketing outlooks. This led to some thinking there was a 'them' and 'us' scenario.

I feel that something drastic needs to be done about that and as I have said to you, some way of involving Crofty more needs to be found.

I honestly feel that this is the best way of doing that and of attempting to unite the team, which after all, must be of paramount importance. I know it could be perceived that I am doing this for all the wrong reasons because Crofty did, after all, refuse to be on the management committee last season, and it could be seen that his 'stirring' has achieved something. But that is a cross I will have to bear, and I will take full responsibility if it does go wrong. All I am trying to do is do what is best for the team.

I am planning on having a management team next season and I would, of course, like you to be on it – there is no obligation whatsoever and please feel free to tell me to bugger off if you want, but I do feel that your input will be most valuable.

I do hope that once you have overcome your understandable disappointment that this will in no way affect our friendship. You know that I will do whatever possible to help your benefit. And I also hope that I can count on your support next season.

Please give me a ring if you want to discuss it further. I really did want to wait until you got back and do this face to face. You may well ask why I did not decide before you went – but I was still waiting for the coach situation to be resolved as I felt I needed to discuss it with him first.

That is not to say that JD was against you – he basically said that it was up to me but I had to do what was best for the whole team. He sensed there was a divided camp last year and that needed to be

rectified immediately. Hope this hasn't spoiled your holiday.
  Jamer

I'm sure it did spoil his holiday; indeed I think it spoiled his whole season. Not only that, I think it spoiled our friendship, for that has never been the same since. It is not that we are unfriendly towards each other, just that there seems to be an awkward edge to some of our conversations. We do not see each other socially so much, and I never feel as relaxed as I once was in his company. We grew up together as cricketers, our careers following remarkably similar paths. We began in the old Three Counties League, where fate should spookily decree that we should share the record for the youngest centurion to the exact day – we were both 16 years and 297 days old when I scored a hundred for Lydney against Cirencester in 1984 and he for Chepstow against Corsham in 1985.

We travelled together to games, shared flats, shared hotel rooms, shared bat sponsors, socialised together, practised together, trained together, celebrated together, commiserated together, and even bought houses next door to each other in St. Mellons, Cardiff. So it is no surprise that Dean Conway, in a piece for the 1991 Glamorgan Yearbook on our pre-season tour to Trinidad, should write: "On arrival at our villa, we were allocated rooms; Adrian Dale and Stephen James were in the honeymoon suite, of course." Typical Conway humour, which while not insinuating anything untoward, was merely stating the obvious fact that we were, indeed, inseparable.

While it can never be denied that Dale has been integral part of the Glamorgan success of the past ten years, I personally feel that he has underachieved in his career. I thought that he was going to make much more of it than he has; something with which Alan Butcher certainly concurred when he was selecting Dale ahead of a host of other hopefuls for the first team around 1990. Indeed, after the excellence of his 1993 season and his subsequent selection for the England A tour to South Africa, I was surprised that he did not kick on to full international honours. Mike Atherton mentioned at the time that Dale was the type of cricketer – a top order batsman who bowls – that England were crying out for; someone in the Steve Waugh mould, as Waugh was then, before injuries restricted his bowling. Of that South African tour party, which enjoyed unequivocal success against strong opposition under the captaincy of Hugh Morris, only Dale and Mal Loye, then of Northamptonshire and now of Lancashire, have not won a full England cap.

Dale, like me, has never possessed the most pure or aesthetically pleasing of techniques; he favours the leg side – "you can't bowl there to Arthur Daley" resounds around the dressing room whenever an opposition bowler strays on to his leg stump – with a predominantly bottom-handed grip, resulting in a closed face pick up, which is not as pronounced now as it used to be. But I think the essence of his problem may lie in the conversation I had with Andy Flower in that Harare restaurant. Dale was there, too. I said that my ambition was to play for England. Dale said his was to be a county regular. Maybe he has not set his aims high enough. Maybe he is just more of a realist than some others. Only he will know that, but it has led to a career where he has become known as a 'nuts and bolts' cricketer, the epitome of the honest, hard-working professional. He could have been more. Of course, he has won games for Glamorgan, but more often he has played a secondary role when I think he might have played the major one.

He should have been Glamorgan's number three in first-class cricket throughout his career, but instead has been catapulted up and down the order. It says much about his character and devotion to the team that he has done so uncomplainingly, but I have always believed that you need to bat in the top four for your county in order to achieve England recognition as a batsman. Dale did enjoy significant success in the seasons of 2000 and 2001, winning the player of the year award each year, whilst batting at number five, and has made it clear that he feels that is his best position – resulting in some added angst when he batted higher up with less success in 2002 and 2003.

There had been no frustration, just intense rivalry, when we met in a club match in the early nineties. It is a day I have never been allowed to forget, and with much justification. For Dale got me out that day. Bounced me out. Caught square leg. Might well have been 'done' for pace. I mention it because I was coming on to Dale's bowling. He is a 'dobber'. I can say that now I've made my confession. But he is a mightily effective 'dobber', especially on the low and slow wickets at Sophia Gardens, where he stymies batsmen with his wicket-to-wicket accuracy. Now that he has emigrated to his wife's native New Zealand, he will be a difficult man to replace at Glamorgan. When he looked like missing the start of the 2003 season because of a minor shoulder operation, I suddenly realised how valuable a member of the side he was, especially of the one-day side. Without him we would have had to play either a specialist batsman or a specialist bowler in his place. His absence would have unbalanced the team. It is to be hoped that one of the young brigade of batsmen who can bowl – Ryan Watkins, Jonathan Hughes or Richard Grant – can work sufficiently on their bowling to fill Dale's capable shoes.

Team selection proved one of my biggest problems in my first year. I followed Maynard's example and took sole responsibility on this, albeit with advice from Hammond and Dale. This led to some awkward confrontations, not least with Owen Parkin, who regularly asked for meetings with me and came armed with mountains of figures purporting to validate his claims for a place. One such meeting degenerated into such an ugly stream of expletives from both sides that we might well have come to blows if I had not departed. I faced some difficult decisions regarding Steve Watkin, in his final year and not as penetrative as before. I should have heeded more closely Hammond's recommendation that he only play on "Watty" pitches – in other words, those that afforded seam movement. I did follow Maynard's example of the previous season by leaving Watkin out of the majority of the National League matches, but lacked the courage to deal more forcefully with the general situation.

I found Darren Thomas a difficult player to captain; his waywardness with the ball early in my first year forming the crux of most of Parkin's gripes. But Thomas is a dangerous all-round cricketer – during that period he hit an innings-resuscitating century against Essex – and an excellent fielder to boot. Parkin, now retired, was an honest swing bowler for whom a major back operation rendered that swing less threatening and affected his ability to come back for later spells. Despite full-on commitment, his fielding was ordinary and his batting truly rabbit-like, so more often than not Thomas got the nod.

Matthew Maynard has always described Thomas as "a captain's dream" because of his willingness to bowl long spells, unsurprising given his high level of fitness. Well, for me he may not quite have been the stuff of nightmares, but it has to be said that, now and then, he could cause some disturbance of sleep. Maynard knew how to handle him, but I did not. He rarely took kindly to my suggestions and he was never happy when I wanted him to end a spell of bowling – an admirable stance maybe, but sometimes a bowler has to look at the bigger picture. I became frustrated with his insistence that he always had to bowl with a deep square leg – not necessarily placed for the miscued hook, but more to protect him when he bowled a bad ball. And, during net sessions, he was always full of advice for other players when I thought he should be concentrating on his own game. So I was relieved in my second year in charge

THIRD MAN TO FATTY'S LEG

that Croft became a conduit between the two of us. He was close to Thomas, understood him better and could reason with him. I could not.

But, having said all that, these were captain/player problems not personal differences. Thomas often amused me during a rain break with his batting impersonations. He thinks he is Brian Lara, and mimics the West Indian excellently. He also does a humorous left-handed version of another batsman at the opposite extreme of the art of batsmanship – me and my idiosyncratic style, top hand well behind the handle, head forever looking down and then up, and then the glide down to third man. And all this preceded by my ridiculously superstitious kicking away of any loose turf or mud around the crease. Don't ask me why. It is something that developed over the years and was incorporated into my routine.

In my second season, I changed my selection procedure to incl-ude Croft – whom I thought was an excellent vice-captain – and John Derrick. I always had the final word, but, tellingly, Croft helped me unite the dressing room, with Maynard, Dale and Darren Thomas all allowed their say in our Fletcher-style management team. Croft's advice on the alcohol issue was good. "Let them have the responsibility. Tell them that if they step out of line, they are letting everyone down – themselves, the team and you as captain." He was always full of suggestions (he has an excellent cricketing brain) and I'd like to think that most of our selections were proved right.

I remember Tony Lewis saying in his book, *Playing Days,* that, as captain, you can never be one of the boys. While I do not believe this to be always so, I was soon to discover in my first year at the helm that there are times when it pays to keep one's distance. Some team-bonding nights became exercises in escape and evasion for me, as disaffected players sought to bend my ear. And the awkwardness of the relationship between disgruntled player and captain was brought home to me when

I found myself travelling with Alex Wharf, whom I had just left out of the side. At the end of the journey, he said to me: "I think that it is best for both of us that we don't travel together." He was right. Not because we were not able to get on (I think we do get on) but just because there were too many pregnant pauses and awkward phone calls to answer (for both us – people were asking him why he wasn't playing) while together. It was better to travel with someone more established in the side.

It will doubtless come as little surprise to learn that I was not the most talkative of leaders. My natural reticence saw to that. As I have said, I am not in favour of too many team talks. 'Only say something if it is really worth saying' was my mantra as captain. And, as an opening batsman, I found it nigh-on impossible to talk before we batted anyway. I was too immersed in my own batting for that. This begs the awkward question of how best to divide personal and team interests. That ugly word 'selfish' rears its head. All cricketers, indeed all professional sportsmen in my view, possess a degree of selfishness. One has to in order to succeed. But in a captain it can be a dangerous quality, which needs to be curbed.

However, I can begrudgingly reveal that I can remember three occasions on which I was selfish as a skipper. First, at Cardiff in 2002 in match against Durham, when the opposition were nine wickets down and nearing the close of play, I bowled Croft when I should have turned to Darren Thomas. Croft was bowling well but the pace of Thomas was what was required to dismiss the number 11. I did not want to bat that evening and let that influence my decision.

In a similar situation at Chelmsford later that season, I did not push hard enough for the final wicket for the same reason. We eventually had one over to face and I decided to go in with night watchman Dean Cosker, ordering him to take all the strike and demoting young Dan Cherry to number three, about which he was rightly unhappy. What's more, Cosker hit his first ball to deep midwicket for what would have been an easy three but we cantered a leisurely two to prompt ferocious abuse from Ronnie Irani and Andy Flower, who chided me for my cowardice. Thirdly, in the final game of 2001 after Surrey had arrogantly batted on when they should have pushed for victory, I declined to bat in our short second innings of 14 overs. I was tired after a couple of benefit events, but, more likely, the reason was that I did not want to face Martin Bicknell. What was most selfish was that Ian Thomas had to bat on a 'pair' and Mark Wallace, also on a 'pair', was next in. I was not proud of myself on any of these occasions, even if, by some perverse psychological logic, I did go on to score centuries in the first two instances.

Overall, my second season as captain was a breeze compared to the first. There was dressing room harmony, with me much more relaxed as a leader. And the side played some good cricket, culminating in lifting the National League Division One title, courtesy of winning all eight away matches. Predictably, I missed the denouement at Canterbury, having broken my little finger in the previous match against Worcestershire, necessitating a double operation on finger and knee to add to the other five performed on my knee during my two-and-a-half-year tenure. This was another Canterbury Tale I could not bear to watch, this time from the dressing room balcony as opposed to on video, as we clinched a last-ball win. Croft allowed me to collect the trophy then, and again the following weekend at Cardiff, when we celebrated despite losing to Warwickshire. I had been heartened beforehand by this e-mail from Tony Lewis, though.

Steve

I have checked on your health with Mike Fatkin. I am sorry you fell apart at the end. If we can nick the Norwich, however, you will be considered to have led a side to the top, and that is always exciting.

I am sorry I cannot be with you at Canterbury. But here is the omen. In 1993 I missed Canterbury because I was on holiday playing golf at St. Andrews. This time I am playing golf at St. Andrews and moving on for a week's golf in Portugal.

In the between years, I stayed at home hoping that we would storm through to victory in September! Fine, except that in 1997, when we won at Taunton, I was in Kent on the Saturday with E.W. Swanton's Arabs, intending to get to Somerset for the final day on Sunday. Too late.

What I am saying is this: my absence always makes victory more likely.

Best of luck,

Tony

It did. And then this missive afterwards;

Steve

Well done! Not only your own performances but the way the side has learned to win a few matches. You do not have a great deal of talent at your disposal and so it is all the more reason for you to feel comfortable with the captaincy. It is even more difficult to be convincing as a captain when you are carrying an injury or a condition that requires deeper medical attention and prolonged recovery.

Tony

Too right it is hard to be convincing when you are injured all the time. But at last I felt comfortable with the job. I had no idea how deep Lewis' 'medical attention' would be, or that I would only have one more match as Glamorgan captain.

CHAPTER ELEVEN

OVER?
IT IS NOW

What a way to go. lbw Cork for 14. April 21, 2003. That was my final innings in first-class cricket, after just two innings of that season. It could not have been scripted worse. For a start, Cork is certainly not the bowler I would have chosen to have taken my wicket for the last time. He may be an excellent cricketer, but, as you may have gathered, he is just not my type of chap. Later that season he attempted to mimic the rather more iconic David Beckham by wearing an Alice band through his hair during a televised match against Gloucestershire. Late in the innings it kept falling into his face as he bowled. I have rarely laughed so much while watching a cricket match. It was ludicrous. I was reminded of my Test debut when I had walked to my car on the second evening after play. Cork was in front of me. "You're nothing but a wannabe," were the words directed at Cork by a chap whom I thought had been partaking a little too heartily in the corporate hospitality. On reflection though, he was pretty perceptive.

The location of Derby speaks for itself – soulless, windy, and cold. Even though it has been spruced up a little, for me it is still a joyless place to play cricket. To add further insult, Derbyshire are the only county against whom I never recorded a first-class century, joining Alan Jones (Surrey), Hugh Morris (Surrey) and Matthew Maynard (Middlesex) in a list of

Glamorgan batsmen with just one county left unconquered. Gilbert Parkhouse's record, as being the only Glamorgan cricketer to achieve that feat, could well stand for ever now with the advent of two divisions. Maynard is sadly running out of time now that Glamorgan and Middlesex are in different sections.

The knee had become progressively worse against Derbyshire. As I had set off for my first run – a clip to square leg – in that final innings, I had felt a sharp pain on the outside of it, causing me to shout "Shit" loudly. Cork probably thought I was having a go at him. "How the f**k did you get that there? That was off middle stump," he moaned in his characteristically theatrical fashion. He thinks every time he hits a batsman on the pads it is out lbw. He does bowl 'wicket to wicket' as the saying goes, but I could hear coming from the Glamorgan dressing room "Oh, for Christ's sake this is not the Cork show" as he began performing again. But I could not move my front leg properly and Cork kept hitting me on the pads. He had snared me leg before many times previously and it was inevitable that he would do so here. It was almost an unfair contest.

Two days later, on April 23, we were scheduled to play Hampshire at Cardiff. I could barely make it down the stairs that morning. I had to use the banister and go down sideways. Could I possibly play first-class cricket in this state? I went to the ground and had some throw downs with coach John Derrick. I barely timed a ball. I was using a new bat, which I blamed for my ineptitude. But deep down I knew differently. I kept deluding myself that it would be okay. Next came a gentle jog around to warm up. I hobbled a lap of the ground. Derrick called me over. "You're not right, are you?" he said.

All I could think was that if I pulled out of this game, it would almost certainly be the end of my career. All the conversations I had had with various surgeons had pointed to the fact that there was little they could do to fully rectify my situation. The problem was that my patella (knee-cap) was rubbing against my femur (thigh bone), all the hyaline cartilage having worn away. I just had to try to manage my knee as best I could. I had done this all winter, scarcely doing any running. All my cardio-vascular training had been confined to the bike and the rowing machine under the excellent guidance of our most recent fitness guru Huw Bevan, the former Bridgend, Swansea and Cardiff hooker, now conditioning coach for the Neath/Swansea Ospreys regional side.

But now it had deteriorated dramatically. I had played in two warm-up matches and, while in no way pain free, it was manageable. I probably should have known that the writing was on the wall when I struggled to beat Derrick (on as a second substitute) to a ball in the outfield in that Derby match. No disrespect to him but, while a talented all-round cricketer (and an underrated coach) he is not the most fleet of foot or the most naturally athletic person around. "It's no good," I said forlornly and walked off the Sophia Gardens outfield for the last time as a player. I immediately saw Professor John Fairclough, who suggested an MRI scan and draining the knee of excess fluid. Within a day it had all returned. Next, he suggested another arthroscopy to clean out the joint in the hope that I might be able to struggle through the season. Four to six weeks is the usual recovery period from such a minor operation. After six weeks, there was still no chance of my running. The knee felt worse rather than better. It was obvious that I was not going to play again that season. It was just a question of what the long-term prognosis was. Fairclough thought that the only alternative was a tibial tubercle transfer – a major operation, which involved moving the knee-cap by literally breaking the tibia. The recovery period was six months.

He thought it best, though, that I sought a second opinion. He sent me to John Newman in Bristol, who had previously advised David Lawrence, the former Gloucestershire and England fast bowler, who had shattered a knee-cap during a Test match in New Zealand. "You've dislocated this patella, haven't you?" he kept saying. "No, not to my knowledge," I replied. "Well, either that or you must have had a nasty blow to it," he retorted, incredulous at the "degeneration around and under the knee-cap" he was witnessing on the MRI scan. That blasted day at Bristol 2001 was the only explanation. I had been writing a diary for *Wisden Cricket Monthly,* which they somewhat humorously altered from 'Dressing Room Diary' to 'Waiting Room Diary'. The entry for June 16 read:

A day I will not forget. I present Mark Wallace with his county cap. I wanted to do that before I resign. Then Glamorgan have their first sighting of Twenty20 cricket. They are disappointing and naïve at times against a Northamptonshire side whose savvy is derived from having already played one match. In the BBC Wales commentary box I was breathless and the players confirm that the evening was like a training session. After the match I tell the team that I am standing down as captain to have the knee operation which I hope will save my career. The surgeons rate my chances at 50-60%. It's an emotional speech but the cheeky Wallace lightens the mood when he asks "Have you got any bats?" I won't be using them for a long while.

Indeed never. Wallace also said to me: "All that training and you're in this state." It was an opinion I knew many were holding. Had my obsession with fitness been my undoing? I don't think so. I think it was my making. "I wouldn't have scored 300 without it," I replied to Wallace. Indeed I do not think that I would have scored the majority of my runs without it. The conversion to weight-training had certainly had a dramatic effect. Maybe I had done too much road running as a youngster. Some of my team mates thought I did too much cycling, which can shorten your hamstrings. Others thought I did too much weight-training and had become too big (if only!). Theories, theories.

Not long afterwards I watched a video of Jonny Wilkinson, the England rugby player. His obsession with training is now legendary. Clearly his performance levels are many, many different planes above mine, but I saw much of me in him and his fanatical training. But I wish I could have been as single-minded as him. My wife will probably tell you that I was anyway. She has had to put up with the crankiness during a day if I have not trained; the unending desire to fit in a training session whatever the circumstances (I even trained on our honeymoon) and the constant narcissistic-like moans of "I think I'm putting on weight." But still I could have been more, I reckon. I wish I could have said 'no' a few more times when peer pressure took me towards an alcoholic haze. People will probably say how boring, as they do about Wilkinson. But what's boring about being a top international sportsman playing in front of thousands of people?

I was an international sportsman briefly. I would have loved to have been so more often. Maybe more so as a rugby player than as a cricketer. I would have needed to have beefed up both my body and my self-belief, but you never know. Imagine singing the national anthem before a rugby international? That must really be something. As I once heard Wilkinson say: "I've got the rest of my life after I finish playing to get pissed." He probably didn't actually say 'pissed' because he is far too polite, but you get my drift. Indeed, some of my Lydney mates once christened me Steve 'Interesting' James after the snooker player Steve Davis. That was manifestation of a dangerous habit we have in this country of fearing to be seen to be trying too hard. Even Wilkinson has fallen foul of this, his obsessive nature resulting in one mischievous journalist asking him prior to the World Cup semi-final against France in 2003 if he was in danger of becoming a basket case. Of course he is not. And hopefully that wonderful success will go a long way to altering people's mind set.

It may seem a fatuous comparison but often when I was playing club cricket at Lydney, I would turn up a little early in order to stretch and warm up. I could hear the titters and caustic comments, mostly from the opposition, but not exclusively confined to them. 'Poser' was the drift. And my training attracted similar comments, even as a professional, to such an extent that, quite often, I preferred to train on my own away from other people who might carp or take the mickey. That actually brings me on to a much wider and serious point. The culture within our club cricket needs to change dramatically if we are to succeed as a national side.

Club cricketers do not practise as a rule. They turn up every Saturday, make all the same mistakes, get pissed, forget about it and then turn up the following week to do exactly the same. Even when I was in Zimbabwe, the norm was for a club side to practise at least twice a week and, if you did not attend those practices, you were not considered for the weekend game. It is the same in South Africa, and, of course, in Australia, where they have an excellent system in which a path exists from the bottom to the top. You could work your way up from fourth grade club cricket all the way up to Test cricket. That is unlikely in this country. The professional game is too divorced from the recreational one. Professionals rarely play club cricket once established in the first team. I did not play for Lydney for the last 10 years of my professional career. My mind set in that respect is actually quite instructive, albeit in a negative sense. I admit that I did not want to play, even when the exhausting county schedule might have allowed. I did not want the hassle because I felt that I was in a no-win situation. If I scored a hundred then people would say "so he should." If I did not, the comment would be: "How has he made it in professional cricket? He's no good." But none of that was on my mind when

I entered the BUPA Hospital in Cardiff on June 27. I think that it is best to refer back to that *Wisden* diary.

July 1, 2003.
After four nights in hospital only now can I write. The surgeons had to break my tibia in order to re-align my patella. But I did not expect a six-inch break. I am in agony.
My addiction to chocolate is fed by my Glamorgan colleagues...

Indeed, coach John Derrick arrived the morning after the operation with two huge boxes of chocolates. The ensuing months were difficult, painful both mentally and physically. I was, of course, extremely fortunate that my wife is a physiotherapist, even if initially, while I spent a couple of weeks bed-ridden, she was little more than a nurse. Every morning before she left for work she would faithfully prepare a flask of coffee and various foods to keep me going throughout the day, as well as plenty of ice to attempt to reduce the grotesque swelling upon my always-elevated left leg. This left me to the writing of this book, which kept me busy, issuing my mind with the strongest of challenges, until I was able to begin my long, laborious series of rehabilitation exercises. I was warmed by the many letters and messages I received, most notably one from Rita Lang, a fervent Glamorgan supporter whose cards and letters of congratulation, commiseration and encouragement have long been part of every Glamorgan player's life.

Dear Steve,
I was about to send thanks for your latest Wisden Cricket Monthly *article but turned on Ceefax and was much saddened by the latest news of the knee's progress. All along I have been looking for information and praying for your recovery. We all realise that anyone on the outside can have little understanding of the pain you and your family must be suffering but we all care a great deal. You*

are truly special and much missed. Believing in miracles I still have huge hope and will continue to "Storm Heaven" and burn rows of those night-light efforts which my church has recently put in place of good old-fashioned candles.

Thank you for so many great innings, I recall with special joy your being first to 1,000 runs and those super efforts at Colwyn Bay – it will seem weird not having you batting there this year. Whatever happens you have been a wonderful part of Glamorgan's history but I refuse to think that the mighty bat must give way to the mighty pen just yet. Every best wish for whatever the future brings.

May things be good.

Rita Lang.

When you read something like that it brings home to you how seriously some people take county cricket; how much it means to them; how much of their life it consumes. It would be easy to dismiss such correspondence as being from 'another mad supporter' and sometimes it is because there are many such 'weirdos'. But not this.

There was an interesting entry in my *Wisden Diary* on July 13.

My first outing to Sophia Gardens since the operation. A curiously nervy experience. I felt like an outsider, an ex-player even.

I was. I knew I was, really. And Rita Lang did too, I reckon.

Sportspeople rarely receive the farewell they desire when they finish their careers. Sir Donald Bradman is the most famous example, with a duck in his final innings. My ideal ending would obviously have been a match-winning hundred in front of a packed Sophia Gardens crowd, saluting with my bat to all four corners of the ground in one final gesture to the wonderful supporters of Glamorgan. Ah, those dreams again. Hugh Morris ended on some note by scoring a century in that Championship *denouement* in 1997, but even he was not sure that it was definitely his last innings. And I'm sure, in an ideal world, he would have chosen Cardiff as the final destination.

It is a quirk of fate that none of the trophies won in my time at Glamorgan were decided at home. Canterbury 1993, Taunton 1997, and Canterbury 2002 – the slight exception being the National League Division Two title in 2001, which was actually decided between games when other results went for us. Don't get me wrong, the celebrations on all those occasions were special, but they might have been even more special if conducted in Cardiff. Indeed, Tony Cottey remarked to me after helping Sussex secure their first ever Championship at Hove in 2003 how special it had been to have achieved it at their home ground.

When you are a youngster making your way in the game, older players' retirements do not really register. They did not with me anyway. I did not stop to think of the torment and pain that might be involved. I was too wrapped up in my own world for that. Indeed one such retirement (Alan Butcher) had opened the door for me. I was too excited to feel sorry for him. Ironically, John Fairclough had advised him to retire because of calf problems, a decision with which I remember Butcher did not necessarily agree. "Just go," I recall thinking. How selfish. Butcher had done much for Glamorgan cricket and was an excellent player.

Maybe youngsters Dan Cherry and Ian Thomas, the two most obvious candidates to have taken over from me as opener, were thinking the same when I was dithering about my retirement. They would never have said so, but deep down I would not have blamed them. Of the two, I think Cherry is the more natural opener. He reminds me a lot of me at the same stage of my career – generally possessing a good attitude and temperament, but sorely lacking in self-belief. I thought he shaped up well when we gave him the opportunity to open with me in 2002. He just needed to kick on and get a big score from which he could have gleaned confidence. Thomas is a feisty character with plenty of attitude, but I think that if he has a future in county cricket it will be lower down the order, although his lusty hitting has been effective at the top of the order in one-day games and can continue to be used there. Mark Wallace has also been tried as an opener, but sadly none of these three has made the opening spot his own.

When I was captain I can at least lay claim to having been involved in ensuring one Glamorgan cricketer received a cricketing valediction, commensurate with his exceptional talent and his loyal service. For at Cardiff in 2001 Steve Watkin received a rousing send off in that National League match against Middlesex after the title had been decided. He bowled the last over of the day and was cheered by a packed crowd, leading the side off.

As I mentioned in the last chapter, Watkin did not feature in many National League matches that summer. But as the title had already been secured, it was glaringly obvious (and the Glamorgan hierarchy nudged me in that direction in case I was not already on that path) that Watkin should play in the final match of the season. It was not that Watkin was not good enough to merit a place, just that the others had won the title and deserved to finish the season in front of their home crowd. So who to leave out? Unfortunately, Dean Cosker made the decision for me. On the Friday night, I had a benefit dinner in Cardiff to which he was invited. He clearly had a late night. At 9.30 the next morning he still had not arrived at the ground. I phoned him. "I've had enough," he said, clearly unaware of where he was, less so of what he was saying. He quickly came to his senses and apologised. Unfortunately some action had to be taken. A one-game ban seemed like a good idea, allowing Watkin his swansong.

What made the decision all the more awkward though was the fact that Cosker had actually been doing me a favour by attending the function. It is not always easy to persuade team mates to do so, even though, throughout my year, my colleagues were unstintingly helpful. I was thankful that Cosker had given up his time, even if he betrayed the extent of his revelry by having little recollection the next day that he had successfully bid for an auction item. He is a most personable fellow, without a trace of malice, although his laid-back attitude can sometimes infuriate, and I felt bad about having to use him as a pawn. But the bottom line was that he had erred.

So that is it for me. Time to look forward to a future career in journalism. That began in 1993 when the Newport-based newspaper, the *South Wales Argus*, was looking for a new cricket columnist. I pipped seam bowler Mark Frost for the job, though I was later told that there had been some debate on the sports desk about the viability of running a column from someone who might not be guaranteed a first-team place. Their lack of confidence mirrored mine at the time. They probably never dreamt that 'At the Sharp End', as it was called then, would become 'Steve James – the Glamorgan captain (or at one time the Glamorgan and England batsman) speaks his mind every week in the *Argus*'. But I am indebted to Paul Tully, their cricket writer, who backed me and set me on my journalistic path. The column, now year-round, continues today.

My writing fires had been ignited a year earlier in Zimbabwe by Neil Manthorp, a journalist I had first come across at Fenners in 1989. He was then the Warwickshire correspondent for CricketCall, a sadly defunct service which used to provide excellent telephone updates for county cricket fanatics. He stood at the top of the stairs in the Fenners pavilion with telephone in hand and said "Steve, your county captain would like a word." It was Hugh Morris, congratulating me on my hundred that day. So when in 1992 Zimbabwe's best cricketers were suddenly thrown from the friendly intimacy of their limited club cricket system into the cut and thrust of an inaugural Test against India at Harare Sports Club, I was racking my brains to ascertain the identity of the congenial journalist whom I had just met at the pre-match press conference.

For that momentous occasion I had been curiously appointed the Zimbabwe Cricket Union's official press officer. The Lord only knows why. I think the suggestion came from my Asian club side, Universals, who were acutely aware of my well-paid sloth (notwithstanding my daily gym ritual) between weekend matches and twice-weekly evening practice. It was chaos. I had been told that my primary duty was to ensure that no one should make an outgoing call on any of the telephones in the press box (if a sheltered annexe of the main pavilion with a door leading directly into the kitchen can be termed thus) without my permission. In other words, I was a glorified security guard. And I knew that was no easy task given the archaic and erratic nature of the telecommunications system in Zimbabwe. I had already been shown the simplest of manoeuvres, which sometimes led to an overseas call being charged at the local rate.

Press officers are supposed to be well versed in the machinations of journalism. Clearly I was not. Matthew Engel asked me, "Are you *the* Steve James?"

"Well, I do play cricket, yes," I stammered with a smile, realising that my callow incompetence at this hastily-imposed post might not be the best way to increase my profile. But I did eventually work out who Manthorp was. He had seized the opportunity of South Africa's re-entry to international sport to begin building a media organisation called MWP, which today thrives as the Republic's foremost agency. And he was soon extolling to me the virtues not only of his company but also of journalism in general.

"Your cricket will not last forever and what better way to earn a living than doing what I am now," he said over one of many Castle lagers we shared that tour.

"Right, where do I start?" I asked enthusiastically.

"Do a piece on the Flower brothers and I'll get it published for you."

I wrote it, but it got lost in the post – no laptop then – and I thought Manthorp was full of empty promises. But Peter Deeley of *The Daily Telegraph* was not. He must have presumed that, because I was the press officer, I was an experienced journalist. He asked me to do a piece on my time spent coaching black schoolchildren. I think he soon discovered that I was no old-timer. But at least it was published. An article in a national newspaper. And Manthorp proved his sincerity by putting me up in his Cape Town home later that winter when my season finished early in Zimbabwe, and getting me some press work too, coincidentally sending me back to Harare to report on the Zimbabwe v. Pakistan one-day international.

I also began writing for the *Western Mail*. My first rugby match between Treorchy and Newbridge was called off due to a waterlogged pitch. When I arrived at the ground, Treorchy were training on it. Fishy. An experienced hack would have made something of that. Not this tyro, though. Later I began writing regularly for *The Sunday Telegraph*, first about cricket, through the assistance of Scyld Berry (when I did those Zimbabwean profiles during the 1999 World Cup), and then about rugby. I had met Peter Mitchell, the assistant sports editor, after that World Cup and had mentioned that I was interested in doing some rugby reporting. As well as seeming a fine fellow, he seemed genuinely interested and said that he had liked my stuff so far.

I thought little more of it. Then, on Tuesday, 9 November, 1999 (the date has left an indelible mark in my memory), Mitchell called. "Would you like to make your rugby debut for us? Bath versus Newcastle this Saturday?"

I did not sleep properly for the next four nights. This was something I had always wanted to do. Paul Ackford, *The*

Sunday Telegraph's rugby correspondent, later asked me why. "Because I love rugby and cricket, and reporting on them is my idea of the next best thing to playing them."

That week I did an interview with Tony Lewis for a question-and-answer series I was doing for *The Western Mail*. "You'll do that; a piece of piss," he told me about the rugby reporting upon which I was about to embark. Urine did, indeed, play an important part in my anxiety about my first 'big' rugby match and my first brush with the Saturday night deadlines. The traffic in Bath is always heavy and slow-moving, but in my blissful naivety I had not accounted for this. For an hour I was stuck on the road into Bath, scarcely moving, and with my traditional Saturday morning cocktail of coffee and Diet Coke tugging at my bladder. Eventually I could resist the urge no longer. I pulled up on the pavement and ran down an alley to relieve myself. Not the most dignified of beginnings for *The Sunday Telegraph's* newest rugby reporter, who then drew scowls from pressmen and spectators alike as he read the teams to the copy taker during a minute's silence for Remembrance Day. My scribbled notes did not quite add up to the 420 words that had been asked for but an obliging sub-editor tagged on a quote from Rob Andrew, Newcastle's director of rugby, to make up the deficit. I was up and running. And, while not green enough to think that I probably would have been given the opportunity in the first place had it not been for my cricket, I have been glad that *The Sunday Telegraph* has never mentioned who I am when writing on rugby. Of course there has been a by-line and even, sometimes, a photo, but no mention of cricket. Some people know, many don't.

Jon Ryan, the sports editor, eventually told me that if I did have to give up playing, there would be a contract waiting. I promised him a decision by November 2003, but I ducked it until the following February. I never thought that it would be so difficult to make that final decision, even though I had probably known in my heart of hearts ever since the major operation that I would be forced to retire. But that did not make the final announcement any easier – to make or to take.

In all essence, it was made for me. My rehabilitation had been an extremely thorough process. For the first time ever, I had done all the prescribed exercises precisely and religiously – never easy for a sportsman when they are so pernickety and often embarrassingly easy compared to those of which you are normally capable. But in January 2004 it was decided that it was time to step up the training in order to gauge how the knee could cope with extra stress. It lasted little more than four sessions. On Sunday 25 January, I began doing some light jogging around the outfield at Sophia Gardens. I could not complete the session due to the pain. In fact, I could barely walk without a limp for the rest of the week. It was over.

The announcement of my retirement was clumsily managed. That was mainly my fault. With all my media contacts, I tried to keep everyone happy and only ended up in making a pig's ear of it. I wanted to be finished on Sunday February 8 because that was what *The Sunday Telegraph* wanted. But as it was, I was gone on the previous Friday due to a rash of speculation stories. I was surprised that *The Sunday Telegraph* wanted the story. I wasn't sure my status warranted that. But I was chuffed with the piece that my old mate Mike Atherton produced. I know I will stand accused of hypocrisy, because I said in the preface to this book that I did not seek eulogies from others, but please forgive me for repeating some of it here. For it caught me a little unawares with its emotional nature and warmth.

Professional sportsmen and women are a unique breed: only they know the sadness that comes with the realisation, in the prime of life, that you are too old to do the one thing you love and, often, the only thing you know. So spare a thought today for Steve James, the former England batsman and Glamorgan captain, whose wonky left knee has forced him to call time on his first-class career.

Retirements, like football agents' fees, come in many guises and the hardest of all to accept is when injury forces the issue prematurely, before complete fulfilment. James has had plenty of time to come to terms with the possibility since the pain caused by the patella rubbing against the femur restricted him to just one appearance last year.

Nevertheless, there is regret in his voice since he sensed there was just a little more left in the locker. "Yeah, I wouldn't have minded playing for another couple of years," he sighed. And if you know him, as I was privileged to during two happy years at Cambridge, you know him to be understated and therefore you know that comment to pass for real desire.

He gave himself every chance of playing on by having an operation to shift the position of the patella and by setting aside the whole winter for recuperation. Last week he stepped up his training for the first time and the knee swelled so badly that he could hardly walk. "The decision was made for me." Not, you sense, that it was any easier to take.

When I asked him whether he had any regrets, he said something that will give you an indication of the type of player he was. "When people look back and say they have no regrets, I find that strange. Professional sport is about trying to improve and better yourself all the time. In that sense there are many things I would do differently with what I know now. Regrets, yes, but no bitterness."

James was a professional in the truest sense of the word: supremely fit, never satisfied and determined to make the most of more than average talent. All told, there were 15,890 runs at a shade over 40 with 47 centuries – a fine record – the runs mostly scored off the front foot in an arc between mid-off and cover-point. In a different era he might have earned more than the two England caps he now treasures.

Both his England call-ups in 1998 came in fraught circumstances as a last-minute replacement for injuries. Each time he dashed down the M4 with little or no chance to practise or acclimatise to his new *surroundings. His second Test coincided with the birth of his daughter, Bethan, and no sooner had he rushed down the motorway than he was rushing back up it, on the first evening of the match, not to miss the moment.*

It wasn't really an England career to speak of, but the honour was well deserved and his only gripe is that he was not given an extended run.

He will miss cricket badly, but because he is a rounded man he will find his way.

He will continue to write perceptively about cricket and his other passion, rugby, in these pages. As well as a first-class cricketer he was a first-class rugby player and since his team, Lydney, lost 91-0 a couple of weeks ago, do not be surprised to see a comeback by a full-back on one leg trying to spark a revival.

As a dual first-class sportsman, James was a throwback. He was old-fashioned in cricketing terms as well – a good player and a good man in an era when many complained of slipping playing standards and of feckless youths. It is always sad to see a good man go.

Pretty emotional stuff from the dour, grumpy Lancastrian – well, that's how the majority still view him. I know a different side to him. But still this surprised me. Warmed me too, mind, for it was a sad time. Atherton also made reference to the writing of this book in his piece and even alluded to the fact that his continual ribbing of my predilection for scoring runs down to third man might have been unfair. He was being overly kind there. There was a time when it warranted unlimited ribbing. He knows that. He must remember that innings against Northamptonshire at Fenners when he was *en route* to Lord's.

But I suppose the article also brought home to me that I had managed to advance from those dark, early years and had become respected within the game. Maybe I could play a bit. I always thought that to average over 40 in a long career was the benchmark. If you could manage that, you could play. So I passed that test, despite all my insecurities and quirky foibles. Very few players during my career averaged over 40 and did not play for England. The only ones I can recall are Andy Moles of Warwickshire, Alan Fordham of Northamptonshire and Peter Bowler who played for Leicestershire, Derbyshire and Somerset. I must have deserved those caps then.

Upon retiring I received many heart-warming letters and calls; the overwhelming gist of most of them being: 'I will miss looking for your scores on Ceefax and in the paper.' It should never be underestimated how many people are interested in county cricket from afar; they may not actually turn up to the grounds to watch, but they are interested nonetheless. I hope those friends of mine will still take an interest. I'm sure it was not just me they were keeping an eye on. Remarkable if they were.

But my favourite call was from my ex-opening partner, Hugh Morris. "Hey, mate, you know what – between us we got 100 first-class hundreds and had 12 knee operations." Must be an arduous business opening the batting. But what he did not, of course, mention was that he has also had to fight that wretched cancer. As I mentioned earlier with Gwyn Jones, a sense of perspective was soon restored and that sadness I was feeling soon passed when I began talking about that to him.

Before I end this book, it is probably pertinent that I take a quick look at what the future of the county game in general might hold. When I look back, so much has changed during my career. I still used buckles to do up my pads when I started. No Velcro then. I have seen the introduction of four-day cricket, coloured clothing, floodlit cricket, two divisions, and varying lengths of one-day games, ranging from 60 overs to 55 to 50 to 45 to 40 (with limited run- ups) and now, most radically, to 20. Central contracts have come in and county wages have spiralled. And people say the county game is too traditional and resistant to change! Some of these initiatives I agree with, some I don't. As I have said, nothing quite irks me as much as the current EU player situation, and I recognise that the county system has its failings – some serious ones at that. But it also has its merits and, anyway, you will not find me overly disparaging of a system that has been so kind to me and provided me with such a wonderful livelihood.

I initially agreed with the principle of two divisions, but recognise that it might have thrown up other problems, maybe even the EU conundrum because of the pressure upon counties to succeed. There is no doubt that they have increased intensity and competitiveness, but whether they have had the same effect on standards is more of a moot point. I know that three-up, three- down is too many. Three out of nine is too high a proportion, whichever direction you are heading, and I can find nothing similar in any other sport, anywhere in the world. It is obvious that this number of movers was passed by the First Class Forum (in other words, the counties) because some were afraid of what prolonged presence in the lower tier might bring. The end for some, maybe. And I wrote this about the possible advent of Twenty20 cricket in 2002:

My hesitancy about short-form cricket has been apparent since we played Worcestershire in a pilot 25-over match in 1999. It is a venture unashamedly driven by the marketeers, with little intrinsic cricketing value. But I do understand the logic behind it (the Benson & Hedges final has not sold out for five years) and will back the project and give of my best - not that I can see that a quirky batsman who scores most of his runs down to third man can be of much use in such a power-dominated game!

I know that I would have struggled to summon up sufficient motivation for it, mainly because I think I would have been fairly ineffective at it. I hated that game in 1999 and in truth was glad I never had to play in the Twenty20. But I could never have envisaged the enormous support and interest which the competition enjoyed in its first two seasons. It certainly attracted a new audience. Sustaining that is now the key.

County wages are a worry. There are some county players, not internationals, on over £100,000 a year now, which I find ridiculous. County salaries have improved dramatically in recent years. And they needed to. In my *annus mirabilis* of 1997, I was the leading batsman in the country for much of the summer and I was on £23,500. Not that this is a poor wage, just that by the modern standards of professional sportsmen it must seem pretty meagre, especially for one who was enjoying considerable success at the time. It was not that Glamorgan were being thrifty, just that that was the going rate.

What I needed to do was to play for England in order to bump up my salary, and by doing so I was immediately upgraded to £40,000 a year. And by the end of my career, I was on somewhere near £60,000, which I think that was about right for someone of my standing (I was captain, remember). I like the Australian system whereby no state player can be on a more lucrative contract than the lowest paid Australian Cricket Board contracted player. But the advent of two divisions has meant that some counties are oblivious to that commonsense formula and are paying way above the odds in their quest for success. And the county circuit is a very small place when it comes to gossip and rumour, especially about wages; so, as a result of these ill-conceived packages, there has been many a beleaguered chief executive who has had players knocking on his door asking for a rise. The result? Increased salaries across the board. The problem? There doesn't seem to be the cash available to sustain them.

County cricket is now ever-changing, with a new one-day structure in place for the 2006 season. But at least the short-term financial situation looks secure with the new, if controversial, television deal. There have been rumours of financial difficulties at Glamorgan – the buying of Sophia Gardens plus the wonderful new indoor centre have naturally been costly – but with a new chairman in Paul Russell with such a successful history in business, and such an industrious chief executive as Mike Fatkin, things are in good hands. They have already declared their ambition by announcing that they intend Sophia Gardens to be a Test venue within a decade, as well as installing floodlights for the 2005 season. I must admit to some surprise at that announcement, as it was only 12 months before that I, as captain, was refused a second overseas player (approximate total cost: £80,000). And now they were talking of raising £12m. Not all at once, admittedly, but nonetheless an enormous sum of money, beginning with an initial phase of development costing £4m. But good luck to them. I would love one day to be able to report on an England match there, especially if it featured a Glamorgan player. I hope they will have a new pavilion by then. The changing rooms at Sophia Gardens are not the most luxurious, and the showers undoubtedly the worst on the circuit.

On the field, Robert Croft has taken well to the captaincy, with the 2004 season being very successful, albeit with the senir players to the fore. But there is a crop of youngsters coming through with every bit as much promise as the likes of Maynard, Watkin, James, Dale and Croft had all those years ago. They just need to start realising it. Quickly.

At the annual Player of the Year presentation in September 2003 a fan remarked to me that he thought I was on "happy pills", such was my relaxed demeanour. I realised then what a grumpy bugger I must have been all these years. Opening the batting professionally can do that to you. But I was probably happy then, because I knew, deep down, it was all over. No more worry. No more fretting over scoring runs. No more superstitions. No more avoiding looking at ducks. Bethan could have them in the bath now – how ridiculous that I fretted about that! I could relax. And now I feel totally at ease. I still love the game dearly, and there are certain things I will miss badly – like the indescribable feeling of scoring a first-class century – but I won't miss all that worry.

Just before I retired, I spotted a question in the recently united *Wisden Cricketer* magazine. It asked the identities of the batsmen who had made the highest individual score for each county. In the answers my name appeared alongside W.G. Grace, which brings us neatly back to that History O-level project, but, more than that, it made me think what my Glamorgan team mates, with their typical ageist humour, would have made of it.

"What was he like, Sid, that Grace bloke? Good player?"

Silly, I know. And I probably would have replied: "Don't know, but Matt (Maynard) coached him and reckoned he was useful."

I do know I'll miss all that.

APPENDIX

THE VITAL STATISTICS

CAREER BATTING RECORDS

Matches	Innings	Not outs	Runs	Highest	Average	100s/ 50s	Catches
In all first-class cricket							
245	424	33	15890	309*	40.6	47/58	173
In Test cricket for England							
2	4	-	71	36	17.75	- / -	-
For Cambridge University							
19	34	2	1298	151*	40.56	6/7	7
In first-class cricket for Glamorgan							
213	367	30	13888	309*	41.21	41/48	162
In one-day games for Glamorgan							
250	243	29	7453	135	34.83	8/51	59

CENTURIES FOR GLAMORGAN IN FIRST-CLASS CRICKET

106	v Oxford University	The Parks	1987
152*	v Lancashire	Colwyn Bay	1992
111	v Oxford University	The Parks	1992
105	v Surrey	Neath	1992
138*	v Lancashire	Old Trafford	1993
150	v Oxford University	The Parks	1994
138*	v Cambridge University	Fenners	1994
116	v Worcestershire	Cardiff	1994
116	v Young Australians	Neath	1995
230*	v Leicestershire	Leicester	1995
101*	v Nottinghamshire	Cardiff	1995
102*	v Cambridge University	Cambridge	1996
110	v Somerset	Swansea	1996
118	v Gloucestershire	Bristol	1996
235	v Nottinghamshire	Worksop	1996
148	v Warwickshire	Edgbaston	1996
103	v Hampshire	Southampton	1996
131	v Surrey	Cardiff	1996

109	v Yorkshire	Headingley	1997
153	v Durham	Cardiff	1997
152*	v Lancashire	Liverpool	1997
162	v Nottinghamshire	Colwyn Bay	1997
130	v Worcestershire	Worcester	1997
103	v Northamptonshire	Abergavenny	1997
113	v Northamptonshire	Abergavenny	1997
227	v Northamptonshire	Northampton	1998
152	v Worcestershire	Cardiff	1998
147	v Essex	Chelmsford	1998
121	v Nottinghamshire	Trent Bridge	1998
153	v Sussex	Cardiff	1999
103	v Kent	Canterbury	1999
259*	v Nottinghamshire	Colwyn Bay	1999
111	v Northamptonshire	Cardiff	1999
166	v Warwickshire	Edgbaston	2000
109	v Gloucestershire	Cardiff	2000
309*	v Sussex	Colwyn Bay	2000
156	v Essex	Chelmsford	2001
121	v Durham	Cardiff	2002
118	v Middlesex	Cardiff	2002
249	v Essex	Chelmsford	2002
184	v Nottinghamshire	Colwyn Bay	2002

CENTURIES FOR CAMBRIDGE UNIVERSITY IN FIRST-CLASS CRICKET

151	v Warwickshire	Cambridge	1989
117	v Nottinghamshire	Cambridge	1989
116	v Gloucestershire	Cambridge	1990
104*	v Nottinghamshire	Cambridge	1990
131*	v New Zealand	Cambridge	1990
102	v Sussex	Hove	1990

SEASON-BY-SEASON FOR GLAMORGAN IN FIRST-CLASS CRICKET

	M	I	NO	RUNS	HS	AV	100/50	CT
1985	1	-	-	-	-	-	-/-	-
1987	8	13	1	246	106	20.50	1/-	4
1989	7	12	0	347	53	28.92	-/1	10
1990	5	10	0	79	47	7.90	-/-	4
1990/91	1	2	-	62	58	31.00	-/-	-
1991	11	19	3	461	70	28.81	-/2	8
1992	24	39	4	1376	152*	39.31	3/6	20
1993	16	30	1	819	138*	28.24	1/4	18
1994	16	28	5	877	150	38.13	3/1	18
1995	15	28	3	1011	230*	40.44	3/2	12
1995/96	1	2	0	20	18	10.00	-/-	2
1996	20	38	1	1766	235	47.73	7/6	15
1997	18	30	4	1775	162	68.27	7/8	14
1998	13	24	1	1268	227	55.13	4/5	9

SEASON-BY-SEASON FOR GLAMORGAN IN FIRST-CLASS CRICKET
Continued

1999	16	25	1	1017	259*	42.38	4/3	9
2000	17	28	2	1070	309*	41.15	3/2	5
2001	9	15	3	568	156	47.33	1/4	5
2002	14	22	1	1111	249	52.90	4/3	7
2003	1	2	0	15	14	7.50	-/-	1

BATTING RECORD IN FIRST-CLASS CRICKET AGAINST EACH COUNTY

Opponent	M	I	NO	RUNS	HS	AV	100/50
Derbyshire	11	18	0	494	96	27.44	-/3
Durham	10	17	1	576	153	36.00	2/1
Essex	13	22	0	839	249	38.14	3/2
Gloucs	13	23	4	640	118	33.68	2/3
Hampshire	12	21	0	738	103	35.14	1/4
Kent	9	15	1	532	103	38.00	1/3
Lancashire	6	10	3	593	152*	84.71	3/-
Leicestershire	8	12	2	496	230*	49.60	1/2
Middlesex	12	23	1	726	118	33.00	1/3
Northants	14	27	3	957	227	39.88	4/3
Notts	11	18	3	1336	259*	89.06	6/1
Somerset	8	16	2	458	110	32.71	1/2
Surrey	12	22	1	590	131	28.10	2/2
Sussex	13	20	3	1051	309*	61.82	2/3
Warwickshire	15	25	1	912	166	38.00	2/6
Worcestershire	13	21	1	814	152	40.70	3/2
Yorkshire	10	19	1	642	109	35.67	1/4

BOWLERS DISMISSING S.P. JAMES MOST AGAINST
GLAMORGAN IN FIRST-CLASS CRICKET

8 times	M.P. Bicknell
6 times	S.J.E. Brown, A.R. Caddick
5 times	P.J. Hartley, M.C. Ilott, D.E. Malcolm, T.A. Munton, R.D. Stemp
4 times	A.P .Cowan, A.A. Donald, P.A.J. De Freitas, A.R.C. Fraser, E.S.H. Giddins, D.W. Headley, P.W. Jarvis, A.L. Penberthy, P.C.R. Tufnell, N.M.K. Smith, C.A. Walsh, A.E. Warner.
3 times	C.E.L. Ambrose, G. Chapple, D.M. Cousins, J.E. Emburey, K.P. Evans, K.D. James, D.A. Leatherdale, J. Lewis, J.D. Lewry, M.J. McCague, D.J. Millns, A. Sheriyar, G.C. Small, A.M. Smith, A.P .Van Troost.

BATTING RECORD IN LIMITED OVERS COMPETITIONS FOR GLAMORGAN

COMPETITION	M	I	NO	RUNS	HS	AV	100/50	CT
Nat/Sunday League	152	146	20	4292	107	34.06	2/32	35
Benson & Hedges	39	39	5	1067	135	31.38	2/6	9
NatWest Trophy	30	29	3	1140	123	44.00	3/6	9

CENTURIES FOR GLAMORGAN IN EACH ONE-DAY COMPETITION

135	v Combined Universities	at Cardiff, 1992 (B&H)
107	v Sussex	at Llanelli, 1993 (SL)
102	v Durham	at Hartlepool, 1994 (SL)
123	v Lincolnshire	at Swansea, 1994 (NWT)
121*	v British Universities	at Cambridge, 1996 (B&H)
109	v Essex	at Chelmsford, 1997 (NWT)
118*	v Warwickshire	at Cardiff, 1999 (NWT)

(Steve also scored 100 against Oxford University at The Parks in a limited-overs friendly in 1999)

SEASON-BY-SEASON FOR GLAMORGAN IN EACH ONE-DAY COMPETITION

Year	M	I	NO	Runs	HS	AV	100/50	CT
1987	2	2	0	32	26	16.00	-/-	-
1989	3	3	0	30	13	10.00	-/-	1
1991	2	2	0	34	23	17.00	-/-	1
1992	19	18	0	588	135	32.66	1/3	3
1993	20	19	1	661	107	36.72	1/5	3
1994	18	18	0	605	123	33.61	2/2	4
1995	25	25	6	1263	93*	66.47	-/14	7
1996	21	21	2	531	121*	27.94	1/3	5
1997	19	17	5	438	109	36.50	1/2	10
1998	16	16	0	436	78	27.25	-/3	1
1999	19	19	2	560	118*	32.94	1/2	3
2000	25	24	7	589	88*	34.65	-/5	10
2001	15	14	2	368	93	30.67	-/2	3
2002	17	16	3	368	86	28.31	-/3	2

RECORD AGAINST EACH COUNTY IN ALL ONE-DAY COMPETITIONS

OPPONENT	M	I	NO	RUNS	HS	AV	100/50
Derbyshire	14	14	1	238	60	18.31	-/2
Durham	15	14	2	592	102	49.33	1/5
Essex	15	13	1	465	109	38.75	1/2
Gloucestershire	13	12	2	358	78	35.80	v-/3
Hampshire	15	15	2	482	91	37.08	-/5
Kent	12	12	0	308	69	25.67	-/3
Lancashire	4	4	0	65	29	16.25	-/-
Leicestershire	9	9	1	340	80	42.50	-/3
Middlesex	16	16	3	611	94	47.00	-/5
Northamptonshire	12	12	2	341	93*	34.10	-/1
Nottinghamshire	10	10	0	255	91	22.33	-/2
Somerset	13	13	1	158	46	9.63	-/-
Surrey	13	13	2	343	80*	31.18	-/2
Sussex	13	12	2	362	107	36.20	1/1
Warwickshire	11	11	1	356	118	35.60	1/2
Worcestershire	14	14	1	293	68	22.54	-/1
Yorkshire	10	9	0	155	51	17.22	-/-